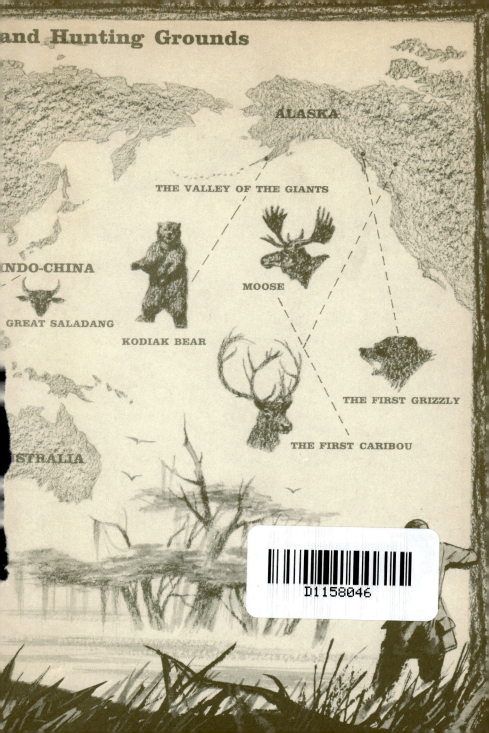

and Hunting Grounds

ALASKA

THE VALLEY OF THE GIANTS

MOOSE

INDO-CHINA

GREAT SALADANG

KODIAK BEAR

THE FIRST GRIZZLY

THE FIRST CARIBOU

STRALIA

D1158046

THE HEART OF THE HUNTER

BOOKS BY EDISON MARSHALL

NOVELS

The Gentleman
American Captain
Caravan to Xanadu
The Viking
The Infinite Woman
Gypsy Sixpence
Castle in the Swamp
Yankee Pasha
Benjamin Blake
Great Smith
The Upstart

SHORT STORIES

Love Stories of India
The Heart of Little Shikara
The Elephant Remembers

NONFICTION

Shikar and Safari
The Heart of the Hunter

EDISON MARSHALL

THE HEART OF THE HUNTER

New York   Toronto   London

McGRAW-HILL BOOK COMPANY, INC.

Library of Congress Catalog Card Number: 56-10323

Published by the McGraw-Hill Book Company, Inc.

Printed in the United States of America

To my good neighbor,

Samuel H. Swint,

Who, to win his trophies,
Climbed many a mountain

CONTENTS

1. Northern Wilds

One

IT is hard for me to believe that a round-faced, chubby boy of eleven, pale with pleasure and pride over the birthday gift of a .22 rifle, in an Indiana town in the first decade of this century—a boy I remember as in a dream—was once myself. He has journeyed up such a long road. So many crowded years have sped back, in the way that the banks of a mountain stream appear to rush backward as the boatman shoots the rapids. I know now that the picture of that urchin with his new gun was the first scene of a strange story rich with change and color and events, with its last scene thirty-five years later. To millions of young men and old, and perhaps to many women, it might be an exciting and significant story. Believing that, I am impelled to tell it.

3

This is to be a deeply personal record. It must begin with an intimate portrait of its protagonist and his surroundings.

Our part of the valley of the Iroquois River, a tributary of the Kankakee, was a gently sloping plain, rimmed by low ridges hardly tall enough to call hills, the land in plow or pasture except for patches of woods and small swamps along the waterways. It was as American as America could be. It was as Middle West as Middle West could get. It was beautiful, I think, in a quiet way; I presume that it still is, although some of the quietude I knew has passed—some, but not all. It was thrilling too, in a way I must try to make you believe. In the fall, when the corn was in shock and all the colors had turned to yellows and grays and browns, and pumpkins ripened in the rows, I could not go into those fields without my heart bounding. Not so much out of appreciation for the beauty of the scene, but rather because the cornshocks were favorite hiding places for rabbits. One might come scuttling forth at any minute. If so I could shoot at it with my new .22; if I hit it, I could have it and keep it and take it home and help eat it, my first hunting trophy. Thereby I would find happiness almost past measuring and come to great glory.

Thousands of people cannot possibly believe what I say about a boy's happiness and glory in killing a rabbit, but thousands upon thousands more can understand it perfectly well. The latter are those who have been swept, almost all or part of their lives, by one of the most powerful and mysterious of human passions— the passion of the chase. I was its plaything for thirty-five years, its puppet, often the victim of its illusions and extravagances, yielding up to it great portions of my allotted time, my energies and treasure, and still so haunted by it that I cannot look calmly upon a sporting arm. I never really knew its cause, its true source, why it came upon me, or what it did to me at long last.

I did not inherit it. My father, the publisher and owner of a small daily newspaper, had shot a few wild pigeon and waterfowl when a boy, but he did not own a gun, let alone worship one. My only brother, much older, liked to "go hunting" and had the seed of the passion in him, but it never grew—at least not as it did with me. If you had looked at me among a group of boys, you would have chosen me as the last among them likely to become a fanatical hunter. But it should be noticed in passing— it might be significant—that often you could look at a group of boys of my age and neighborhood without finding me with them. Even then, at the age eleven, when a boy usually feels that powerful need and longing for membership of a group, I was very often alone.

At that early age I had not yet isolated the fact, although I had seen its signs, that hunting is a lonely sport, that the hunter is essentially a lonely man, more often than a "lone" man; and the bigger the game, the lonelier it gets.

The echo of the guns of the frontiersmen in that part of Indiana had died away decades before my birth. There was no tradition of hunting in the town to take hold of me and mold me. The atmosphere and talk around our house had nothing to do with sport; my father followed none, even in the newspapers; he was an inveterate reader of heavy books; my mother wrote poetry and painted pictures. Now I come to a singular fact, to the making of a startling disclosure. I also wrote poetry. By age eleven I had written quite a number of poems—at least they were verses with an unmistakable poetic quality—and had not succeeded in concealing the fact from my friends. I lived in terror of being laughed at on that account, but, although they grunted and made faces, I can't say they ever laughed at me.

Perhaps I had some other strikes against me. In an excess of enthusiasm for the genius of the times, my father had named me after two benefactors of the human race, Thomas Edison and Nicola Tesla. Edison Tesla Marshall was a good deal of name for a chubby boy—diffident, absent-minded, slow at learning sports, not knowing quite how to get on with his companions—

and it was soon lumped off as "Tess." This, alas, is a girl's name. I bore it until I was past thirteen, when my father, well along in years, sold his newspaper and took his family to Oregon, where he expected to find a peaceful old age growing apples and pears in the Rogue River Valley. There I promptly and finally dropped the "Tesla."

Oregon was a different kettle of fish from northern Indiana. The valley itself was, at first, well settled by old Oregonians called mossbacks; and we had hardly caught our breaths before we began to watch a great inrush of orchard buyers, a great many of them of a social class which we unsophisticated Hoosiers hardly dreamed existed. They came from the great cities of the East. A few were retired professional men on a rather grand scale, but many were rich younger sons and some were remittance men; and of course there were many adventurers and touts taking advantage of the boom. At this point they had nothing whatever to do with my dreams and development as a hunter. I saw almost nothing of them. The passionate hunter to whom I was drawn in high school was the son of a saloonkeeper down by the railroad tracks.

When, in Indiana, I had gone all alone into the woodsy patches with my .22 rifle, and had felt perfectly safe from being laughed at, and my imagination could flow full-tide, I had looked there for wolves, bears, and even catamounts, let alone the far-scattered wildcats that were still actually to be found in the less settled parts along the Kankakee. In Oregon, within thirty miles of our home, wolves—at least coyotes—and bears and mountain lions actually existed, roaming the great forests of pine and fir. But I sought them very little there, and not for long. I had found another, particular object upon which to vent my passion. I had been given an old Winchester hammer pump gun, and I fell in love with ducks.

Since this affair was so ardent, and since I know now it is

rather common among fanatical hunters—often indeed the seeming root of their fanaticism—I must describe a few of its symptoms. It is the only sport that I know—God save the mark in my calling it a sport, because often it becomes an obsession—that is so engrossing, so beautiful in many of its aspects, so thrilling, so mysterious as to interfere with and in fact often prevent the natural pursuit which teen-age boys and young men make of girls. Fishing and football will do so occasionally; but duck hunting is a real and frequent cause of celibacy in its broadest aspects among its followers.

Or perhaps I have got the cart before the horse. These striplings and young men are drawn to beauty and mystery, and are greatly thrilled by both; but it may be they would not seek with such ardor that swiftly skimming pencil line across the winter sky if they were not largely failures in the more sensible and natural and common chase. Neither Dingie, my hunting mate, nor I made a go of it with the girls. On the other hand the boys who played football, or who fished sometimes, or who could hunt ducks or leave them alone, seemed almost invariably successful ladies' men.

Ducks are the big game of small game. Not ruffed grouse, not wild turkeys, not wild geese—no, not even if all the hunters of grouse and turkey and goose in the country rise in their wrath—none of these can invoke the poetry and the passion wakened in the human soul by wild ducks hurtling over a pass or volplaning down into decoys—provided of course the hunter is introduced to them when still quite young. I was fourteen when I shot my first wild duck. Boys of eight do so in North Dakota, and how they can ever bring themselves to follow any other occupation I can hardly imagine. My first wild duck proved to be a merganser—a fish-eating, saw-billed, hardly edible variety—but by decapitating her, I concealed her deficiencies; and my mother gave her a thorough roasting. Evidently she had been living on shellfish instead of the finny sort, because my brother partook of her without complaint, and with a little help from my imagination, she seemed to me delicious.

So far I had only read or heard tell of decoy or pass shooting, where the thrill and poetry of the sport reaches its zenith. The few ducks at which I shot I had stalked and flushed along Bear Creek or sometimes from "potholes" on the desert—a great stretch of treeless hardpan close to our town of Medford. Almost always I missed—to my bitter shame—yet Dingie and I persisted, driving twenty-five miles a day behind an old plowhorse in a bone-shaking cart—from before sunup till long after dark— and the day came when I shot my first mallard drake. I held him up by his yellow bill and looked at him. I had never seen anything as gorgeous. His wings were heavenly blue. His head had the shimmering green of new-sprouted wheat. He weighed more than three pounds; and when I had carried him into the house under my coat, then brought him forth with a flourish, my mother's eyes shone in her happiness for me; and as he looked up from his book, an expression I could not read stole across my father's face. I think now that he wondered what in the devil life would hold for me, with my vast longings and flamboyant dreams.

That life came nigh to a sudden end when I was barely seventeen. I had gone forth to Little Butte Creek, not this time with Dingie, but with a schoolmate named Nolo Lindsey, and not in our old farm horse-and-buckboard, but in Mr. Lindsey's auto. I was armed with the same old pump gun, but its works had been damaged years before by a summer's lying in the mud of a river bottom, and what was called its half-cock, the safety device of this particular model, would not hold. That is, I had to carry the hammer against the firing pin, which any fool would know was a dangerous practice. If I knew it, I ignored it.

The episode, apart from its very real and serious outcome, has a strange and creepy side which I need not try to rationalize or

explain. As Nolo and I were walking back, empty-handed, toward
the automobile, we came on a fence, beside which I saw whom
I took to be an old farmer with a rather long white beard. I say
that I saw him with every inward conviction that I did so, and
I can still, despite some odd future developments, take him for
that. I had climbed the fence and started to draw the gun through
it, when he spoke to me. At least I am under that very sharp
impression.

"Don't ever drag your gun muzzle foremost through the fence,
young fellow."

I think I thanked him for the well-deserved reprimand, and
brought the gun over the fence with great care. Approaching
the car, I rested the butt on the running board and turned to
talk to Nolo. The next thing I knew was the blasting roar of an
explosion, intense pain, and inability to keep my feet. I staggered
and fell, knowing I had shot myself.

"How bad am I hurt?" I asked Nolo, when my sense came
back. "Look at me close." I remember the words perfectly.

"The side of your head is all bloody. You've shot off part of
your ear."

"Go down to the creek and get some water and wash it off."

He found a bucket in the car—such as was almost always carried for overheated radiators in those days—and went off to the
creek. In his absence I happened to lower my left hand, with
which until now I had covered the raw wound against the sting-
ing air, and to my great shock, the thumb was missing at the
middle joint. It was not bleeding; the flesh had been seared by
the flame from the muzzle.

"Look me over, and see if I'm hurt anywhere else," I said to
Nolo, when he returned and he had dashed water in my face.

"I can't see any other hurt," he answered.

In due time I was able to guess what had happened. The butt
of the gun had slipped off the running board, permitting it to
fall through my hand. The distance was just enough to bring

my hand to the muzzle the precise fraction of a second that the back of the hammer hit the board, and, flush against the firing pin, exploded the shell. The charge had blown off my thumb, sent one or two bullets through my middle finger, rushed by my chin within shaving distance, up along my face, to rip off the upper rim of my left ear, leaving indelible perpendicular scars on my temple, and lodge birdshot everywhere under the skin against the cheekbones and the eye socket. No escape from death could hardly be more narrow. The fact my left eye itself was not blind, not in the least injured, was a miracle.

My parents wept on hearing of the accident. My main trouble was not the immediately forthcoming operation on the stub and lacerated cheek and ear, but the fear that they would no longer let me go duck hunting. If they did not, I thought darkly, I might as well have been killed.

This is the strange aftermath to the accident. When I went back to high school I asked Nolo what became of the old man standing by the fence.

"What old man?" he demanded.

"An old fellow with white whiskers who told me not to drag through my gun."

"I didn't hear him. In fact I didn't see him. Edison, he was some one you imagined when you lay there groaning. There wasn't any old man."

I let it go at that. It seemed the most sensible course. But I was not done with the old man.

And my fear of the gun's being put away and my being forbidden to go hunting came to nothing. In fact my father had the gun repaired, and made arrangements with his nephew, who owned a big cattle ranch in the duck-thronged Klamath country, for me to cross the mountains in a wagon and visit him at every break from school. A new and glorious gleaming world opened before me.

II

When I stayed at my cousin's comfortable ranch home I would get up about three and walk two miles with my gun and shells to the house of a man living at Lost River Bridge who kept boats to rent. I would hire one long before dawn and row downriver, but I dared not go too far because the river quickened its pace and finally poured over a dam. As the light cleared, a good many flocks of ducks passed up and down on swiftly beating wings. I would see them hurtle out of the grayness—their necks stretched, their wings throbbing rapidly, their unbelievably thrilling shapes in silhouette against the brightening sky, and sometimes—more and more often as my practice lengthened—my charge would carry true and they would check in mid-air and hurtle down.

I am still unable to explain, by power of reason alone, any marksman's ever hitting a fast-flying duck, let alone doing so four or five, or maybe seven, or once in a while nine times, out of ten tries. The bird is traveling, say, sixty miles an hour, an easy pace for a mallard, a loitering-along for a redhead or a noble canvasback, or for the darting dot that is a teal. That means ninety feet a second. The column of shot may be six feet long and two feet wide. How can any man find the bird over his front sight and touch his trigger at the precise fraction of a second which will cause a collision between the rushing shot and the hurtling target? He must "lead" the bird, but how far, and how soon?

The last part of the question is easy to answer—he must fire the instant that he sees her with all his eyes, sees her with an intensity, a sharpness, that is almost preternatural. Every hunter knows when that instant occurs, but often he fires a hundredth of a second too soon or too late.

But if the duck is clean-killed, she crashes. Death comes to her in the middle of a wingbeat, the water or the marshes no longer leaping beneath her, her piercing vision instantly darkened, the sudden undreamed-of spilling of her brimming life. But only rarely does her blood soil her beautiful plumage. She remains an object of beauty, as still-life painters discovered centuries ago. The hunter—not the sportsman, in my case; this was too much work to be sport; this was the relief of a rending passion—holds her by the feet and looks at her and his heart glows.

Big gaudy mallard drake, for example, and his brown hen, or male sprig in his dress suit, and, wonders beyond these wonders, bullnecked canvasback that you glimpse in the middle distance, who is over you, too near for you to spread your shot in his path, before you can raise your piece! He has a receding forehead and a streamlined bill. It is not uncommon for him to weigh four pounds. But when the hunter cannot find these princes of the duck kingdom, he may shoot the swiftly rising widgeon, or bluebills and ringnecks—greater or lesser scaups according to the books—with canted wings! There are the beautiful flying blue-winged teal. There are the rank-flavored spoonbill, who fly bigger than they are. There are little ruddies that will hardly flush, and now and then a whistler, or a bufflehead. I have rowed half a mile to retrieve a fallen green-winged teal, hardly bigger than a jacksnipe.

Once I hired a boat whose oars had no pins to secure them in their locks. When I stopped rowing to shoot at a passing flock the oars slipped out into the water. By the time I discovered their loss they had floated thirty feet behind the boat, which was being driven much faster than they because of a tail wind. A good swimmer might have stripped off his heavy hunting clothes, kicked off his high boots, and, oblivious to the icy chill of the river, swum and retrieved them. But I had never been able to learn to swim. I could only see them dropping farther and farther behind—and somewhere below me, I did not know whether at the end of the next reach or of the second mile, the river roared over a dam.

The boat was big and awkward. I tried lying on my belly and guiding it with my hands. This had no appreciable effect, and I was equally powerless to steer it with the butt of my shotgun. I was closer to panic than I would have liked to confess. Then, in the mists of morning, I saw another boat, the first I had ever seen in these waters. It looked oddly short, and its single occupant was a bewhiskered old man.

He drew up in easy reach of my voice.

"I've lost my oars," I shouted to him. "Would you please pick them up and bring them to me?"

He did not answer with words, but he retrieved the oars and brought them to me. Although I knew a good many of the settlers in the valley I did not recognize the old man, and still did not feel free to ask his name. However, since he had an unlighted pipe, I asked if he would care to try my blend of tobacco. He accepted gladly.

Meanwhile we were both rather busy with our oars, stemming the drift of our boats. I turned back upstream; and when my scare had passed off, I turned to wave at the old fellow. However, the river had rounded a bend, an early-morning mist had blown in over the glinting waters, and I could not see him.

When, safe at the ranch house, I recounted the incident, a very odd expression came into my cousin's face. There was perplexity in it, I thought, colored by embarrassment.

"Edison, you're not stringing me, are you?" he asked.

"You should know I'm not."

"I do know it, from the look of you. But I know every settler in this part of the country, and there isn't any old man with whiskers."

"Then he came in for a visit."

"It would have been hard to manage it, without me hearing about it. If you'd been asleep since then, I'd take my oath that you'd dreamed that old man."

"Anyway, I got back my oars."

"That saved you a big scare, but I don't think you'd have gone over the dam. That water backs up and gets almost still, farther down."

I remembered the old man by the fence at Little Butte Creek. I went so far as to try to recall whether the two looked alike, and could possibly be the same. There was one point somewhat similar: the first old man played no actual part in my accident; the second—according to my cousin—only saved me a big scare, or possibly some panic-driven act in what my cousin thought was largely a false alarm. It happened that on a third occasion when I was to be greatly frightened, this time certainly with full cause, an old man with a white beard made his presence eerily known, but again played no actual part in the forthcoming accident. Maybe he was a guardian of some sort, or a comforter! But even my idly asking the question shows how coincidence may cast a glimmer of the uncanny over unrelated episodes, or even betray the mind.

The fact remained that in three crises in my youthful life, an old white-bearded man entered upon the lonely scenes—or else I was the victim of mirage. Perhaps the mathematical chances against the occurrences are no greater than those against the dealing of a straight flush in poker.

III

In college soon after the Klamath visits, I received the first compliment of my marksmanship. One of my mates had gone with me on a pheasant and duck hunt along the Willamette River. On our return I eavesdropped on a report that he was making to some other students.

"When Edison raises that ol' shootin' iron," he was saying, "something's goin' to drop."

Did it matter enough for me to repeat it, nearly forty years later, in a book intended to be a serious report on my hunting career? God only knew how it mattered!

In my first year in college, at eighteen, there came to me a sign, an omen of the future, almost as incredible as it was bright. Writing a phantasm of the imagination in the form of a short story—for I had no experience of any kind on which to base a factual story—I sent it off to *Argosy* magazine and received a real, cashable check, in two figures. I must say, knocking on wood, I was never again bereft of high hope and confidence in my capacity to earn a living, and almost never again without funds. With these in my pocket, I was able to hunt ducks not by trudging up Bear Creek or rowing down Lost River, but in the ways of which I read in outdoor magazines—the ways followed by the great sportsmen.

Here is the scene. Perhaps my boat is hidden in high reeds fronting a lake shore in the great Klamath country, or farther east in Lake County, in those years an empty wildness except for a few cattlemen and homesteaders. I have crossed the mountains to get there in my Model T Ford; the chances are that, in these early years, I am alone. Perhaps I am at one end of a pond that is part of a chain of ponds down which the flocks pass in autumn flights, and my blind is my boat dressed with reeds, or a heap of tumbleweed, or even a carefully erected stand with a wooden floor. In front of me, the nearest about forty feet and the farthest about a hundred, float my duck decoys, sometimes substantial shapes of wood, or, in inaccessible country, painted canvas that I have inflated with my lips despite their vile taste; or perhaps I have only outlines of cardboard. But the ducks come

on. If they are sprigs—pintails in Midwestern parlance—I have
identified them at two furlongs by some action of their wings;
I can spot the steady, purposeful, down-to-business flight of
mallards. I might confuse canvasback with redheads at this distance, but only for a second or two, for at once, immediately,
in one climactic rush, they will be over my blind; but I do not
confuse them with long-winged ducks, such as those just named
or with widgeons or gadwells and of course not with teal, or
even with their cousins of the scaup clan, which have action all
their own.

It is perfect duck weather: gray, cold-looking clouds and a
cold wind that bends the reeds and, except for my heavy cloth-
ing and my youth, would bite me to the bone. It suits me as a
still, warm, moonlight night suits lovers. The water ripples and
looks gray.

It is a beautiful sight to see ducks making into a pond to
light. But they almost never light among the decoys. Often they
skim down out of range. More likely they will circle and re-
circle the hunter's hiding place, looking down, regrouping, sometimes streaming one by one or two by two, until at last they
either take fright or bend their wings in expectation of lighting
—always coming in, like airplanes, against the wind—when they
are met by the cruel blast of shot.

Ducks are gregarious birds. Thus they travel in flocks, and the
members of any one flock are inclined to act similarly, unless
they are made suspicious or alarmed. This means that their actions are a beautiful thing to see. Scaup, especially, are likely to
advance like a squadron of cavalry horses, in file or abreast, their
spacing about equal, their wings canted at the same angle, and
their heads turned the same way. But they are not such noble
ducks as canvasback, that positively belt over the blind, coming
in so fast that you can stand and wave your hat without their
being able to change their direction or their gait. At their first
alarm, their first glimpse of the hunter, too late for them to veer

away, widgeons will climb like rockets. Before you know it, they are out of range. Teal will scatter and dart. In an instant they are gone. Mallard are wondrously good at changing their direction when flying full tilt, and at gaining distance by any means that comes handy. If there is any living thing more vivid in the instant of its nearness than a flying flock of green-head mallard ducks, it is a tiger. The simile might seem extravagant, but I hope to show you, before this book is through, that it is not.

Two

AGED twenty-one and done with college, I was given an honor which afforded me deep satisfaction, and changed the course of my life. Bob Ruhl, only a few years older than I but editor of the morning paper, asked me if I would like to be a member of the Rogue River Valley University Club.

No amount of traveling about, living and looking and judging and taking such honors as came my way, can ever diminish this one. The club's membership consisted almost entirely of wealthy men who had settled in the valley as orchardists in the years of the big boom. The great majority had gone to Harvard, Yale, and Princeton, with a sprinkling to Williams and United States military academies. Measured by the yardstick of social accomplishment and experience, I did not belong in their company. My roots in America were extremely old and deep; my family had produced lawyers, editors, schoolteachers, judges, and soldiers in all our wars. But I had never heard of the Hasty Pudding, the Porcine, or Skull and Bones; I thought Old Nassau was an island; I did not know the difference between a liqueur and an *apéritif;* although I had had a dress suit for college affairs, I had never in my life worn a dinner jacket, while such was standard evening apparel with my fellow members even when they dined alone. If this was a little leaning backward toward émigrés from Versailles, if it suggested the lonely sahib on his tea plantation in the Assamese hills, the fact remained that on the whole they had the aristocratic viewpoint, they lived up to it with a minimum of ostentation, and most were widely read, highly cultured fellows. On the other hand, in the town where I lived until my fourteenth year, no one ever heard of keeping a maid. The use of the word was considered highfalutin; we kept a "hired girl," but she could sit down at table when she pleased. And my highly educated father still used the frontier "ye" for "you," and employed the term "aristocracy" to refer only to the upper class in Europe or ancient Greece.

The most distinguished member of the club at that time was probably Dr. Louis Salade, retired from a successful practice in gynecology in Philadelphia. And one evening, as I was sitting there in a dinner jacket like other members, trying not to imitate them and at the same time not appear gauche, I heard Dr. Salade refer to a sheep hunt he had made in the Canadian Rockies.

When I caught him alone one afternoon, I questioned him as boldly as I dared. He was willing and eager to tell me about the trip. His eyes gleamed and his voice rang with enthusiasm. So it came about that I too saw great ranges running, their gleaming peaks and dark ravines, precipices, ledges, and, atop a boulder, a magnificent ram gazing across his kingdom.

My passionate interest persuaded him to tell me other stories of his hunting days—after moose in Quebec, caribou in New-foundland. He spoke of Indian guides, of campfires he had known, of great silences and nights of glittering stars, of defeats and victories. I could do nothing about them now. I was writing every day, pushing into new fields, finishing my first novel, trying to save enough money for a bang-up wedding to the girl of my choice in faraway Georgia and for the home I had promised her. My terrible (for it would have frightened a psychologist) enthusiasm for the outdoors, transmitted from my heart through two fingers to the keys of my battered typewriter, caused these dreams to come true. And in the September of Agnes' and my first year of marriage, I added up some figures and told her what I longed to do.

She could go home and visit her family and friends, while I would take off for British Columbia, where dwelt a grizzly-mauled mountaineer, who would guide tenderfeet to the hunting grounds. I wrote to him in a state of high excitement, but it happened that before I committed myself to a trip with him, I heard of a man named Dean Cochran, the younger brother of a local insurance agent, who had gone to the Caribou to become a trapper and shake the dust of civilization from his heels. At Agnes' insistence I telegraphed Mr. Cochran—an old telegraph line meant to cross Alaska and all Asia before the Atlantic cable was laid down passed close to Cochran's trading post—as to the reliability of the grizzly-mauled guide. From Barkerville I received the following hair-raising reply:

> KIBBE ALL RIGHT BUT I WILL TAKE YOU MYSELF. WITH GOOD LUCK WE WILL GET MOOSE AND CARIBOU, PLUS MOUNTAIN GOATS AND GRIZZLY BEARS. BRING WARM CLOTHING BECAUSE OF THE LATE START.
>
>   DEAN COCHRAN

It happened that the telegram arrived only an hour or so before a man and wife whom we had invited to dinner. I was still electrified by it, walking and talking in a trance, and at the first chance, showed it to our guests. The man was rather handsome, and rather pompous, and through his speech ran an habitual mocking tone. Still, I thought he would shake off his affectations for once, and I would see him tremble with excitement. Mr. Cochran had telegraphed me about grizzly bears. There was the word on the paper jumping to the eyes. But this half-petrified ass handed it back with the merest murmur of comment. As evidence of the reality of the passion that overswept me, I tell you I could hardly believe my ears.

The day came when I set forth, Agnes and my sister Lucile going with me as far as Vancouver. From there I traveled up the Canadian Pacific Railroad as far as its junction with the Caribou Road—a name that rang with trumpets and gongs and drums—up which mail-carrying autos carried passengers two hundred miles to Barkerville. Its course followed the valley of the Fraser River, the chief river of vast British Columbia, seven hundred and forty miles long, but navigable (other than by canoe) for only a hundred miles. At a Fifty Mile house on the road we began to see the outskirts of that vast forest of which I had dreamed, over whose existence I had exulted and about which I had written words of fire.

At the Hundred Mile house I saw caribou horns, taken from a stag that had drifted from his range farther north. Here too I made a fool of myself at dinner, mistaking tea for coffee, praising it highly as such, and embarrassing everyone at the table, especially our driver. Only the driver had the heart to set me straight, and that on the following day. The only possible explanation was, I was not in my right mind.

At the Hundred and Fifty Mile house I saw moose horns. The Caribou was not naturally moose country—they had come in from the Stikine, our driver said—but now they were usurping some of the feeding grounds of the great white-maned caribou. From this point on, we never left the forest. It was closing around us in awe-inspiring depth. The trees were almost all spruce, which had a silvery sheen close by and in good light but which darkened with distance until, on cloudy evenings, they looked almost coal-black. Scattered among them here and there were little spinneys of quaking asp, their ever-trembling leaves turned golden by the frost; and sometimes a solitary aspen stood alone in a deep-green ocean. These strays from some less somber forest only emphasized the poetic gloom of the spruce.

This was the great North Woods. True, our present latitude was only about fifty-four, barely "North of Fifty-three," as in Kipling's rhyme, but the forest stretched almost unbroken, changed only a little by different altitudes and climates northward to the barren lands, eastward to Quebec. Where prairie intervened out of its lawful place north of the Dakotas, it was only wilderness without trees. The little towns on the passes and at river junctions were only trading posts. With the forest crowded about them, they seemed queer excrescences of the forest rather than the work of man. No smoke rose, almost no sound; unless you knew the trails you could hunt a year without finding one of them. The same could be said for the trapper's cabins, sometimes strung a day's march apart throughout his "lines."

When we could see at all beyond a stone's toss, we saw the skyline of spruce. There must be no other such skyline in the world. Spruce trees, at a distance, have an enchanting shape; a whole ridgetop of them in silhouette against the evening sky becomes the epitome of all that the North Woods mean—unmeasurable vastness, solitude, God at once infinite and at hand, a cathedral dimness. I had come to the North Woods and I could never escape from them. I would be paroled to wander the plains and the tropic jungles, but in my dreams they close around me still.

II

Dean Cochran met me in Barkerville. He was a tall, rather lean man, with a resolute countenance and keen gray eyes. I had sent him a copy of my first novel, *The Voice of the Pack* (meaning the wolf pack, as *The New York Times* had pointed out in its friendly review), and I think he was greatly surprised if not disappointed in my appearance. I did not look like an authority on wolves. At looking like an outdoor man, I was a flat failure. Fully stretched, I stood five feet six and a half in my stocking feet. I wore a mackinaw, but also glasses for astigmatism; my boots were authentic-looking, but I gaped too wide and stared too long. Later he told me that at every first view of something I had not seen before—even a trapper or two whom we met early in the trip—a look of what might be idiocy came into my countenance. But he wouldn't have told me except for some other kind of things having happened. . . .

He took me to his house where I saw his pleasant wife and bouncing baby; also I met there a kind of hostler who would accompany us to our permanent camp; I recall his name as Brown. However, he shook hands with me rather stiffly and I soon discovered that he was disgruntled over something, and prepared to dislike me. Not until the following day did he tell me the cause of his peevishness, and then only after solicitous questioning on my part, and several false starts.

He too had read *The Voice of the Pack*. In it I had stated that a plainsman could not understand the wilderness as did the mountaineer. He himself was a plainsman, he would have me know —from Saskatchewan—and the misstatement had cut him to the quick!

Between dawn and sunrise I saw a wonderful thing take shape. About a dozen dispirited horses standing in their halters, amid saddles and bridles and saddlebags which Brown called "Alforkes," and boxes and bundles of kits and supplies, became slowly but solidly a bang-up pack train, including riding horses for Dean, Brown, and me. We set forth up a narrow, wet, dark trail winding through the spruce thickets. In just a moment I lost sight of the roofs in the little clearing and soon there came into the air a smell—although I seemed to feel it with my lips and through my skin as much as with my nose—that I would part with again and again in months and years to come, glad to get shed of it in exchange of the comforts and seeming safeties of civilization; and also unite with again and again, always with a load dropped from my heart, a thrill up my backbone, yet with a kind of awe and a kind of peace.

It was the breath of the wild, as undefinable as it was unmistakable. Not of all the wild—the tropic jungle has a different feel—perhaps a scent rather than a smell; this breath was of the Northern wilderness where comes, every winter, the great purifying cold; where the waters are chill as long as they can flow and then change to deadly ice; where the whole land lies in sleep under the snow.

I began to see animals, almost all of them pointed out to me by Dean, riding foremost in the train. He would have let me ride first, deep and deeper into the forest, had it not been for the maze of deer paths and sometimes moose and caribou trails that would have caused me to wander off our course. The commonest animals were brightly marked chipmunks, and my heart glowed to think of them tucked away all last winter, curled up in their snug dens under the deep and silent and almost trackless snow, only to waken to such a joyous frisky life—and just now a mightily busy life—as they prepared for their long sleep. In contrast to them we saw lackadaisical Franklin's grouse, perched on the tree limbs and unwilling to fly even when shot at with our pot-hunting .22. They were neither beautiful nor bold, but blowzy and stupid, and how they made a go of it in the rapacious North I could hardly imagine. True, calling them fool hens, Dean tossed them a fool's chance to escape the pot. I had to shoot them through the head or not at all.

Shades of my boyhood! I could still look straight down a rifle barrel. I shot six in a row at thirty feet, three for supper tonight, three for breakfast tomorrow—along with rice and gravy just a well-filling meal for three hard travelers. Whereupon Dean

worried less about my behavior when I would be face to face
with a bull moose with big flat horns, or a caribou stag with a
white mane. But though pleased with the feat, I became more
uneasy than before about the future. With just a trace of
nervousness I could have missed six times in a row. I had
enough sense—just enough—not to get nervous over pot-
shooting birds that would not fly; but what would I be when
great antlers tossed?

Dean showed me a marten, whose high-priced fur he coveted,
dashing through a fallen treetop. Often he pointed down at
game tracks in the moist earth—most of them of deer, one of
a black bear. I had resolved not to kill deer on this trip unless
needed for meat. I could have got them much nearer home; I
had made some sort of deal with the gods of the wilderness, to
take big game or none at all. Deer, although wonderful quarry,
were betwixt and between. Also I would kill no bear unless it
be a grizzly. This was a less superstitious, more sentimental
ideal, for I had once seen a black bear in the Oregon woods and
was glad I had had no gun, such a clown he was, such a fum-
bling, bumbling old chap.

In my middle boyhood I had become an easy, never a
crack rider, and had thought I had forgotten even that; but the
prowess never really leaves the body, and I made out better
on that hard, rough trail than I hoped. My back grew lame
and my legs ached and my hands felt raw, still at the trail's
end I got down stiff-legged but happy and hungry. Our refuge
for the night was one of the huts on Dean's trap line, containing a little stove, and enough floor room for three men to lie
side by side. Just before bedtime we went to the door and listened to the wind.

"Mr. Marshall," he said, "you didn't get here any too soon
this year."

Early on the next day's march we began a long, arduous
climb to gain the top of a plateau. Happily, Dean did not have

to ask me to spare my horse instead of my own legs; on the
first sharp steep we hit the ground at almost the same second.
He looked pleased at that, and highly pleased that I saw a buck
mule deer in a distant beaver meadow before he did. Of course
he was watching the trail and I the scenery; still it was a victory. The truth was, my eyes were becoming awake. They
were sound eyes to start with and this balsam-scented country
of sudden, brief, exciting views was making them snap. And
now the views too were getting wonderfully better. We were
gaining the heights.

Although I did not know it these heights had been famed for
their beauty since the gold rush fifty years before. We were
getting into the park lands—open spaces varying in size from
a few acres to a square mile or more—strangely parklike with
their rich, green short grass—enclosed in black forest. We
looked up at them first, then across, and finally down on them.
We were following a high ridge, with the parks spread out below us on either hand. And just a little above us now was a
row of glimmering snow peaks.

"We're in caribou country," Dean told me, with a note of
exultation in his voice. He loved this aloof and lonely land, so
sparing of every favor except beauty.

"Had I better slip a shell into the chamber?"

"Yes, but be sure of your safety."

I remembered an old river-soaked pump gun whose safety
would not hold. Not so this made-over Springfield of .30 caliber.

"You see, Edison, there is a lot of game in this country, but
sometimes you don't see much. Weeks go by, sometimes, without seeing a decent head. We have no time to spare on this
trip. If we run into a handsome set of horns, I want you to
take it—don't try to wait for a better."

Maybe I would see no head at all, and the winter would come

down, and I would have to go home empty-handed and hollow-hearted.

We were way up now, the hard climb about over, and I could get back into the saddle. We rode about an hour without any change in the tenor of our way. The land had become a little forbidding. I had gazed out across a hundred green parks, the feeding ground of caribou this time of day, and all were empty and all looked lonely and cold. Without my noticing it, for there was nothing yet to draw my attention to it, we were approaching a rather thick clump of spruce trees. When we were hardly sixty yards from it, there entered upon this silent, austere scene a dynamic figure. It was a little like looking up from one's idle stare to discover a flock of canvasback arching their wings to light among decoys—except that the impact of the visitation was a hundred times magnified.

Running and bounding, his horns tossing, his white mane shining, pranced a great bull caribou. I had seen deer in the woods at home, but I had never known that an animal large as this could be so wildly alive. If he had run steadily away he could have been out of my reach before I could get down from my saddle and raise my gun; instead he stopped and tossed his horns and flashed his mane. His scientific name was Osborn's caribou; but I had never seen one before. It was indeed my first sight of big game. I saw it and longed to possess it with a great, perhaps an evil longing.

The stag still danced and pranced. He still shone like the morning star. But I had got down, now—tumbled down—and the gun was coming up; the butt plate was jamming against my shoulder; the barrel was coming level. Then, yielding to my great yearning, perhaps cheating myself of its prize because of its awful urgency, my finger pressed back and the gun roared.

The next I knew the caribou had got his big feet under him to run—and he was running—he was flying—he was bound-

ing high but far at every bound—he was getting away untouched. In a few seconds he had leaped into cover and disappeared.

Dean rode up to where I stood, and got down. He was trying
to hide his profound disappointment, but did not quite succeed.

"I told you there were caribou in this country," he said, man-
aging a grin.

"Was that a fine head?"

"Since you ask, I'll tell you. It's the best I've seen this season."

"We won't see any more as good, will we? Or maybe we
won't see any more at all—period."

"It can happen so, but I don't think it will. I'm going to take
you to the best caribou grounds in all B.C. And look here. Don't
cuss yourself any more than you can help. Of all the stags, caribou are the most electric. Elk and moose seem more bovine.
Caribou upset a man's nerves. Almost all big wild animals are
glorious, but caribou are out of this world. I can't describe 'em.
I don't need to, now you've seen one."

Someday I was going to get that very one, or one as good or
better. But I didn't tell Dean that. It would sound too boastful,
too green.

III

As Dean was my first guide, I made the mistake of thinking
that most guides were somewhat like Dean. They are, in one
respect—almost all are rugged individualists. That common factor alone causes them to differ greatly in most other respects.

Dean was not unique among them in being a great reader. In
fact the most heart-warming tribute to good books I ever heard
was made by a guide, of nothing like Dean's education, the following year. But none other than Dean knew Goethe or could
quote at great length from Faust; none other had read and loved

to discuss such widely diverse books as Gibbons' *Rise and Fall*, and the *Thoughts* of Pascal. Happily we both loved poetry and found it creeping into our talk every few minutes in this poetic land.

"I'm increasingly glad I gave you the hard trip instead of the easy one," he told me by the campfire we had built outside the tiny hut, for me to mourn by and find comfort in, on the night following my grand miss of the caribou bull.

"Why? I'm certainly not showing myself a hardy mountaineer."

"Let me explain. The other trip is by canoe through the chain of lakes. I make a good deal more money at it, and my sportsman gets as good a bag; in fact, he's almost certain to get a better moose and his chance of a grizzly is as good, if not better. The chances for a fine caribou are not as good, but that isn't why I rejected it. I think the main reason was it's softer—you don't get the feel of the North Woods when sitting quietly in the boat that you do riding mustangs through these snow-wet thickets. This is your first big-game hunt—and I want your maidenhead to be broken with a bang."

He considered awhile, and I was struck by the thought lines on his still-young face and by the outcroppings of granite in his nature. Many of the men you meet dwelling in the woods are a pleasant sort of renegade from the busy world. Dean could have done well in that world, but he had wanted greater freedom and more primitive adventure than it could afford him. He had turned his back on it to live in the great dark spruce forest and among the mountains.

"I told you I'd take you to the best caribou country in B.C.," he went on presently. "Well, I'll do better than that; I'll take you to the best neck of the woods in that country. We'll have to reshape our plans a little. Brown was going to leave us tomorrow night at what I call my outpost, to go to see about his own trap line. Instead he'll help us pack in the morning, then bid us good-

by. Instead of making for that big camp, we'll hit for Lost Camp.
You'll think that a good name for it, before we get there. And
we can't make the long marches with a full train—too much time
is lost loading and unloading. Also there are several places that
only my best horses will cross—without taking them through
one by one. So we'll have to make out with as little gear as possible and a diet of mostly meat."

I went to sleep and dreamed of horn-tossing, mane-flashing
caribou stags that ever escaped my aim. Dean wakened me in
the chill light of breaking dawn.

Brown went on his way with half our pack beasts. Ready to
go, we took down a steep incline, forded a rushing stream in the
valley, and then began to cross a series of ridges. None were as
steep as the long mountainside we had climbed yesterday to gain
the plateau, but the trail was narrower, the sharp lash of spruce
boughs harder to avoid as we rode through thickets. There were
far more fallen logs, each of which must be bounded over, not
walked, lest my horse catch his feet and fall. It was a tiring thing
to force my will every two or three minutes, make him pull himself together, hasten his pace, and jump. A greater strain on man
and beast were the brooks, creeks, and almost-rivers that we
forded in every valley between the countless ridges. They were
all white water with beds of shifty gravel or water-worn stones.
Once you made up your mind to ford, there was nothing to do
but lash your horse and keep on forcing him, never letting him
slack, until he was out of it. And worst of all were the occasional
bogs where you had to haul up on the horse's head with all your
strength to help keep him from floundering. Pack beasts stuck
in these plagued places again and again, and had to be pulled out;
and one of them whom Dean called "a yellow cuss" simply gave
up in the middle of one and appeared to sit down on his tail.
Still, the sight of him there gave Dean and me a picture to take
home.

I saw more game than before, including a cow caribou with

a calf of that season, a flock of mountain goats on a distant cliff face, perfectly pick-up-able with my powerful binoculars, the billies and nannies and kids easily distinguished, black horns and white beards clearly discernible through the mistless mountain air.

"If we were on your way back, with our heads and horns and maybe a skin, and you wanted one for your bag, we might go after an old billy," Dean told me.

"I don't think I want one on this trip," I answered.

"He'd not be as imposing as a fine ram, or nearly as hard to get. Still he would make a fine trophy, and the rams are way across the range, out of our reach."

"I don't know. I think he's sort of in the class with black bears, a little bit too human. Still I'll make this deal with you. If I get a good caribou and a fair moose and any kind of a grizzly worth shooting, I'll pass up all mountain goats, even if one walks into my sights."

"That deal is not with me. It's with what Kipling calls the red gods. But I'm witness to it. Although they're perfectly fair game, I haven't shot one of these old white-headed philosophers for ten years."

On that same day's ride I saw a small zoo's worth of secondary beasts—a badger, a porcupine, weasels beginning to turn to snow-white ermine, a snowshoe hare, a family of otters on a creek bank, a beaver swimming near his house in his home pond. On the following day we ran across a trustful flying squirrel, a mink, a coyote. We also saw a wolverine, known also as a glutton, and by the worst names which Dean and his fellow trappers' tongues could lay on them, and we would certainly have shot him if we had got our guns out in time. The wolverine is the demon of the forest. He will follow a trap line, killing and tearing to pieces every animal he finds in the traps, and then, when he comes at last upon the trapper's abode, he will cry, "Aha!" Now the devil-ment is really going to begin. He finds his way in, by tearing a hole in the roof or forcing a door—he is stronger for his weight than any animal in the North—and starts idly by ripping apart all the bedcovers. Then he will dump all the edibles in the middle of the floor, fixing them so neither the trapper nor even another wolverine can eat them. Then he will wind up by tearing down the stove, and ripping into ruins the skins the trapper has drying on their boards. Then he will wave his tail and go on his fiendish way.

We got to Lost Camp about three o'clock in the afternoon of the second day. There were several salt licks about, Dean said; still this alone did not account for the great amount of caribou sign. One trail winding down from the hillside across the little valley looked clean-cut as a man-made sidewalk.

With my rifle, a sandwich, a canteen of coffee, and plenty of smokes, I made up the trail until it came out on a park broken by clumps of black spruce. It afforded an almost clear view for about two hundred yards. Then I found a comfortable seat, with my back against a spruce trunk. I was ready for a long watch.

The forest life began to stir about me. A flock of grouse only a little bigger than quail, yellowish-colored and fuzzy-looking, ran by me; I took them for some mountainous variety of ptarmigan. A snowshoe hare almost walked over me before timidity conquered curiosity and forced his reluctant withdrawal; an animal which I did not see plainly had a wolfish outline but appeared coal-black; I still think to this day he was an extra-large wolf, hanging around in hope of a caribou calf. He probably would not attack a cow, at least without help from his wicked comrades. Alone of all the deer tribes of my acquaintance, the doe as well as the buck caribou wears horns, not as heavy as her lord's, but long and sharp-tined. Besides, she has sharp front hooves with which to strike, and she can carve a wolf's chest in two. However, I never did get a clear view of the beast, and since wolves are stealthy beyond belief and hence almost never seen by the human eye, Dean thought it unlikely that my visitor was a wolf.

I dared not shoot at him lest a big caribou bull might be making his way down the trail and would be scared out of the country.

I went back to my cigar, not in the least afraid that its fumes would warn this same hypothetical caribou of my presence. I knew of hunters who would not smoke even in a duck blind, but the old gray hunters whose accounts I had read had never told of a single instance of big game's being frightened away by to-bacco smoke; the idea being that while it might be unknown and hence regarded with suspicion, it was such a pleasant smell to animals compared to the natural man-smell that it could almost act as a perfume. The terror and disgust awakened in almost all nose-minded animals by the frightful taint of man is one of the marvels of the wild. I can hardly believe we smell as bad as all that, but the behavior of deer and bear, buffalo and elephants, proves it beyond question.

I finished the smoke and looked at my watch. The time was just five, and the short October day was beginning to fade. Already the distant timber looked darker, and the view was less sharp. I felt the wave of melancholy that sweeps over most men when a dimness comes upon their eyes and they know that they have done all, or about all, they can do today, and their hope of better things must be deferred until tomorrow—for most men die a little, late in the afternoon. Perhaps night-roving animals have something like the same feeling in the dawn hour, when the light that signals them to go to their lairs breaks in the gray east.

But a little movement far up the trail, beyond the first thicket that blocked its view, caught my eye. It disappeared, then re-turned to my field of vision as a great, thrilling movement. It was made by a band of caribou. It contained cows, a calf or two, and a young bull, but its leader was an old bull. On his head were great projections, which to my bulging eyes looked as tall as

those of the lost bull. Certainly his mane was as fine, his neck as
burly, his form as stalwart. Now small thickets intervened, but
he passed them all and came into plain sight less than a hundred
paces from my watching place.

Perhaps because I lay in ambush and he didn't see me yet. I
controlled my nerve. I raised the gun with slow, steady movements and, bracing it strongly with my left arm, got the big bull
in my sights. Just in time I mastered the fatal impulse to jerk at
the trigger, and instead pressed steadily.

The gun roared, and the great bull, one of the lords of the forest, fell to the ground. Down went his crown, the white mane
ceasing to glimmer in the failing light.

Dean came on the run. "Did you get him?"

"I believe so."

"Is he a big one?"

"He looks pretty big to me."

We paced together, my gun ready. The bull lay where he had
fallen; apparently he had been killed instantly by the ball's breaking his spine. Too high to be a good shot—if a few inches higher
it would have been a miss—it was a lucky shot.

"What do you think of him?" I asked, my voice shaking.

"It's a big bull. I can hardly remember seeing a heavier bull.
The horns are not as long as those we saw yesterday, but very
massive and impressive. And—I'll be damned! He has a double
eye-guard."

"What does that mean?"

He showed me two prongs, one from each antler, thrusting
forward over the eyes. Ordinarily there was only one. He had
never seen a pair of these before.

"On the whole it's a fine head—a noble head."

I would take it home and have it mounted, and hang it in a
place of honor over the fireplace. Some of my friends would
admire it, and think of me as a big-game hunter, but Dr. Salade
would make no such assumption on evidence as slight as this, nor

would I myself. I knew about big-game hunters. There were some, professionals more or less, by nature mountain men or jungle men, the type usually called sourdoughs in this part of the world, whose prowess I could never hope to match, but even to be a good amateur was a goal distant from me by hundreds of days of trying and hoping, up trails in forest or plain, muskeg or jungle, hundreds of miles long.

I V

Two mornings later, while I lingered over my coffee and bacon and eggs, and a luxurious shave in water Dean had heated for me, he went off looking for richer grass on which to picket the horses. He came tearing back to tell me there was a caribou bull in a salt lick only a quarter of a mile from the cabin.

"He's not as heavy a bull as yours, but his horns are a good bit longer."

"What would we do with the meat?" I asked as we started walking.

"You needn't worry about that. I'll ride over and tell Salt Fish Ole about it. He'll have his squaw and whole family of half-breeds here first thing tomorrow. They'll make good use of it, never fear. And you can browse all day in my library." In spite of Dean's grin, the part of his library that he kept at Lost Cabin was carefully chosen and extremely readable, especially on winter nights.

We sped swiftly along, and presently he motioned me to be silent. Now we walked stealthily, and at last he held back a bough of young spruce. "Look through there," he told me.

Hardly sixty yards distant I could see a fine caribou bull, his head down to what looked like puddles of gray water. He never dreamed of our deadly scrutiny; he was at his magnificent and graceful ease. His antlers were obviously longer than those of the bull I had shot, but not as massive, and his body lacked the mature bulk of the other.

"I'm going to let him go," I said.

Dean heaved a big sigh.

That day we rambled where I could not have gone alone, through a maze of trails and wildly running ridges. We were looking, Dean said, for a moose; the black monsters often came to the heights this time of year. Yes, and if we found one of sufficient spread of antler, I would shoot him and take his odd-looking—almost grotesque—yet immensely impressive head. But our chances were far better in a valley not far off, with beaver meadows and ponds strung along like emeralds and sapphires. What Dean really hoped to run on in this rambling was a grizzly bear, digging for marmots perhaps, or edging near a winter den; and if I could shoot him and take his fur, it did not much matter what fell to us in the way of trophies thereafter. We would have found the Golden Fleece.

Dean and I spent a happy week in the quest; then the darkening clouds, and a shrieking in the wind that rose and died away in the middle of the night, and signs too obscure for my untrained eyes, warned him that we must go moose hunting in all seriousness, and nearer home than this. Sometimes the snow pelted down before its time, and blocked the passes.

So we packed up and made for Beaver Valley. It was a pleasant spot, the cabin one of Dean's best and the country alive with small game and deer. There was plenty of moose sign too, and we saw one or two every day we hunted—but only cows as yet, and immature bulls. Here, to my great excitement, we came on the tracks of a grizzly bear, and spent the whole day trying to follow them and to get a shot at him, but we lost him on the first stony ridge. The track of his rear foot was ten inches from tip of heel to claw-tip.

We could not stay here, either, very much longer. Even I, a rank tenderfoot, could smell the wind, and knew that winter was

on its swift way. Already we were using days we had meant to
spend hunting grizzlies, but we used them well, and most of the
time my step and my heart were light. Then there came to pass
an encounter on a game trail that even old sourdoughs would
not soon forget.

It was a game trail circling around a beaver pond, in a country
of birch-tree thickets. Trusting now in my vision to see game,
Dean let me walk in front, directing me now and then in a soft
voice. Suddenly we met someone. He stood seven feet and he
was black, and his distance from us was not more than fifty feet.
All three of us had been moving with stealth, or such a close
meeting would hardly have been possible.

He was a bull moose with every mark of a big bull, at least on
the side at which I had the best view. The gun leaped up and
blazed, and the bull dashed off with a great throwing of mud.
I was quite sure I had missed. The fact that he stood so close was
no guarantee of a hit—once a hunter pulls off, his bullet can
fly unbelievably wild—and would only multiply by many times
the offense of missing. And just as my racing bolt had jammed
home another shell, and I was trying to get a clear sight on him
bounding through the golden-leafed saplings, he bounded on
higher than before, and farther, and fell in a heap.

Dean and I made toward him, in case he sprang up for a last
fight. But his last fight was over, and he would battle no more in
the autumn days with other bulls for the lordship of the wood
or for a mate. He had fallen on his left side, giving my first clear
view of his right side. And the antler on this side was not nearly
as heavy as the one I had seen.

It was as massive, but the palm was not wide-spread.

"If you aren't the greatest fellow for getting these off-pattern
heads," Dean said. And if he felt any disappointment he didn't
show it.

I refused to be disappointed. The bull himself was old and
massive, and his time had been about out; indeed the malformed

horns on both the caribou and this bull moose had been signs of senility rather than youth. But he was still impressive, and his head would look fine in our dining room at home. And now we could turn to hunting grizzly bears.

And no one could ever charge us with not hunting them. We were up early and late and rode wide and far. And the riding was not as easy as it had been a fortnight past, when we had ridden out from Barkerville. A cold rain fell every day. Often it turned to light sleet or snow, enough to whiten the evergreen boughs before it melted, and often beating into our sleeves and the collars of our coats. The streams rose higher. One really great early snowfall—two feet or more in the valleys, six feet in the passes—and we would have a hard time getting out. We would not stay here three months before we could find a way, but we might be snowbound for three weeks.

There came a night when the wind soughed, and when I went out at midnight on an errand its knives scraped my bones, and a soft, wet snow was falling. In the morning Dean took one look at the coverlet six inches deep, and one at the white, cold-looking clouds.

"The hunt's over for this year," he told me, "And we're going to try to make it down from the plateau to my number one cabin in one day's ride."

He began to pack the horses in great haste, and instead of standing about, looking at the scenery, I threw together our breakfast of bacon, eggs, and pancakes. He called to me to not spare the grub box; we would need all the stout provender we could hold before the wicked trek lay behind us, and our lunch would be a stick of dried caribou gnawed in the saddle. In hardly an hour we set forth into the snowy forest.

Dean is a good and lively talker, and since then he has told many hunters of our race against the weather. It stood to reason that Dean must ride in front. He knew the trails and the best crossing of boggy ground, and the easiest fords through the rising, rushing streams. This meant I had to ride behind the pack horses, to hurry them on; and that meant riding so close to the hind beast that when the long bough of a snow-heavy tree would catch in his saddlebags and bend forward until it pulled free, it would come swishing back at me, a blow hard enough to knock me out of the saddle if I did not fend it off. So my coat sleeves were soon full of snow, as was the neck of my shirt. It was impossible to stay dry on that rough trail, and hopeless to stay warm.

We crossed uncounted ridges. We forced our saddle horses to jump numberless logs. Again and again one or another of our pack beasts floundered or fell, and one or both of us had to dismount to get him going again. On the whole, though, they were brave creatures, patiently bearing their heavy loads. Once they snorted and stamped in alarm, and the wild thought struck me that a grizzly might be near, making for his winter bed. Both of us could not leave the horses, but I told Dean I wished to go alone to see, and that I would not be gone five minutes. He looked me in the face, remembered I had done well enough with my last two bullets fired, and grinned and nodded his head.

I got down and walked up the wind a little distance from the trail. I found no bear, but I did find tracks suggestive of a cub bear, that I thought had been made by wolverine. And I found too, a greater discovery: the loneliness of the North Woods. In less than five minutes it closed around me, deep and still, and I knew I could never live the life Dean lived, defying that bitter loneliness, somehow changing it to a balm by resources within his own nature. Could I ever become a big-game hunter? I had come a little way nearer my goal, but not very far.

I followed my own tracks back to the pack train, reported to Dean, and the punishing journey went on.

I knew cold and cramp as I had never known them before, discomfort that did not fall short of misery, uneasiness, great yearning for shelter and fire, and finally deep fatigue. But at last

we were down off the mountain; the danger of serious accident
was greatly reduced; and although the woods were thicker, the
way was shorter.

We passed the last three wicked hours. Then Dean shouted—
we had been riding in a miserable silence—and I too saw the roof
of the trapper's cabin. We fell out of our saddles and as Dean
unpacked the horses, I carried the bags we needed tonight into
the shelter. The twilight had come down. Before he could hobble
the beasts—they would not stray far tonight—the darkness closed
in, bitter and chill. The wind began to rise. Tonight would be a
night of heavy snow.

Dean built a fire in the little stove. Such blessed warmth came
forth; then such heavenly scents as he cooked supper. By now
the wind was raging at the roof and we were amidst a blizzard.

"Will we be snowed in?" I asked.

Dean gave me a searching glance. "One reason we had to make
this camp," he answered, "is yon pair of snowshoes."

He pointed to them fastened to the wall.

"There's only one pair."

"That's all we need—for me to get to Barkerville and get a
sled. You'd have to cook and lay up till I came back. But as far
as I know, we'll be snowed in only as long as this storm lasts.
Then if the drifts aren't too deep we'll go back together in the
saddle."

That satisfied me, and after a great meal of rice and meat and
stewed apples, Dean got a small phonograph and low stack of
records out of a box. He began to play them, the pieces he par-
ticularly liked—I could fairly say loved, for he wouldn't have
labored to bring them here, this many unbroken in the rough
pack train, if they had not been close to his heart. All were
pieces that reflected his own dreams and imaginings—they did
not relieve his loneliness but told him its meanings. The *Peer
Gynt Suite* wailed of the mystery and sadness of death, and sang
of the joy and grace of the dance, whether the flying dance of

the cranes over the great lakes or the dance of the leaves through
the birch forest in the fall of the year; or it echoed the passion
of the storm that broke on the mountainside, or the drums of
the thunder and the pipes of the wind, like sounds of a king's
pageantry in a mountain hall.

Strangely it was the soft and tender *Souvenir* by Drdla, much
beloved by people of common taste like Dean and me, that thrilled
and touched us the most. Perhaps because it was a song of love
and beauty and remembrance, and hence in such dramatic contrast to our present scene. There was beauty of a kind in the little cabin, and warmth and fellowship, and now there was music
and distant scenes, while outside the storm raged, and the snow
swirled before the wind in wan clouds, and the wild animals
sought what shelter they could find, and the young trees moaned
and bent down with their white loads.

I was much more tired than Dean, from lack of knowing how
to save my strength and husband my endurance on such a day as
this, so after I had got into my sleeping bag he played the records
again. So it came about that I went to sleep listening to the death-
less songs of Stephen Foster, sung long ago and always, here in
this trapper's hut amid the blizzard, as well as in the bright fields,
far away.

In the morning Dean called me to "Come and get it." He had
already prepared our breakfast, fully as nourishing as last night's
supper; and the storm had died in the night, and I felt the deep
silence of the snow. But it was not very deep as yet, Dean told
me. The horses would know that we were going home, and
would conduct themselves well. With even fair luck, tonight we
would bed down in Barkerville.

This came to pass, and on the second day I caught the auto-
stage for the journey to the railroad. On it were two other hunters, from Chicago, both on their first trip, but by some counting
they had better luck than I. They showed me their two sets of
caribou horns, each longer than mine, moose horns of greater

breadth and far more symmetry, and rolled up in salt two grizzly skins.

By some counting, yes, and for a little while I was prey to that black, sick passion—jealousy. To judge from the trophies, the only legal evidence, the only record, they had had a better trip. Yet there was another counting that only Dean and I knew. By that counting, made up of failure, success, dreams, facts, snow on mountaintops or beaten into my face, firelight and dawnlight and starlight, in truth countless imponderables, my trip was one to cherish all my life.

Three

AT the next year's summer's end, I began to long for the North Woods.

I wanted to go again with Dean—and never miss a shot when his eyes were on me—but I knew that the company of some other guide would widen my knowledge of men and nature and enrich my experience in life in general, for there never was an old road that holds quite the wonder and surprise of a new road. Since I especially desired a caribou head as high and noble as that I had missed on the mountain—in fact was obliged to take one to get square with myself, somehow—I chose the same general country as before, where Osborn's caribou comes to unsurpassed growth and glory, although in the region of Quesnel Lake instead of back from Barkerville as before. In this case, although I knew it not, my correspondent did not intend to take me out himself. He had gone into the outfitting business in a rather large way, and had hired two men of the country to go with me.

Arriving there, and seeing a coyote on the lake shore the first morning, made my blood quicken in my veins. Then, on meeting my two fellows—for both turned out to be truly my fellows in the happiest sense of the word—I had premonitions of good fortune. One of the two I called Jim—I remember him as such, perhaps wrongly; his last name I have forgotten. He had great respect for book-learning. He told me of a youth who had "a crackerjack education"—snapping his fingers in enthusiasm—only to throw it away. And it was he who spoke the marvelous tribute to a good book that I have mentioned earlier.

"There ain't nothin' like a good book, especially when you're runnin' your trap line, and putting up at night in a cabin all alone. Every night you read the limit you've set on yourself— and you dasn't go beyond it, no matter how you ache to, for the book will be through too soon. At last you got only about thirty pages left. You go all day and all that night thinking about the story, but you don't open the book until you're in camp the next evening, and everything snug, the fire blazing, and the cabin warm, and the skins well fleshed and stretched. Then you light yourself a smoke, and finish the smoke. Then you say, 'Oh boy,' and sit down and finish the book."

He did not know what he did for me, a book writer, in telling me this. Since then, when the blue devils gather 'round, and I wish I had written realistic books of social significance for a select audience instead of tales of love and adventure to carry away a whole multitude of readers, I remember Jim's words, word for word, and I rejoice that my fate moved as it did, and my heart glows.

My other companion was Mauffett Hamilton, a quarter-breed Indian, tall and lithe, with a slow, humorous way of speaking.

For fellowship of itself, its warm and wonderful and indefinable essence, I had never before or since met any man who possessed such a gift. Actually his pedigree would have rocked a society of genealogists to its foundation. This is what he told me, and with apologies to all the other impeccable descendants of the great man, I believed it. He said that his great-grandfather was a British duke, and the duke's son, Lord Hamilton, loved life in the wilderness and had taken a wilderness wife. Mauf had a Norman nose. Also he had an air about him, which if I must account for in some logical way, I think I would guess at the crossing of bloodstreams of a to-hell-with-it aristocrat with a young and beautiful squaw.

It happened that my outfit crossed trails with the outfit of a young Floridian, and its bull cook and head wrangler was Mauf's younger brother. He was an odd-looking chap, with a slow, infectious grin. I remembered that I asked him to fix the minute hand of my watch, as it stuck on the hour hand every time the two crossed. He handed it back to me with a solemn look befitting a bishop. "I fixed it," he told me. "They won't stick any more." I looked, to discover that he had broken off the minute hand altogether. However, I could tell the time within about five minutes by the position of the hour hand, and could now understand perfectly how early clockmakers long put only one hand on the faces of clocks, saving a lot of machinery and work, wear and tear, and still letting their patrons tell the time quite well enough.

The young Floridian was a most social and agreeable fellow, like so many Southerners of French descent, and I was so taken with him that I accepted his invitation to pitch camp beside his for a few days. He never strayed from our environs. His idea of pleasant camp life was to sit and smoke with Mauf's brother, and to cook delicious meals for all hands, served with plenty of toddy. Meanwhile, with either Jim or Mauf, I was tramping the ridges.

Once I looked down from a ridge top to see at first what I thought was a young caribou bull about a hundred yards below me. Then I discovered, to my amazement, that it was a very large buck mule deer, wearing the biggest and handsomest horns I had ever seen on this variety. I could not walk on and let the old buck live; if I had reached that point of mature and civilized feeling in a time like this, it would be down a long, far trail and I might as well put my rifles in a box and become a camera hunter. I thought the head was very near a record, and our camp needed meat.

At my first shot he stood perfectly still, and I thought I had missed. At my second shot he dropped. When we went down to see, we found both bullet wounds in the chest, each positively mortal. I don't know why he refused to drop at the first shot and I don't know much about animals anyway, except from tales and personal experience and what I read in books, but I venture the wild guess that he stood erect awhile by what would be, in a man, a feat of will. One bullet had clipped off a small spur of horn near its base; except for this minor defect the head was well-nigh perfect and of great beauty and impressiveness.

When I had returned to camp, I had come to what I have since felt was a good decision in regard to the trophy. Jeff, my camp mate, was not going to get any trophies, at least on this trip. At the same time he did not wish to go home empty-handed. Greatly afraid he would refuse me, I asked if he would accept the magnificent deer head as a gift.

"Edison," he told me, his fine eyes shining, "I'm overwhelmed."

I heard later that the head was a source of great pleasure and pride to him for many years. Then, forced to give up his home, he had it put up in a barroom in his native Florida city, where it became the subject of a "yarn" known to barflies and retold to every newcomer who would listen. It was to the effect that the buck was shot by the bartender in the Everglades, and was the world's record Florida deer. Were he indeed one of that variety, it would have been another case of "Eclipse first, and the rest nowhere." I have never been able to disavow the wild surmise that he was the world's record mule deer.

II

It was to be expected that Dr. Salade, my mentor in this passionate pursuit, had not been impressed by the moose and caribou horns I had brought home the preceding fall. But they had called to his mind a flood of moose and caribou-hunting stories, and I had listened spellbound. In the forests of New Brunswick and Ontario, it was the custom for guides to "call moose"—by imitating the mating call uttered by the cow, or—even more effective—the bull's challenge to battle.

"And one time," Dr. Salade told me, "I asked the guide to pass the birchbark horn to me and let me call."

"You'll only scare the moose," the guide had replied. "It takes years of listening to the old boy before you can imitate his war cry."

"It's my moose, and I'll try it."

Dr. Salade took the horn and imitated the challenge to perfection.

"How did you do it?" the guide asked, after the moose had come up, shown a mediocre head, and had gone his way.

"As an obstetrician," Dr. Salade replied, "I've heard a precisely similar sound six days a week for the last twenty years, when my patient was in the second stage of labor."

Oddly enough, neither Dean nor my present guides had ever "called" moose. Indeed, the belief persisted in those parts that only the eastern moose, not the far-western moose of British Columbia, would come to the call. Since the two were of identical species, this did not stand to my reason. I resolved to be the first hunter hereabouts to hunt moose by calling.

I would not attempt a cow call. But the bull call, as given by our guides, sounded easy enough. Through a rolled magazine in lieu of a birchbark horn I was soon able to achieve a reasonable facsimile. Still I warned myself that I could not hope for results without long practice.

It happened that in a few days Jim and I heard a bull call in a birch forest across a small, shallow pond. We found a hiding place in a thicket and I began to give my version of the call. After my first big grunt, there fell a long and, as if startled, silence; and I—and I'm sure Jim too—imagined the bull depart-ing in a hurry. Then to our great and beaming joy—and it is a dreadful thing to feel joy while waiting and trying to kill—we heard a reply from the forest.

In a few seconds I called again. Now the return grunt came quickly, and it sounded nearer. It did not seem quite fair to be waiting in ambush for my great horned quarry. I remembered that I had slain my caribou, the preceding fall, by waiting on a trail; but I could not look ahead to other ambushes, some of them ten thousand miles away, or foresee that was where I would shine, that I possessed a deadly patience, perhaps a devilish cun-ning. I was young now—conscience is more active in a young man than an old—now was the time to stop the dubious business, the pitting of my sophistication against the bull's innocence, but the thought of his coming—perhaps with great horns that he had to guide between close-growing trees, tall, black, with a big black bell, spoiling for a fight with a rival—reduced me to a savage with little power of thought, only a great lust to conquer and kill. If he came on, his only chance was that I would miss.

Presently he came trotting out of the woods, and plunged into the water. Swiftly he came through the shallows, seeking battle, but my cruel bullet was not a rival's horns, and it knocked him to his knees at its first brush. He rose again and came on, and I fired again. And as he fell, then struggled a few seconds before his great life could pass, the thought came to me I was using too light a gun. What was two hundred and twenty-five grains of lead against half a ton? But the thought came and was almost lost amid a wave of joy that the bull was mine.

It so happened that the horns turned up rather steeply, instead of spreading wide as with most bull-moose heads; even so their spread was forty-eight inches—fair but not in the least unusual. Many fifty-four-inch horns were taken in these parts; on the Kenai Peninsula in Alaska, sixty-inch moose horns were counted good but not excellent; the record heads measured well over seventy inches.

In the way of aftermath I thought again of light versus heavy rifles in pursuing such heavy game as moose. My rifle was a made-over Springfield .30 caliber. Yet the old, gray, tried, sun-dried, half-crazy white hunters in Africa did not carry guns of this power when they went forth after lions and buffalo—the first animal far lighter than a bull moose, the second not twice as heavy. They fired rifles of .40 caliber up to .60, firing balls of from four hundred to six hundred grains. Yet it was almost heresy to hint that a made-over Springfield bullet often did not deal death quickly enough to heavy game; place your bullet well, said the gun cranks and the expert marksmen, and the rifle will do the rest. The trouble was, many of us dubs were too excited, in that climactic second of firing, to place our bullets well.

Jim skinned out the head and bore it to camp, while I was afraid some hunter would see it coming through the thickets and mistake it for a live and intact bull moose. There were more hunters here than in the wastes behind Barkerville, more than I liked. More than they liked too, no doubt, for hunting is essentially a lonely passion.

The head was much admired by Jeff and his stalwart; and I had become fond of Jeff; yet I thrilled when Mauf hesitantly told me that the "boss" had come by; and Mauf and I were to hunt alone in the "high mountings." Jim would help carry our light outfit up to the heights, then, to my deep regret, go his way.

Soon the thrilling thought struck me that it was not how far you went up the Caribou Road, or how far North, or how far from civilization, that determined the scarcity of hunters and the degree of beauty and wonder of the land, but how steeply and long you climbed. Above all these dark woods, profoundly thrilling in themselves, there was an extension, a balcony for the favored, a kind of speaker's table above the multitude, indeed a hunter's heaven, made up of green parks amid the forest, and snowy peaks. I carried my own gun, shells, binoculars, camera, candy—I was a great candy eater on the trail—reading matter that it happened I never opened, and first-aid kit. These together made a weight of something like twenty pounds, and it was all the burden I wanted on that sky-leaping trail. Jim and Mauf each had eighty pounds, including my sleeping bag and rainproof cover, Mauf's quilt and tarpaulin, cooking gear, and a grub sack containing bacon, rice, and dried apples only. The country had to do the rest in the way of feasting us. To my quiet pleasure—for I would not speak of it for the world, letting Mauf think I took it for granted—he did not bring a rifle. If we should meet a belligerent grizzly bear, that would make it more complicated.

III

These highlands were just as lovely as those in Dean Cochran's domain, where he had brought me, a trembling tenderfoot. My feet were still tender and I still trembled, and I doubted if I would ever get over the condition. But if I did, some of this wonder might not come upon me. This plateau was no more wonderful than the other, but the season was earlier, the weather better, and we had more time to enjoy it. And in an entirely different way, Mauf was as charming a companion as Dean had been, and as heart-warming.

All day we roamed the ridges and the park lands spread out

below, and we talked and laughed as happily as two urchins playing hooky from school. Mauf was immensely amused by a vast variety of things. Once he found out that he could call up moose by cupping his hands over his lips and grunting prodigiously, he did so for the fun of it; we would lie perfectly still until the moose almost walked on us, then spring up with a great *"Boo!"* We were rather lucky not to have one of the victims of our jest take it in bad part, or think we were a rival bull, and pass his horns at us.

There was one rather young bull whom we found every day in the same neck of the woods, and he could not learn that our "call" was a snare and delusion. He was rather lean in the rump, and Mauf called him "a peaked-assed bugger." Because he was a good hunter, we saw a great variety of game besides moose, including black bear, a yearling grizzly that, thank heaven, I could not bring myself to shoot, deer, and once a long and eerie view of five wolves, running in single file across a far-distant park. They were chasing deer, Mauf thought. We saw many caribou, too, cows and calves and young bulls and old bulls with commonplace heads, and all were glorious, and all shone in the autumn sunlight, and all were wildly alive. But so far we had not found a bull with a mighty crown, the equal or superior of that great bull I had met and missed on the mountainside last year, and I almost believed it could never happen. I almost dreaded its happening, if it were in the lap of fate, because that would mark the real end of this hunt.

Since, if we were to live well, we must live on the country, and I had no intention of our starving ourselves in this game heaven, I had shot a yearling bull caribou. There would be no loss to the country thereby; one mature bull could serve as many cows as he could capture from his rivals. Also the meat was quite possibly the best that the Northern wilderness provides, its only rival being young mountain sheep. Mauf carried a lunch of thick meat sandwiches in his knapsack, which we ate with great relish at our noon rest. But our best meal, and one of the greatest joys of the day, was our supper.

When Mauf had built the fire, he would cut two immense steaks from our caribou carcass. These he would set to broiling while our pot of rice boiled; meanwhile I had washed for the night and shaved to save myself the chore in the chill of morning. We now had about twenty minutes to wait the stewing of a mess of dried apples, so into a tin cup I poured each of us about an inch of Hudson Bay rum. As the drink took hold we sat facing the fire, our backs to a log, and recalled all the adventures of the day and told with great merriment such jokes and incidents as were appropriate to the occasion, and reached a sociability such as I had rarely ever managed with others. . . . By now the steaks were ready and the rice was done. In the hot skillet Mauf melted a good quantity of the caribou fat, which he poured directly on our great helpings of rice. This gargantuan and delicious meal, topped off with a tin cup each of stewed apples flavored with canned milk, was our stand-by every night, and I have never eaten any other meals that were at once so delicious and so satisfying.

Immediately afterward we crawled into our beds, and knew nothing more but the cool of the mountain air and the soft sounds of wind and of the wild weaving through our dreams, until morning broke.

Mauf was one of the most complex people I have ever met. Give him the merest bath of cultural and academic education and he would have fitted into the most civilized society in the world; on the other hand he was the best woodsman I ever knew. Yet one afternoon, well after sundown, when we should have been entering camp, I saw him in a pickle.

He and I had been sitting on a ridge top scanning the parks below. As we rose to leave I had the vaguest impression that he took another direction than the one I expected. After a few minutes he began to walk very rapidly, and since I am short-legged, I could hardly keep pace with him. Suddenly he stopped with as sheepish a look as I had ever seen on a human countenance.

"Supposin' I asked you which way was north, what would you say?" he muttered.

"Well, I'm very flattered you asked me"—actually I was troubled—"and, as you know, I have no more notion than a newborn babe—but as a wild guess I'd say it was over there."

"It couldn't be over there," he told me gravely. "It must be over there."

I got out my cheap pocket compass, on which I placed small reliance. Its needle quivered and presently pointed in a direction neither of us had indicated.

"That compass is wrong," Mauf said.

"All the books say that when you're turned around, believe your compass."

"I couldn't be turned around. But that mountain is in the wrong place."

"Well, let's sit down awhile, and think it over."

"We will—but the trouble is, it's getting late. Mark you, we can spend the night out if we have to, but I'd be the laughing-stock of the whole Caribou country."

Five times in the next five minutes Mauf asked me to repeat the compass reading. Then he would stand with his arms extended north and south—according, that is, to my compass—and instantly forget which arm pointed to which. When he finally admitted that we were lost, I felt that the victory was half won.

"Let's go back to where we were sitting."

But Mauf did not know the way—to his tremendous ill-hidden amazement—and of course I did not know either. But there was something he did know—and that was enough to make a fire for the night, in case we must spend it here. Presently he found a rotted stump, and together we pushed it over. It was soon blazing cheerfully. I could almost forget the creeping, darkening shadows.

Then there came a wonderful sign from heaven. There was

nothing miraculous about it, except for the world and everything in it being one big miracle; and thousands of lost people, and millions more of lonely herders in all ages and all climes had felt their hearts lift to it as the twilight revealed it. It was only the young moon, bright and deeply bent as Diana's bow—and the young moon, of course, is visible only in the west.

"Well!" I said, grinning. West was west, exactly as my compass had told us.

"Mr. Marshall, I sure did get turned around, but I'm all right now."

Yes, we were all right, and in the dark, among the maze of ridges that seemed to run every which way, across open parks, through forest, across mountain streams, Mauf and I made our way almost as straight as crow flight to that needle in the haystack—our tiny camp amid the wilderness—guided by that beautiful and luminous queen of heaven. It seemed to me I could never again feel a moment's sorrow that I had been born. The adventure of living was an adventure beyond the power of words to tell.

IV

One afternoon when Mauf was scanning with my glasses an outlay of mountain parks below a distant ridge, he held his glass in the same place a long time and focused it with great care. Then he handed it to me.

"See what you see directly over the top of that quakin' asp, in the clump of birch trees."

After many more directions, I finally muttered, "Mark!" It was a bull caribou. I could make out his horns, and they looked very tall.

"Is that him?" Mauf asked.

"I think so."

"The fellow you missed last year?" Mauf's lips were smiling but his piercing eyes glittered with excitement.

"If not, I believe it's his twin brother."

"Well, he's a long way from here, and only with luck are we going to get to camp by dark. With just a little bad luck, we might have to stay all night. But the last time we thought so, we got home."

So we began the long march. Almost instantly we lost sight of the caribou bull, then of the quaking asp that had served me as a pointer, then the clump of birch trees, then the meadows flanking it, then the great gulch of which he was a denizen. We traveled a good three miles—and then Mauf came out on the very point of land he had started for. It was the most wonderful piece of orientation I had yet seen.

Again he squatted down and searched the forest with my binoculars. The search took ten minutes, and the shadows were creeping fast.

"Well, there he is!" he burst out. "Look at him, and say if you want him. If there's any doubt about it, we'll turn back now."

Mauf told me how to level my glass. In a minute or two I found the stag, still half a mile distant, but brought up to one hundred yards by the power of my lens. His horns looked incredibly tall. I could see the gleam of his white mane as he moved his head. It was the brightest spot in this spreading world of shadows.

Mauf and I made the long stalk, I pacing in his footsteps. At last we came upon birch thickets where we had seen him last. I crept through them. The vista opened. Then when I thought he had become suspicious and stolen away, he burst upon my sight. Even now, in this grayness, he seemed preternaturally vivid. Every movement was superbly animated. He browsed not more than eighty paces distant.

For not the first time in my life I was caught up in a kind of reverie that, for these seconds—perhaps longer than that, perhaps

too long—made me unable to shoot. I was not debating inwardly;
I did not even seem to be questioning. Rather it seemed I was
waiting either to shoot, or to grant him his life and go away. I
knew that the latter course would be a noble one. I have always
had a love of noble actions, regardless of how few—perhaps
only one, in my life's book so far—I had ever practiced. It might
be that if I did so, I might never need to go big-game hunting any
more; the great compulsion would be over.

Then I knew something else. I did not have to dig it out of
my brain; it came to me as a revelation. It would be a noble thing
to spare the great caribou I had hunted so long—the equal, possibly even the superior of the one I had missed, conceivably the
same bull. But I was not a noble man. I had known noble men,
but I was not of their company. The lusts and the longings of
ordinary humanity were so strong in me that most of the time I
could not rise above them. I was not sure that I wished to. I
wanted to live in the valleys and on the hillside, not on the moun-
taintop. I wanted the big horns to attest my victory—even this
present victory, if I could win it. Mauf looked at me, but did not
speak or move. The drag on my arms lasted a few seconds more.

Suddenly they were free. The rifle leaped up. But I did not
hold steady—I shot too fast—and the first bullet struck too far
back. The bull made a great bound—and I had to shoot, it seemed,
for my life. Actually I was not in the slightest physical danger,
but inimical forces gathered thick about me in that split second
as I threw in a second shell—forces of great power. If I missed
this chance, the third of three and the last, now given me after
two failures, I would take great harm. I knew it as well as I
knew the surging flame of my life. Now that I had decided to
take his life, in common human strength, I must not fail through
common human weakness.

There was no time to aim—yet I did aim. As though he were
a canvas duck belting by my blind, I caught him in my sights. I
saw his great horns in front, his gray neck, and his white mane,

and the powerful heaving shoulder. At that point I touched the trigger.

The bull burst through a sapling and crashed down.

"That was a good shot," Mauf said in the big silence.

"Thank'ee," I told him, trying to smile.

"It was worthy of an old-timer."

"I'm way short of an old-timer. I'm a long way from being a big-game hunter. But by the great horned spoon"—for men swear mildly in moments of great emotion—"I'm on my way."

Four

THE Stikine River rises in the Stikine Mountain Range, a great broadening of the Rockies in northern British Columbia, and it flows in a big loop to come out upon the coast of southern Alaska at almost the same latitude where it was born. In more settled lands it would be called a large river, for it flows more than three hundred miles with many a cataract and many a long stillness, but although a great naturalist wrote marvelously about it, my *Encyclopaedia Britannica* did not give it a single paragraph. However, I learned about it from other sources, and toward summer's end I determined to make its lower waters the scene of my next visit to the wild.

There were great numbers of grizzly bears in the forests front-ing these waters—and this is what drew me. There were no ar-rangements for hunters here, but I thought I could make my own. So I took ship to Alaska, up behind Vancouver Island, crossing Queen Charlotte Sound, to come into the Inside Passage. This is perhaps the most beautiful coast in all this world, with its count-less deep-green islands climbing steeply from their own perfect images in the water; deep-cut fiords, inlets, bays, and distant deep-blue, pale-blue, or snow-white mountains.

I disembarked at the town of Wrangell, close to Stikine's mouth. Here was the summer home of the trappers who trapped her lower waters, and I did not think I would have trouble en-listing one of them to take a greenhorn on a canoe trip along his line. I met a rangy, dark young man whom the men around the store at the trading post recommended highly. I will call him Joe, for I have forgotten his name. Had I been a better judge of character—but I would have lost something by it too—I might have looked farther.

"Do you feel pretty certain you can bring me up to a grizzly?" I asked.

"Three or four, I 'spect. Then it will be up to you."

One would be enough, provided I held closely enough when I touched the trigger. Even that would be more glory than I could take lightly. The grizzly's true name is *Ursus horribilis*, the most dangerous of all bears, his only rival in size being the polar bear. This statement would seem to dispute the vast size of the Alaska and Kodiak bear, to which many a hunter could attest. Actually these were grizzlies, too, more uniformly brown, and found in an environment more favorable to growth. Our own West, with which I was strongly bound on my father's side, rang with tales of grizzlies' ferocity and strength. They differed from black bears not only in size and color and length of fore claws. They were not tree climbers. They were not humorous old gentlemen or rather distracted ladies or fussy cubs. They attacked frequently when wounded, and occasionally for the devil of it. And then they were killers and maulers.

But I had not traveled three days with Joe when my hopes took a great fall. As long as we kept to the waterways, Joe was in good command of the situation. We made good progress; our camps were comfortable; the meals satisfied me; and he talked cheerfully, though sometimes windily. But the moment we left the canoe on the river bank—we were traveling up a great tributary of the Stikine and, in turn, its ingressing creeks—we got into, to put it mildly, difficulties. The country was the thickest I had ever seen. No jungle under the tropic sun could hardly be more dense. It was hardly possible to move at all. I could not see thirty feet ahead, and the whole infernal tangle was beset with devil's club, whose long, pulpy leaves bore three-inch thorns— the most devilish plant ever invented by Mother Nature to keep people out of her forbidden grounds.

The bitter truth, which my reading had failed to make clear to me, was that this part of the Stikine Valley was northern rain forest, practically impenetrable by man except by the use of a machete to chop out a path.

How did the trappers manage? Simply, they made no attempt to enter the forest except when the undergrowth was covered by deep snow. They ran their lines along the banks of the rivers, the tributaries, and the creeks. Beavers, otters, and minks, all water-loving, comprised their main catch, but they caught a few marten, fisher, and fox, and once in a while, using what looked like a medieval instrument of torture, they trapped grizzly bear.

But no great chain would hold the trap fixed to a tree. The grizzly would either break it, or tear out his foot, or tear it off. They must let him drag a log called a "toggle" until they could come up on him and shoot him. They were dealing with giants. Some of the men I had seen in Wrangell hardly seemed worthy of the battle.

I wasn't either, by many a count, but at least I held my quarry

in reverence and awe. The fact remained that I was not going to
come up to him—never see his great shaggy form in the open and
close—and soon I would have to go home empty-handed, except
for the greatest stroke of luck or some drastic change of tactics
of the hunt. True, the monsters occasionally came to the water's
edge to find salmon, dead and dying after their rush from the sea.
They would even ramble here awhile, but one bound took them
into the woods, and that was where they usually lay and loafed.
Suppose we happened to spy one in a long bend in the river. If
the wind was blowing in our faces, we might scull up to him in
deadly silence and get a shot. If our scent blew to him he would
be gone at our second or third stroke. I had read that, next to
an elephant, a grizzly bear has the most wonderful nose on earth.

Joe was not greatly disturbed by all this. He was doing the
best he could, as any man could see. He had thought we would
run on some bears, but if we did not, it was the luck of the game.
He was not a regular guide. He had no reputation to lose, although he might have to stand a lot of kidding. As he faced
the prospect manfully, I yearned to attack him bodily. I did
not, and instead put my brain to work on the problem. It had a
capacity for "low cunning"—my sisters had always told me so—
and I needed it now to fill the cup of my soul.

I was well acquainted with the principle of baiting grizzly, to
hold them in one neighborhood, but what could I do for bait?
To enter the locked-tight woods and shoot a deer would be as
impossible as shooting Bruin himself. Well, could I collect
enough salmon? I had seen an old net, with great yapping holes
and tears, in the trapping cabin. Only rotting carcasses remained
in the shallows, but behind us in the creek was a good reach of
deep water, where I thought a few of the fish might be spawned
out but still alive.

Although he had no faith in my plan, Joe agreed to try it.
We stretched the net across the neck of the deep blue stretch,
then, drifting to its lower end, we paddled up through it, splashing

with all our might. To my amazed joy, the net began to swing and dip. Out of it we took about twenty salmon.

These we piled on the bank, just below a peninsula stretching out into the stream, affording a perfect screen for our approach. A bear would certainly smell the bait, I thought; would come in the night, and we would likely find him there just before dark tonight or in the gray of dawn tomorrow.

At sundown the bait lay undisturbed, and we returned to the still and lonely cabin. It was not warmed by human companionship as Dean's and Mauf's had been. I wished I could tell Joe how I felt about my quest for a grizzly bear; and after a while I resolved to try. Almost always I had found more, rather than less, response in my fellow human beings than I had expected, regardless of the personal nature of my talk. I was trying to warm him a little first, by talking with him about half-breed and quarter-breed Indians. He was about to marry a pretty half-breed girl.

"I don't suppose you ever knew Mauf Hamilton?" I asked. It was a foolish question; even in this thinly settled land. Mauf was a Canadian, not an Alaskan, and Quesnel Lake lay some five hundred miles from the Stikine.

"I seen him one time, when I was trappin' out of Fort George," Joe answered, without the least amazement.

"I was with him last year, in the Caribou."

"Well, you won't go with him again. Gallopin' consumption swept through them Indian settlements last winter—my girl was kin to a lot of the people. Mauf's brother died, and so did Mauf."

I sat very still and listened to the ripple of waters, discernible in this deep hush. Mauf, without my going where you are, I wish I could sit with you one more time, our backs to the blaze and a tin-cup inch of rum in our bellies, and talk and laugh over the day's events. They were not events. They were only incidents which our fellowship and avid appetite for life magnified into events. I could tell you how I want the grizzly, but you would know without telling.

Where in the devil have you gone, Mauf? That's the way you expect me to put it, if you are listening. Where go so many of the beautiful and the best?

I take a little drink, and forget about Joe and these surroundings, and remember the peaked-assed bugger. I remember the rice with melted caribou fat poured on it, and I remember the spread-out parks and the white peaks. Didn't you cut a figure, that night you got lost? Then the moon showed up.

Maybe another moon has shown up since. I can't stand the thought of you being ever in the dark, but I can get used to it. Mauf, do you remember the caribou of the tall horns, the objective of our trip, the Silver Fleece of his mane? I shot well that evening; you said so. I resembled the big-game hunter I wanted to be.

Well, if I find the grizzly tomorrow, I'll shoot well again. I'll do it for you. I'll feel you are looking at me. I'll put him in the same room with the caribou, and you will come into that room, and sit down, and grin, and tell me something funny, and I'll be aware again that we are brothers. You a quarter-breed Indian, I a conquering Nordic, God save the mark. But we proved our brotherhood on the trail.

The trophies will be finely mounted. You will be proud of them, and of me.

II

I was awake before dawn, and hurried Joe as much as I could. He had no faith in the undertaking and was inclined to dawdle. "And while we're up there, we'll see if we've caught a beaver." I had suggested that we put out a trap near a beaver house

behind a little dam the preceding day. I had remembered that
the gustatory passion of grizzly bears for beaver was one of the
mysteries of the wild; I had read it, and both Dean and Mauf
had told me so. The grizzly would tear down the beaver's house
—when he could get at it—and even try to catch him swimming in his ponds, making quite a ludicrous show of himself. If
we could catch one, Joe could have the skin and I could put the
thirty pounds of odoriferous meat with my bait of fish.

"Now that's a good idea. A bear might come up to a beaver
carcass."

Also, the price of the skin might line Joe's pocket.

We paddled silently down the creek. We came in sight of the
peninsula, and all was quiet. As we rounded it my gun was ready,
but the only comfort I found was a decided diminishing of the
pile of fish. Some very hungry big-bellied animal had been there
in the night. Nearly half of them were gone.

We went on down to our beaver trap, to find a drowned
beaver. Joe skinned it on the spot, and, after setting the trap
again, we brought the white carcass, looking like that of a fat
shoat, to the remains of our pile of fish. Then we returned to
the cabin for breakfast.

Immediately after breakfast we seined the long pool again,
catching only four or five fish. These were discolored and almost
dead; I was in haste to add them to our bear bait, making it well
worth Bruin's time and attention. As we came nigh, Joe and I
stared in disbelief. The skinned white body of the beaver, which
had crowned the pile of fish, had disappeared.

It had vanished without trace in a matter of half an hour.

There could not be the slightest doubt that the grizzly was
still in the neighborhood, had visited the bait during our brief
absence, had snatched up the prize in his jaws, and vanished in
the forest.

If we had waited in ambush only that little while, instead of
humoring our empty bellies, I would have probably got a shot.

"Didn't I see another beaver house about half a mile above the cabin?"

"Yes?"

"Have you got another trap?"

"I sure have."

"Well, let's get it and set it. Beaver meat is the grizzly's favorite."

"Well, the beaver season isn't officially open—and these Canuck game wardens aren't like our easy-goin' Alaskans—but it will be open, time we get back to Wrangell, and I guess you can keep a closed mouth."

I readily conspired with Joe to break the law again. We set the trap, and when we had paddled back to the cabin, there seemed nothing to do but go in, sit down, read a book I had brought, play solitaire. It was two hours after sunrise. Everyone knew that grizzly bears did not stir about this late; *our bear,* the bear that came and went like a shadow, had retired into a thicket guarded by devil's club to eat and digest his enormous meal. Certainly he would not reappear until twilight, probably not until after dark. Well, I would try to get Joe to fix it so I could sit for him. Maybe he could build me a little blind, downwind from the thickets into which the big three-cornered tracks had disappeared.

I was not content with that. I wanted to go back now. I wanted to see if maybe the grizzly had still an empty corner in his gorge—that he still yearned for the high-smelling fish— maybe that he wished to make sure that some other grizzly had not wandered along and was stealing from his store. But how could I tell that to Joe? Even since I was a child, I had harbored a great and secret fear of being laughed at. Well, I was afraid of grizzlies too. They had worked upon my childhood mind— perhaps that was why I hunted them. I rallied my nerve as though for a hard shot.

"I want to go back to the bait for another look."

"There's not the least use."

"I want to go, just the same."

"I ought to be making some skin-stretchers."

"I don't give a damn about what you ought to be doing, when I tell you to go somewhere."

"All right, all right. The most we'll do is disturb him so he won't come back at all."

So we got in the boat and paddled downstream. There was a sharp curve just before we came to the grassy peninsula, and it broke upon my vision, its extremity first, a little at a time, and all was quiet, and it seemed my cake was dough. Then as the view opened farther I saw what looked like a black bow-shaped something, about six feet long, over the grass. I glanced at Joe, and he had turned white.

He dipped his paddle long and clean and still. The boat shot on and rounded the point of the peninsula. And there, standing in my pile of fish, was a grizzly bear.

Could I mistake him from any other kind? I saw his high shoulders, his great shaggy form, his square, broad head. He turned to look at me, not yet frightened, ominous instead. At that instant I fired.

He leaped into the water, but did not try to flee. Not he, this lord of the deep-green wood, this lone baron of the wilderness. The first grizzly I had ever seen gave me my first full charge. He came rushing through the shallow water, with a great rumbling roar of pain and rage. The high-splashing water accented the ferocious scene, and gave him a gigantic aspect.

I shot again, and missed. The distance was hardly sixty feet when the action began; by the time I had thrown in another shell it had shortened to thirty. The bear was right there. He was truly one of the most formidable animals in the world. He was belligerent in the extreme. If he could reach us he would break our boat in two, claw and drown us both, or perhaps crush our skulls. The instant was one of extreme danger.

Indeed it was hardly more than an instant, the time I had left in which to stop the charge. It came, it was passing, and in an instant more it would be gone. I think it was my shame at missing my second shot that gave me that little added thrust of willpower that enabled me to hold steady on my third. I leveled on his great mass and pulled the trigger.

He fell into the water, and was instantly up again, raving and bawling, but now his feet would not work right. He circled and thrashed in the shallows. Once more his eyes fixed on us. He made a brave and knightly effort to resume his charge. Then he rolled over backward, groaned a little while, batted the air twice with his front paws, dropped his head, and died.

III

My grizzly was a mature male, weighing fully six hundred pounds. When we had pulled him up on the bank and rolled him into the canoe his body filled the front half of it. With his head on the bow, and his great front paws hanging over the sides, he made a picture that was subsequently published in *The New York Times*. In due course, with his teeth gleaming and his lips in a snarl, his mounted head and skin made an impressive, luxurious rug.

But Christmas had hardly come, that year, before I began dreaming of the bears to the westward. The main stretch of Alaska is east and west. Technically speaking, Alaska begins on the 130th parallel west of Greenwich, and ends brushing the 180th parallel, roughly three thousand miles. Attu is a lot farther west of Wrangell (the Alaskan town, not the Siberian Island) than Medford, Oregon, where I spent my later boyhood, is west of Boston. As a matter of fact, Attu, Alaska, lies more than a thousand miles west of Honolulu.

Bears were found only a hundred or so miles northwest of

Wrangell, on Baranof and Admiralty islands. These too were of the grizzly clan, but differentiated by being called Alaskan brown bears, and they ran a full size larger than regular grizzlies, and were fully as belligerent. Many naturalists believed that these particular island bears were the most aggressive bears in the world, with the possible exception of the chevron-marked Himalayan bear. They lived in very thick woods; they killed deer as well as caught fish; and their nerves stayed on edge. In the few cases in Alaska where bears had mauled or killed people, sometimes in unprovoked attacks, the rogues were these woods-dwelling Alaskan browns.

But I wanted to hunt under different conditions from before, and by going farther west I could find them. Across the Gulf of Alaska lay Kodiak Island and what was known as the Alaskan Peninsula, stretching southwestward from Kamishak Bay to Unimak Island, about five hundred miles. I knew that this whole territory was open, windswept barrens—mountains and tundra and muskeg—and everywhere through it roamed the famed Kodiak bear. Named for the island where he was first identified, he was the largest bear in all the world, the big bears sometimes obtaining a weight of fifteen hundred pounds.

How could I stop at Baranof Island when, with a few more days of rough sea travel, I could gain the shores of Cold Bay, up under volcanic Mount Pavlof, and get me—who knew?—a full-sized Kodiak bear?

I was a little short of money that year, so I did not write to outfitters around False Pass, who took out sports at twice the cost of my British Columbia hunts. This awkward fact I did not explain to the friendly manager of Pacific American Fisheries, who helped many rich hunters arrange their hunts. Instead I thought to make for Seward on an Alaskan liner, catch the mailboat plying westward, and in one of the little settlements find and hire a trapper who would take me into the wild. The mailboat was named the *Star,* and she was not very big, and the cabins surrounded the mess hall, and the seas were notoriously and villainously rough. For the third time in my life I knew the prolonged agony, just short of torture, of extreme seasickness.

But her hands took a lively interest in my venture, and one of them knew a couple of Swedes, living at Sand Point, who had a gas boat and would not be fishing at this time of year, and who might be hired to take me into Cold Bay. True, they knew nothing about hunting as far as he knew. But they were reliable sourdoughs, who would not drown or desert me readily as would some "Siwashes"—a generic term of contempt applied to half-breed Indians—found along this coast. When I met the two men I was of the same opinion. Neither was a Swede; one was Dane, the other Norwegian, and they swore "by yiminy" and "by Yesus," and both were husky fellows, in the prime of life. I will have to call them Tom and Jerry as on the trip, for I never knew their last names and their first names were something like Ludvig and Wolfgang.

I could tell the worst of that trip in one paragraph, but it would take me many pages—which I will not attempt—to tell all of the best. As the spring tide began to recede, their boat stuck on a sandbar near the mouth of Cold Bay. This meant we could not enter its deep cut to draw near the interior of the country; and many miles of tundra and muskeg separated us from the high mountains where, at this time of year, we could profitably look for bears. We were waterbound except for an hour or two at high tide; and we could not reach the mainland at all except in the boat's skiff, which would hold only two people and no supplies. We stuck there two weeks, the total time my schedule permitted for hunting. Once, after a forced march to the nearest highlands, Jerry and I saw a small moving dot that my binoculars revealed as a Kodiak bear, trampling up a mountainside, his big feet throwing snow like a young avalanche in a reverse direction, but as unreachable as though on the face of the moon.

But when I turned homeward, with empty hands and bag and with a good deal of emptiness in my heart, I found that I knew two men quite well. Indeed, I knew them better than my friends and professional associates, better than any other men outside of my immediate family. It struck me that most of us go through life knowing almost no one. Dean and I, and Mauf and I, had hunted together. Most of our energies were expended in knowing the joys of the sport and the delight of the countryside; and so each pair of us had come through fast friends. In the case of Tom and Jerry, we had nothing to do but eat, sleep, and become acquainted. This last we must do in order to pass the time, so we had talked with a frankness I had never given nor received from any man. They had seemed ordinary fellows, and I suppose they were; but if so, every man on earth is extraordinary. At least he is positively unique. I had picked up a little snobbery around the University Club—not from our better members but from our worse—but I got shed of it quickly, marooned on a sandbar in Cold Bay.

As for Kodiak bears, there was nothing to do but wait for another year.

I V

Meanwhile my writing prospered well; and early in the spring I wrote to the manager of Pacific American Fisheries, who had canneries out to the westward, asking him to put me in touch with an outfitter somewhere near False Pass. He recommended a Norwegian named Vic.

This time the trip was bang-up. In May I sailed from South Bellingham in a comfortable cannery tender, the *Catherine D*, under Captain Knight, a blue-eyed skipper as Boston as Boston can be. Vic was waiting for me at False Pass, with another Norwegian, hired to carry packs, cook, and keep camp. The latter was tall and thin, with a melancholy mien and mustache, and I thought he was too frail for the heavy work; but he could manage his squaw, Vic said, and that took a lot of man. We sailed through the Pass into Bering Sea in a powerful dory and, hoping for favorable winds and tides, turned back eastward. After many hours we ran into a creek mouth and beached the boat. We were now in Izenback Bay, across the peninsula from Cold Bay, and on the north instead of the south side of Mount Pavlof.

We could not pitch our camp at the creek mouth—we were too far from the hunting ground. So in spite of the cold drizzle of rain we must start up the valley at once, our supplies being too short to let us linger. Anyway, at this time of year, Vic said, there were only two kinds of weather on the shores of Bering Sea. One was moderately cold, windy, and rainy, the other awful cold, windy, and dry. Our march was at first over muskeg that lay close to the sea. It was an immense grassy swamp, the water sometimes knee-deep, except where it lay in channels that looped and divided and redivided in a labyrinth of waters. You could not put down your pack and rest your back till you gained the tundra.

According to the dictionary, tundra means "a rolling, marshy, mossy plain in Northern Siberia." On the whole this is a good definition, but in this case the tundra had jumped Bering Sea and lay in western Alaska. I can tell you about the footing. It was an endless series of mossy mounds, on which the foot fell at a different angle at every step. I became footsore and desperately cold and weary. And the sky was gray, and the land gray everywhere except far ahead, where I could see snow on mountainsides.

I felt about the country in a peculiar way. I had thought I had never seen a country so desolate, even Death Valley in California—for tall cacti grew there, and the weather was warm. This was a cold desert with plenty of water flowing. Not one tree rose in three hundred miles; the only woody growth was alder thickets, not yet in leaf. The wind blew all day and all night, all winter and all summer, and most of the time it was raining. When the rain ceased, usually the fog came down. Here the warm Japanese Current met the icy waters of Bering Sea and the result was perpetual foul weather. Here the natives lived in little malodorous mounds of whales' bones and moss called *barabaras,* and they too seemed oppressed by their dark abodes; and the country seemed dead, with only a few ptarmigan flying back and forth across the tundra crying a mournful cry, some foxes that ever preyed on them, wolverines that, being fiendish, had found a suitable environment, and many salmon that rushed up the rivers to die.

Yet there came to me the powerful inkling that although I could not see them, this bleak and eerie land, forsaken by all the gods except some of terrible aspect, was the true home of the Kodiak bears of which I had dreamed before I knew I was dreaming. I would find them here, I thought, and find adventure of great scope, and some hard-to-capture truth.

We came to a possible campsite at four in the afternoon. All we had to put in it was the men's tarpaulin and bedroll, my sleeping bag, and our kits; and the cook—his real name was Ole —would lay out these things, and build the fire. Meanwhile five hours remained of daylight in these latitudes this time of year, so Vic and I headed up the valley. I had asked him to leave his gun in camp. Although he did not like the idea very well he agreed.

Some years later a glacier priest was going to explore this valley and write about it to many people's delight. But he had not got here yet, nor had any *cheechako*—which word roughly corresponds to tenderfoot and means, literally, a newcomer. As far as I could learn, no sportsman from outside had ever preceded me up this big, fast-flowing creek into this savage valley. I began to see sights that only a few trappers and Indians and other inhabitants of this haunted land had ever laid eyes on, and this not once in seven years.

As the valley ascended, the hills on each side became more steep. The rain had stopped; but a thin fog came in from the sea and flung dim eerie clouds and whirling skeins and streamers over the land. Sometimes these cleared away, exposing distant views, and sometimes they thickened, and we could not see our way for a hundred steps. But once I caught a glimpse of glittering peaks far in advance, and then, on the hillside close to us, in a break in an alder thicket, Vic saw a bear.

"Is he a big one?"

"He vas plenty big."

We began climbing the hill, flanking the alder brush. This was too thick to enter, and we would have been blinded; but it had many openings into which the bear might flush. My nerves were on edge lest I fail to get a shot at him, or shoot and miss, and Vic's fear was that I would shoot and hit, but not hard and straight enough. Then the fog settled in heavier than before, or else it was a light thing, and we had climbed up into it.

"We might as vell go back," Vic said.

"I think it's clearing a little now."

"I t'ink it goin' to get vorse."

But it did clear a little, and I looked up and I saw something dark and huge in an opening in the alders. Before I knew what I was doing, I fired at it. At once he gave a great bawl and plunged into the thickets.

"Did I hit him?"

"You vounded him, and I don't know vat happen now."

And I do not know what happened, even now. In general, there followed a running fight in the foggy thickets. The big bear sallied forth from his unseen retreats again and again. Sometimes he was obviously seeking escape, sometimes he seemed coming up to fight, but every time either a bullet's shock and pain or the roar of my piece caused him to turn aside. The wan clouds blew in, and amid their dimness I felt their bitter chill; then a sharp gust of wind would send them flying. Vic and I ran up and down the sides of the thicket, sometimes following broad avenues into its depths; and Vic led the running now, for he was much less afraid than I, and his blood was up.

Once the bear burst out of heavy growth almost on top of us. He was not thirty feet distant. He showed prodigious in the dim light; and perhaps this was partly an optical illusion, but certainly he was by far the largest and most fearsome beast I had ever seen outside of a zoo. He was red-colored, burly, and shaggy, his head was like a ten-gallon keg. It did not seem possible I could knock him down in time to save our lives; and I did not, but the bullet gave him another wound, and he turned a little sideways and ran off, bawling.

After that his bawling became continuous. It was a deep, rumbling, resonant roar, that seemed to shake the rocks. Some was rage, and some was pain, and my heart felt pity for him even as it craved his conquest, with an ever wilder craving. Once the fog blew in bank after bank, and a bush forty feet away turned to a dim smear. The great bear could have escaped us now, had he left the field and climbed the hill. We could not tell where he was by his great roars—sometimes he sounded just at hand, and sometimes far away. It was a strange thing to be standing there, blind, while the great Kodiak stampeded back and forth, roaring, through the thickets.

Suddenly the sound ceased. I stood, greatly frightened, my gun ready, straining into the silence. All I could hear was the drip of water from the alder branches. I glanced quickly into Vic's weathered face. It looked pale, and certainly deeply strained.

"What do you think?" I murmured.

"I t'ink he's dead—or sneakin' off—or sneakin' up on us."

I stayed on extreme alert for a long minute more. Then the fog bank began to break up, to whirl and whisk away, and suddenly the air was clear.

"Ve can look for him now," Vic said briefly.

"Where did the sound come from, just before it stopped?"

"In t'e middle of t'e patch. But I've got to walk ahead, if I'm going to find him. Can I carry your gun?"

I hated to be unarmed for a single second, but the proposal was eminently fair, and I could not refuse. I passed him the weapon and he led the way with a resolute step. It seemed to me that we searched for nearly half an hour, every minute dragging longer and longer. I thought Vic wanted to give up. I waited in dread for his decision—"I guess old Brownie get only flesh vounds, and took off up t'e country"—something like that. I had only scratched the giant with a couple of shots, had missed all the rest, and he was gone. My only chance had gone with it; and no matter where I looked, I would never see such a bear again.

Then Vic gave a great shout. He began to run—and burly men like him usually cut a comic figure when they run. He made for a big dark spot in a nearby thicket. We forced our way into it, and there he lay—this monster of the wasteland, the Kodiak bear.

His skin would be far from a record, but of impressive size— Vic guessed it at ten feet. His great claws were ivory-colored in very striking contrast with his deep-red skin. His fur was long and thick. He was a trophy not to be despised.

V

Before leaving "outside," as Alaskans called the American mainland, I had promised Mr. McIntyre, my publisher, a memento of my trip in honor of his forthcoming marriage. Sitting long and alone by the fire, I thought what pleasure it would give me—and almost certainly him—if I presented him with my bearskin with ivory claws. I could and would do so, if, in my stay here, I could get a better or an equally good skin.

My license permitted me to take three bears. Judging by our

having shot a fine specimen in the first two hours on the grounds and by the number of tracks we had seen, it was perfectly possible. It seemed to me that Vic had brought me to the finest bear grounds I had ever imagined. I decided to put it up to him.

"Vic, with a fair amount of luck can I get another bear?" I asked.

"Maybe so, but if you do, I vant to get him in broad daylight and clear vet'er."

The particular fame of the Kodiak bear lies in his size.

"I want a great big bear. I'd like to try for a record."

Vic explained that the very large males were apt to be found close to the snow. This was June; they had only lately left their dens, and apparently the very large boars were later sleepers than the middle-sized boars and sows. Tomorrow he and Ole would get my skin and salt it down. The next day we would see.

The day broke gray and dismal, but the moderate wind did not shriek in my ears, and I felt the premonition of a great experience. After all, how could I miss it? Vic and I meant to penetrate the secret heart of this wild and eerie land, which he had never seen and whose existence no cheechako like me had ever dreamed. We were going up almost into the shadow of mysterious Mount Pavlof. It was a wild and fantastic region inhabited by giants. And if I could return with the hide of one of them— not one of their common run of giants, but of a super-giant, such as had won fame for the species all over the world—if I could find such a one, and shoot straight, and kill cleanly, and bring back his head and hide with its great claws and stretch it out by my tame home fire. . . .

The day began with a succession of wonders that did not cease until its close. We had not gone half a mile, walking up the creek bank, before we saw a mother bear with two cubs. They were ambling down the valley in our direction, but because the wind blew off the mountains and toward the sea, they had not noticed us yet. The mother idled along, stopping now and then to dig in the dirt—looking for squirrels, Vic thought —and the cubs romped and played. When she had drawn within two hundred yards, I thought it was quite near enough. I knew the reputation of grizzly-bear mothers with cubs, and I was eager to give her a gentle fright. Vic was enjoying her unsuspecting approach.

When she came within a hundred paces she stopped and threw up her muzzle. No doubt an eddy in the air had borne to her the dreadful taint, for the change that came over her was remarkable to see. She bounded forward—as light as a deer, it seemed—and cuffed both cubs on the head with what looked like a one-two. At once they got in front of her—where they were taught to get—and the three started for the hillside as fast as they could run. What did they fear, when in all probability not one of the three had ever seen or smelled a man before?

A little while later we saw a male fully as big as the one I had shot, across the valley ahead of us.

"I wonder if I ought to go after him," I said. "That would make one for me, one for my publisher."

"If you shot him, the shot would echo all through the valley, and we couldn't get t'at big one you said you vanted."

So we kept on. And now, a mile ahead of us, I began to see what looked like a wall of ice, with white spires on top, at the head of the valley. My glasses revealed the whole mass as a great cluster of icy pinnacles, climbing perhaps a thousand feet into the heavens. The mountains shutting in the valley began to look sheer. Yet on one of the sharpest steeps we saw what my glasses told me was a giant bear plodding upward through the drifts.

Small white streams began to hurtle down from the heights, often with bridges of last winter's snow. The whole land took on an eerie and fantastic aspect. I had the illusion of wandering in a dream. I imagined that some scene resembling this in the mountains of northern Norway, a scene of austere cliffs, of bounding streams, of glittering ice, of wailing winds, of giants climbing through the snow fields, and of desolation everywhere, had inspired Grieg to write *Peer Gynt*.

I rejoiced I had come to western Alaska, and would still rejoice—so I swore by what served me for saints—even if my dream of the great trophy did not come true.

We saw more bears in the snow. We passed within two hundred yards of a bear a good deal larger, we thought, than the one I had taken before. He was busy digging, and our scent was blown downstream; although we walked on open ground, he did not notice us. A few minutes later, Vic touched my arm.

"There's a monster, asleep in t'e snow," he murmured.

"Where?"

He pointed. A bank lay close by one of the little leaping mountain brooks that joined the creek, and on top of it, cooling off, new from his den and getting ready to shed his winter growth of fur, lay a tremendous bear.

"Come wit' me," Vic said resolutely.

Swiftly but silently he led me toward our unsuspecting quarry. We gained the edge of a break in the rock.

"Now sneak forward, on all fours, to t'at big boulder, and don't make no noise," he ordered. "When t'e time come, take a good aim."

I did as I was told. In spite of my leaping heart, I did not cause one stone to knock against another. Time loitered, but it moved at last, and I found myself at the boulder. I was within forty yards of the giant. I could hardly believe in him, he was so big. He dwarfed the great bear I had shot two days before.

He was still sound asleep and snoring. Was it like murder, or was it in any way ignoble, for me to lie down on the ground, thrust forward my rifle, and take deadly aim? I did not try to answer the question then; time and circumstance pressed too hard—whatever the guilt was, I took it on my head. When I was ready, I carefully pressed the trigger.

One of the great forearms moved a little; otherwise the giant lay still.

There was no way to determine whether or not his skin broke the record for Kodiak bears, because the skins listed as larger might have been stretched. This much I knew. It was the largest Kodiak bearskin I have ever seen—before that time, and since. Laid out on the ground, it was twelve feet from tip to tip. The rear paw measured exactly eighteen inches from heel end to the tip of the short claws.

Undoubtedly he was a very old bear. Some of his teeth were missing, and the hair had worn off his rump from sliding down mountainsides; and since he was in heavy winter pelage, he must have been bald in those parts for many years. Kodiak bears were said to live to be twenty-five. I thought it very likely this colossal bear might be fifty. He had lived greatly in his day, roaming the huge sharp mountains of his native land, often climbing Mount Pavlof, digging for ground squirrels, in season going down to the muskeg and following the salmon streams, gorging to his heart's content. He had fought with rival boars for the favor of sows. He had seen fiery sunsets, the drifting mists, and heard the strange wild music of the winds; and when the salmon died in the shallows and the dreadful winter began to close down, he had climbed and climbed to some den he knew, where he sank into gargantuan sleep.

He had not felt quite awake when he had left his den this spring, and had lain down on a snowbank. Through no mercy of mine, but rather through my covetousness, he had died in his sleep. Perhaps, though, the gods that understand, the nature gods—of man's nature among the rest—knew no wrath.

2. The Whispering Veld

Five

IN the next few years I did not go hunting for big game. Agnes and I were having babies; our social duties were growing; my career as a writer expanded and money and time had to be watched and conserved. But as I passed through my early thirties I felt a growing restlessness, a deepening revolt against minding my business in this staid way, almost a sense of neglect of a debt owed not to myself perhaps, rather to life itself, on the terms it had been given to me and I had received it. To be too thrifty and sensible was not a good or even a wise thing; it might be a stingy thing.

I got out my rifles and groomed them. I read with black envy the reports of big-game hunters from fields I had never seen. I looked at my great bearskins and high-antlered heads and recalled the seconds of their taking, and they counted more than weeks and months and years of common living. Our house was bigger now, and so was our bank account; there was room in one for more trophies, and the other could stand a sharp reduction in need as great as this.

"If you feel you have to go," said Agnes, "go."

"For four months?" I asked, stammering and turning color.

"Us'll git along." This was in perfect imitation of a rich, warm vernacular she had heard all her days, for she was a Georgia girl.

"Agnes, if I'm going to make these trips at all, I should try to take them when I'm young. They won't hit me nearly as hard when I get old."

"You needn't make any excuses, Edison. I knew it was coming."

The trip out and home to either of the great hunting grounds that I had never seen and had only visioned, took four months. One was the African veld; the other was the Asiatic jungles. Lindbergh had made his epochal flight, but as yet there were no oceanic passenger planes; anyway I would love the long voyage, occupying about two months in all, with two months in the field. Which should I take first?

Deposited in our family archives was my first composition, written at the age of six, which I still think was a succinct piece, full of sharp description and showing a lively sense of dramatic values. It read:

"Lions is bad. Lions is feerse. Lions ete folks."

Africa teemed with lions; they lived in the rocky *kopjes* and hunted in the yellow grass. There were none in Asia except a few on the western deserts. In Asia there were other beasts, not in such vast variety, but with a greatness and a glory of their own—a fact that had dawned on me quite a few years after my first infatuation with lions. So it was not from haste to see, meet, pursue, perhaps slay a lion that caused me to lean toward Africa as the earlier goal of the two. Rather it was a feeling that a tenderfoot hunter, with only a few calluses gained in the forests and the tundras of the North, would do better on that continent. In and about Nairobi lived several "white hunters," whose business was to outfit and escort visiting sportsmen; some of them were organized into a corporation with an imposing name. In southeastern Asia at that time I could not locate a single professional guide.

I did not approach any of the English white hunters. I had been snubbed by some Englishmen I had met in Canada—always my own fault for speaking to them without being introduced—and while I had defended myself as stoutly as possible, I had not liked the experience. I did not want tea in the afternoon or a cold shower before dinner. And having heard of an American from Oklahoma and Texas named Charles Cottar, for whom one hot bath weekly did very well—something of an ivory poacher in the old days, who now guided greenhorns on the wonderful East African highlands for considerably less than the sum charged by the elegant Englishmen—I cabled him and set a date.

In due course I packed my dinner coat—because safari in Africa as well as *shikar* in India often have their social side—and my duffel bag. I put my guns in their cases, wondering for the first time if they would do. One was a .30 U.S., a good positive arm for bucks less than eland, bongo, and greater kudu, and a young English nobleman's favorite piece for lions until, after many clean kills, he fatally wounded a lion that killed him. The other was a 9.5 Mannlicher that I had won on a bet, and shot only a few times at paper targets. I found myself disliking this rifle with great heartiness, although I did not know why.

The date appointed came at hand, and I stepped down from

a railway carriage in Nairobi, the very English capital of Kenya. My first feeling was one of profound dismay. Coming to meet me was an old man with a feeble step. Yes, he was Charles Cottar. He had been down, he said, from a bout with blackwater fever, complicated by a leopard's getting on him, but he was all right now. How could this cripple lead me over the veld, through the grass, and amid the thorn, after big game?

Yet I soon began to notice the old hunter's eyes as he spoke, the light in them and the life and change, and they were not the eyes of a dotard. And there were other signs I could not yet isolate, and then a big plain sign, when he began to curse some hotel porters who had picked up my baggage without permission. His voice had a ring to it. Also it had a Western accent still.

All the next day, as we assembled the outfit for our trip, he walked and talked with increasing vigor. Actually he was well short of sixty, although in town he seemed much older, and only when he got shed of it did his years peel off, and these were beginning to give way at the mere prospect of return to the veld. That was his stamping ground. He had traded for it his old hunting grounds in Texas and Oklahoma, when these were far from tame, and he had lived by it, and fought it, and loved and hated it for more than twenty years. He was tall, big-framed, and once a phenomenally powerful man. His hands were still wolf-quick when they had to be, as I noticed when he drove the lorry to pick up some supplies. My recommendation to him was that I was an American, for he had never forgotten, never ignored, that he was one too. And this meant more to him than I could quite understand at first. It was the keynote of his being, an obligation and a great pride.

He had piercing eyes, narrow set, indescribably blue. Still I did not know then that he was the heir of Jim Bridger and Kit Carson, the very last of that great breed of hunters developed in the American West. A true Mountain Man born after his proper time, and strangely walking the plains of Africa. The knowledge would come to me in due course.

The outfit contained no tea tables or portable shower baths. But it was adequate and carefully assembled, with no vital parts left out. And I liked the look of our corps of "boys." There were not more than twelve—skinners, scouts, camp tenders— whom I would pay a shilling a day each; and an upstanding W'Kamba—or so I remember his tribal name—to be my gun-bearer, who would get two shillings. The latter's name was K'nini. I meant to learn all the others before many days.

My last act before we set forth was to go to the game office and buy a license. Cottar had no patience with governments' charging for a man's God-given right to hunt, but had to stand for it, and I had to put out quite a large sum of money. In fact the fee was so high that I did not buy the extra license for ele-phant, which cost fifty pounds. If I could get lions, buffaloes, leopards, and a rhinoceros, not to mention some of a long list of splendid bucks, all of which were lawful quarry for me, I believed that I would have the most thrilling big-game hunt that I could dream.

II

When one enters upon the lean and sunburned veld a little way back from the houses, he walks straight into the Age of Mammals. You do not see people; you see wild beasts. You do not pass from city to city, from town to town, with service stations and farms strewn between; you move from one wild scarp to another, from one great grassy plain to the next, from wastes of thornbush to the low flat-topped mimosa forest, across the dark-green brush-grown dongas on and on into the Beyond that old Afrikanders call the Blue. There is no experience like it this side of a hunter's dream. Truly it is a hunter's dream come true.

I had read enough animal books and looked at enough pictures to be able, right from the start, to identify a good many of the animals. Herds of zebra grazed or loafed in all directions. No one could mistake a gnu—the wildebeest as he is popularly known in Africa—with his bisonlike fore and horselike rear; these were seen in great numbers in the mimosa groves, and they were given to short stampedes, bucking and running in circles. I spotted the two common hartebeests, topi and kongoni, they were called—the former compact, easy-moving, self-confident-looking antelopes, curiously suggestive of overgrown goats; and the latter long-snouted, taking awkward-looking stances, silly beasts you think until you find them more wary than most of their companions. I knew Thomson's gazelle from his small size, grace, charm, and constantly whirling tail. No hunter was so green as to mistake 'mpalla, because no other African bucks moved with such long and soaring bounds, defying gravity it seemed. They were besides wonderfully beautiful, with their rich brown coats, bent-back horns, and graceful shapes. An ugly figure in the grass, with high forequarters and low rear, and a scuttling motion, was a spotted hyena. There were plenty of these, and plenty of vultures in the sky, because these sunlit plains are ever the stalking ground of death.

Before long we saw a herd of giraffe. They galloped effortlessly beside the lorry for about a hundred yards, then turned off to go about their innocent affairs. It was no skin off my back that they were now protected by law; indeed it was a comfort. I hated to think of one of the beasts falling from his great height by a hunter's bullet. He outtowered the tallest elephant, the very king of Africa, and remained unaware of man's deadly nature, trusting us to approach him within a hundred paces in the wide open.

Away somewhere in the grass or the hills or the scrub, beyond our sight now, but surely to hove into it before long, were eland big as oxen, but dashing as moose in America; heavy roan antelope would cross our path. On deserts not far distant dwelt oryx with rapier horns. And it was not unthinkable to find bongo, which many hunters counted a better trophy than water buffalo, although I could not agree; and we might see stately kudu and even the magnificent, elegant, and most beautiful sable antelope.

All these and many more inhabited the Blue into which we headed. And even now we could begin to watch for Africa's great game, the animals that had fired the imaginations of men since the days of the pharaohs. A leopard might steal out of the grass, beside the road. A herd of buffaloes, their horns laid back, their muzzles thrusting, could cross the middle distance. Not long ago, just about here, a berserk rhino had attacked a Ford car, killing both its riders. A tawny glimpse in the thicket might be a lion.

We encountered none of these mighty beasts on the first hundred miles of our journey. But late in the afternoon of the second day, a black tracker riding in our lorry suddenly cried out in high excitement.

"*Tembu! Tembu!*"

Cottar threw on his brakes and spoke in Swahili. My gaze followed the lean black finger, but at first could see nothing but a patch of thorn trees about a quarter of a mile distant. Then, as I stared, a dark shadow turned into a black form that moved. When I had leveled my glasses, I made out short white tusks, an upraised trunk, and big extended ears.

"It's a young bull, all alone," Cottar said after a long look. "I wonder what he's up to, so far from his pals. It's not a sight you'll see every day, and I believe he'll bring us luck."

Two hours later we had the luck to camp on the veld, beside a brush-grown donga hiding a silver trickle of water, so apart and lost from Nairobi that it seemed we must have dreamed it in the first place. The light of the two blazing campfires seemed to burnish the skins of the black men as they emerged from the shadow, and the carcass of a tommy ram was slung from a mimosa limb. I had walked a little ways with Cottar, and had shot the little buck—an easy shot at fifty yards—with my .30 U.S. Cottar himself was a different man, walking lightly and easily, ten years younger than in town, keen-gazing, and with something magnificent about him that I could not yet define.

The night came down and the stars came out, and Africa began to talk to us in her strange and thrilling language. I did not know it yet, but Cottar told me that a chattering out in the dark rose from a pack of jackals. A whimpering cry like a babe's was made by a fox; a long and eerie howl was the overture, he said, to the chorus of the hyenas. These cries became more frequent, and they took different forms, and reached us from all sides, as though the camp were surrounded. Sometimes a long quavering wail broke into a noise like maniacal laughter. Often the ugly invisible brutes merged their cries in a kind of song, the effect of which was at once eerie and strangely sad.

Suddenly, at its height, it was cut off. I saw old Cottar raise his gray head, listening with an intensity of concentration; and an expression both fierce and poetic came into his face.

"Do you hear that?" he asked, low-toned.

"I hear nothing." Indeed the silence lay as deep as in the North Woods under snow.

"Listen closely."

I did, and far away I heard a low grunting sound, repeated at exact intervals.

"That's an old male lion, going out to kill," Cottar told me. "The lion is not the king of beasts—the elephant is—still, lions are a class by themselves. It's no wonder to me that kings and conquerors have associated themselves with them, and they appear in palaces and temples old as the Great Sphynx. One of the greatest of the pharaohs saw fit to record on his monument: 'I hunted the lion.' "

Cottar raised his big, sensitive hand to shield his eyes from the firelight.

"I have hunted the lion. It's one of the few things in my life that I feel I would like to write down. You'll hunt them too before the moon comes back. You'll know what it is to look into those fierce eyes under that big mane. Don't think he may not kill you, because he may. It doesn't happen often, but often enough for him to live up to his fame. He's a wonderful fellow to be sharing the planet with us. He's the real stuff."

He paused a moment, then he said a word in some foreign language. He said it mainly to himself, and it had deep meaning for him that he could not tell me, and which I must find out for myself.

"*Simba*." It was only the Swahili word for lion.

III

Ranging out from this camp, Cottar and I hunted through the early morning hours, rested and loafed at midday, and took off again in late afternoon. Our custom was to ride in the light lorry across the grass, dodging the thorn thickets and the mimosa groves, until we came on likely-looking ground, then search out the ground on foot. Actually we were almost never out of sight of game. From the watchtower of any mound or anthill we could see from ten to a thousand head. About half were zebras, the standard fare of lions; the rest were almost always topi, kongoni, tommy, wildebeest, and 'mpalla. I would take one of the latter, I thought, because of the beauty of his hide and the shapeliness of his head and horns. But that was also a good reason for not taking one, when the ease of it denied his rank as a trophy. It took no moral strength, or even a sporting attitude, for me to resolve to spare these others, except as we needed meat.

But there were also bucks nearby that we could not see so

plainly. That was why Cottar never walked boldly, in the open; he stalked along on the flanks of the thorn or in the shadow of the dongas, never in a hurry, his fierce eyes darting in all directions. Near the close of our first day's hunting we came suddenly on a very large bay-colored antelope, with a fine sweep of pointed horns and a stiff brown mane. Loafing in the late sunlight, he was a wonderfully vivid beast, and my heart leaped, and I knew that here was big game.

"It's a roan," Cottar told me, in the merest undertone. "Take him!"

Roaming alone, apart from his vigilant cows, he had not seen us yet, or at least had not identified us as enemies. He was walking slowly, his head lowered, not more than sixty yards away. As the Mannlicher jumped to my shoulder, he raised his head, his ears shot forward, and his eyes fixed on us in a startled gaze. I still had plenty of time. I would not shoot too quickly and miss. I aimed almost at the point of the shoulder and pressed my trigger.

He gave a great bound that I could hardly doubt was his last bound, the convulsive leap of death. But instead of falling in a heap, he landed with his legs under him and flying, and straightway he broke into a darting run like a thoroughbred horse. His wits were about him, too, for he aimed for a break in the thicket, and he gained it before I could work my bolt. Instantly there was no sound or sight of him anywhere. Except for my shame and old Cottar's embarrassment, it was as though we had met no roan.

"That was a bad miss," I said.

"Yes, but hunters are likely to miss bad their first few days in Africa. I don't know why, unless the intense light makes them misjudge distance."

"That wasn't the fault in this case. He was within a stone's throw, and I couldn't have misjudged the distance more than a few yards. You may not believe me, but I think it's this plagued gun. I don't mean there's anything wrong with it. It just doesn't fit me."

"Let me shoot it."

He fixed a cigarette paper on the trunk of a tree. Walking off a hundred yards, he took the gun, swung it lightly on his shoulder, and fired, all in one continuous, smooth motion. I had seen animals move as gracefully, but only one human in my immediate remembrance, and he was Chandler Egan, a former amateur golf champion, when he had walked up to, swung at, and lambasted the ball. The paper fluttered down. We walked back and retrieved it, to find it with a neat hole bored through the center.

"I told you there was nothing wrong with the gun," I said, trying to excuse my excuse.

"But there is. It's got the wickedest kick I ever felt. It isn't a big honest wallop like I get from my .470 double. It's a jar that rattles the bones of your head. There's the trouble," he went on, looking at a cartridge. "The bullet's too heavy for the charge of powder. From now on, use my .405 Winchester for big game. It's a lever-action piece, which can't stand the charges of a bolt-action or a double-barrel express; still it deals a hard blow."

I felt much better; and at the next try did wonderfully better —in fact the whole immeasurable distance between positive success and utter failure. About three days had passed, with no trophies on the drying rack but the skin of a cock ostrich that I had shot with the U.S. .30. Moreover, I had more guilty feelings over this kill than almost any I had ever made, without in the least knowing why. There is nothing sacred about an ostrich. He is a brawler of the worst kind, always fighting and squawking, and a vicious kicker. Still, on account of his beautiful plumes— or perhaps his vanity, at once silly and humanlike—I could hardly bear to look at him, laid low.

On a cool, dewy morning, just after sunrise, I saw a large animal standing in deep shade fully two hundred and fifty yards distant. Strangely enough, Cottar had not seen him yet, and evinced immediately excitement as he recognized him as a bull eland with very large horns. I could not hold true at offhand shooting at this range, so I raised my sights a little, took a rest on the edge of a mimosa trunk, and carefully squeezed the trigger. At the shot, the bull rushed forward at a headlong pace for about fifty yards, then crashed down.

We hurried up, to find a magnificent eland shot cleanly through the shoulder. The horns were massive; although not long in proportion to the oxlike size of the animal, they fell only an inch or two short of the record for this species. My gunbearer spoke in proud tones in his native tongue. Cottar replied with quite an air.

"It is not every *bwana* who can kill *pofu* with one shot," K'nini had said.

"Any American *bwana* can kill *pofu* with one shot," was Cottar's nationalistic—if not chauvinistic—answer.

Actually, it was a fine trophy. I would fetch it home with pride. Moreover, eland meat was so prized by our natives that they would butcher and sun-dry every pound that our camp cook could spare.

But the great hunt had not yet begun.

There were signs of it developing when, skirting a donga, Cottar caught sight of something brown in its brush-grown bed. He ran forward, hoping for another glimpse, then called me to him in a voice hoarse with excitement.

"I saw a lioness, and I think the brute with her is a lion. Go where the brush thins out and take a stand. I'll try to flush him your way."

I walked as fast as I could to the place he had pointed out, K'nini behind me bearing the .30 U.S. I did not run, needing all the breath that I could save. When the brush thinned out, leaving deep-cut grassy banks, I found a vantage point from where I had clear vision for a twenty-yard span. Two hundred yards from me, too far from me to be certain of his help in a bad fix, Cottar was fiercely hurling clods and stones into the thickets, meanwhile shouting profanities. About one-third of that distance I heard a distinct rustle of brush, then another considerably nearer. Pleasantly excited until then, suddenly I was in the grip of fear.

I did not conquer it, and as I gazed at the short space between me and the blind bush, it deepened. It was sharper than common fear or even fright. In it was the realization of an impending crisis, which I did not know if I could meet and conquer. I had taken too short a stand. My gun was too new, and beyond that, back of that, my aim was too uncertain, and my nerves yet untried by mortal conflict. The lion might stop and take his aim while he was still out of my sight, then come in one hurtling surge. I wished I had stood farther back. I would retreat now, except it meant lowering my guard.

Then there was suddenly a loud crash of brush, causing a swift, cold prickling on the back of my neck, along with a jump of my nerves. Not from the end of the thickets, not in my direction, but out at one side and quartering from me, broke the lion. I saw him in the sunlight and thanked God he was not charging me, and for that I gladly traded the good shot I would have had for a snap shot. He was scantily maned, but his muscles stood out, and he looked bigger than lions I had seen in a zoo—and this was his own country, his own wild, where there were no iron bars, and all the advantage of the ground and of experience lay with him. I sent a bullet after him. I am not sure that I took careful aim or any aim at all, I was so glad to have the crisis pass.

. . . If it had passed. I caught a glimpse of brown color, curiously vivid among the green, then there was swift movement I could not follow, and in the next second the whole scene had changed. The lion had gone, but at the edge of the brush stood the lioness. I think I saw her the very instant that she caught sight of me. She changed from a runaway to a beast at bay. Through some muscular tension, her body changed shape. It was still lithe, but was like a drawn bow. But she was the bow and the arrow too.

I saw her fix her gaze on me with deadly sharpness. She moved her feet a little, her tail seemed to stretch and stiffen. She dropped her head, and I knew she was going to charge.

I had worked the lever, in the hope of a second shot at a lion, so my barrel was loaded with a live shell. In spite of my wild haste to fire it, the brookless urge to end the danger instantly before it became closer in time and space, I did not let fly without aiming. The potential was in me to do it. I almost—not quite—did it. I had learned enough not to, in the hits and misses I had made on other grounds. And this situation was greatly different from most of the others; I did not consciously think of it but I must have known it, even then, in those few seconds of terror, for I acted on it. Usually the only penalty was the loss of a trophy. Not so when I had shot at the grizzly, nor possibly at my first Kodiak bear; then the cost of missing became unreckonable. And it takes a long time for a grizzly's charge to go home—a matter of orderly seconds, not exploding instants.

I took as quick aim as was aim at all. It was not careful enough to make sure—instead my haste made me take a shocking chance —but the luck of a tenderfoot on his first critical shot in Africa was good. The beast was near and I saw her clearly and perhaps powerfully over the sights; and while I did not aim for the head or breast, which no real hunter would fail to do, at least I leveled on her whole form that was poised to strike. I touched, and she dropped flat.

I uttered some sort of yell. The next I knew gray-faced K'nini was shaking my hand.

IV

Cottar came on the run. I had never dreamed that the gray-haired Afrikander could cover ground so fast. Before he arrived, my eyes had regained their focus, and the green thickets and the brown veld and the tawny lioness and the gray-green mimosas no longer looked distorted or off-center, as things appear in dreams. I was unhurt, and there was no real change except that the lioness who a minute before had rippled and blazed and almost snapped with vitality beyond measure was now a carcass. But it was a somewhat splendid carcass, even though it looked much smaller than it had looked in life.

Cottar and K'nini spoke to each other in Swahili.

"K'nini says you fired very quick," Cottar reported. "He hardly had time to get scared."

"It wasn't that way with me. And it seemed I took all day."

My shot had sufficed—like Mercutio's wound—by no wide margin. My bullet had not centered the target and had missed the low-dropped head, and entered just behind the foreleg, quartering through the rear part of the chest cavity into the opposite flank. A little farther back and the lioness would have lived minutes and perhaps hours, and she had needed only seconds to complete her intended business, to keep her white-hot resolve. You had better shoot straighter than that, Edison! Cottar did not tell me so, except perhaps by conspicuously stepping off the distance between the dead lioness and my ejected shell—just under sixty feet—and by what I read in his face. K'nini said as much, with a touch of humor and high humanity, when he asked Cottar for a cigarette, obviously to quiet his nerves. I told myself so, though, in plain blunt Anglo-Saxon.

My main exploit in the next few days was to shoot a nine-foot black mamba. He had run like a whiplash across the grass and then, very strangely, coiled in an almost open place, where he was easy to see and kill. The thought came to me that he might be the most dangerous large animal—thousands of times heavier than the tsetse fly carrying sleeping sickness or several million times the malarial mosquito—in all the length and breadth of Africa. He did not kill instantly as does the elephant, but he sometimes finished the job in five minutes, considerably sooner than most human deaths wrought by mauling lions, storming rhinos, or goring buffaloes. However, Cottar told me that a close-lying common adder hereabouts, that never sought a quarrel, ended far more human lives than the big aggressive mamba.

Then came a day when one of our trackers found the spoor of a big buffalo and his herd. It led down a hill into a quite extensive swamp watered by springs, rivulets, and small, dark pools. The grass was waist-high, low enough to shoot over, but farther on, reed beds stood higher than our heads, taller than a buffalo, tall as an elephant. Cottar stopped me before we followed the tracks into these blind thickets, and his face looked troubled and his eyes were grave.

"This may turn out quite a shauri," he began. *Shauri* was a Swahili word meaning "business" or "affair." Cottar used it more dynamically to mean a fight.

"Yes, sir," I answered, not only in respect to his gray hairs.

"It's what you're paying for, and I'm willing to take you in. Just you and my bearer and me; I don't want to have to look out for your bearer, for although we might help him, he can't help us very much. That .30 U.S. is too light to drop a buff in time. It would probably make matters worse."

I nodded to all that.

"Are you sure you want to try it? It won't likely be our only chance. We'll probably run into buffaloes in open country, where you can see what you're doing, and shoot at a fair range. That is the way most guides do it, when they take out sports. They don't even show 'em places like this. Their parties get as much game as mine, but not the thrills. If we flush that herd, they may be no more dangerous than so many waterbucks, but again . . ." He paused, and politely looked away, so I could consider this in private.

"I want to go," I said presently.

This was true, but there was more to it than that. I likewise wanted to turn back. Still I did not think that Cottar's and the black men's opinion of me—for everyone would know—was the deciding factor. Pride might be—although, I hoped, of a kind that had no being, at least no expression, outside of my secret self. At the same time there was nothing heroic about risking one's life to kill a buffalo in a nameless African swamp. In my case it took a forced bravery, not quite authentic perhaps, but more than bravado. I would not have needed to do this if I were not, and had always been, doubtful of my common male share of intrepidity. Cottar had been perfectly right; this was what I had paid for, and come for. Hunting nondangerous big game is a test of hardihood, determination, self-control, and certain skill, traits in which the hunter can take rightful pride. When he engaged lions and buffaloes and their ilk he contracted to furnish something more—a defiance of danger, the degree depending on his protectors or lack of them. To go alone after elephants in thick country was tantamount to volunteering for battle, the odds by no means even but enough to make one think, wonder, and daydream.

At Cottar's command, K'nini and the tracker turned back. I felt sorry for them, for it seemed that they had both lost a little face. There is no difference between a white man and a black man, or a brown man or a yellow man or a red man, when it comes to the needs, the strengths and infirmities, of the human heart. We walked on, and forgot they were alive.

The tracks became great holes in the mucky ground. A vigilance came upon Cottar that might be more intense than that I had seen on the donga bank; and that would be natural enough, for the reeds became increasingly higher, and the danger of a charge from close at hand, just beside us, was greater than before. He held his rifle in both hands, across and rather far out from his breast, and I knew he could level it in the twinkling of an eye. The Negro walked just behind him, his head turning slowly as he watched both sides of the trail. Feeling strangely lonely and forlorn but with my heart thumping, I brought up the rear.

We passed through a reed bed, a tingly passage. As Cottar

pushed out of its blind end, he stood quickly to one side, and with the same quickness and lightness, the Negro stepped to the other side. I knew what that meant. I was to come through. I did not look at their faces; I did not need to, to be sure what was waiting for me. My pace quickened and in a second more I saw the herd.

It was ranged in a half circle, about seventy-five yards distant. The beasts were facing us, and in almost every case I could see only the head and horns and front quarters, the hindquarters being concealed. They were standing at the edge of the reeds, not hiding there, but thrusting far enough out for a good view of their pursuers. About fifteen were plainly visible; here and there dim black shapes, all but hidden, showed others hanging back a little from the ominous line. And now I strained with all my powers of vision to be sure to locate the herd leader.

It did not take long. He was taller than the rest, far more massive, and his horns had a far greater spread. And now the mental coaching I had gone through during the advance had unmistakable effect. It was fixed in my mind not to shoot too quick. The gun came up quickly—almost as quickly as Cottar's gun could come up—that was from my being an old duck hunter—and my gaze flung quick and hard along the barrel. The black mass filled my sights and still I did not shoot. Still I waited, a long-drawn fraction of a second, until I distinguished the base of the vast neck. Then, throwing an enormous amount of nervous energy into that small, light action—merely seeing the target with extreme intensity throughout the fraction of an instant that the mechanism worked—I fired the piece.

Cottar and the Negro knew what to expect when the gun roared. I did not know, and underwent nervous shock. Some twenty tons of living might, the strange and hard-to-believe might that big animals possess, hurled into action at once. It was in the nature of a stampede and hence dangerous; luckily it did not come our way. It thundered along the flank of tall thickets, and there was no use to try to fire again, because I could not tell one of the big beasts from another. Water and mud flung up like dirt after a dynamite explosion; the torn reeds made a tearing sound, something like a forest fire I had heard in Oregon years before.

The uproar became less centered and changed to a series of minor outbursts as the herd scattered through the swamp. The beasts were on all sides of us now, crashing through reeds and splashing water, and half of my mind was alert to the danger, and the other half remained preoccupied by my affair with the herd leader. I could not believe I had missed him, although I could not be sure—other times I had felt sure, I had been wrong. There was no dark shape in the grass where he had stood.

An instant later I heard a buffalo plunging through the high reeds a good distance to my left and in front, and I caught a glimpse of him, and he loomed unbelievably large. He was my bull, I thought, and according to his course he would burst out into the grass in a few seconds more, and if I could get on the other side of a close-by thicket, I might catch sight of him. Wildly, without thinking, I ran in that direction. Only after I had gone forty yards did I realize that I had broken contact with my companions. It happened that at that same instant Cottar had run the other way, making for some higher ground that his trained eyes had located. In an instant both he and his bearer had disappeared.

"Marshall!" he shouted above the tumult. "Where are you?"

I had no breath to answer, because the buffalo had broken from the grass and was plunging toward me. Instantly I saw it was not the herd bull, but instead a big cow. Her thinner, sharper horns were no less lethal; more than the bull she was used to charging lions who menaced the calves. I got ready to shoot. I was spared the dangerous act only by a little coolness—I suppose I could call it that—at least a high perceptivity functioning side by side with panic. In seeking my aim I looked closer at the cow, and

then I saw she was not looking at me. Her gaze was fixed a little
to my right. She was only in stampede, and in a few seconds she
came devilish close to me, only to burst into the high reeds and
vanish.

Apparently the cow was one of a numerous band, perhaps
part of the original herd, or of another panicked by my shot,
for several other buffaloes showed themselves in the next few
minutes. They were running in all directions, with that rocking
motion I had seen in farmyard bulls, and faster than I could
hardly believe. At brief intervals one would break from the high
reeds, loom back and huge in the open grass, and disappear again.
I stood swinging my gun from side to side, frequently whirling
as I heard a crash behind me, and cutting an absurd figure of a
big-game hunter.

Cottar called me again, and now I saw him, standing in an
extensive open, his gun ready, its butt plate close to his shoulder,
and his whole figure one of ready belligerence against all comers.
He was neither cool nor calm—far from it—probably cursing in
a low voice to save his wind. I might have known that no real
hunter or for that matter, no real man, only his atrophied semblance—would not be wildly excited by such a scene, either formidable or badly frightened according to his basic chemistry, as
charged with adrenalin as a charging lion. Still I could not get
with him or even answer him, on account of being nearly run
over by a half-grown calf.

Only a few seconds after that I saw the great herd bull. He
broke cleanly from the swamp reeds at the far end of the open
space that Cottar commanded, and plunged straight toward him.
Whether he was charging him in typical buff rage, or merely
running that way in a blind frenzy, I did not know. Cottar would
not let him get near. His gun would swing a little; the butt plate
would jam his shoulder; his gray head with battered helmet would
lower briefly; there would come a deep roar drowning out for

one climactic second every other sound—and the beast would drop.

He would fall dead, and Cottar would cut off his head and give it to me, and I could take it home—but it would not be mine.

None of these things happened. As I stared, helpless, unable to shoot because Cottar and the target were too nearly on a line, the bull did a strange thing. He stopped, reared up like a horse on his hind legs to giant height, dropped back, then toppled on his side. He gained his feet, trotted off in another direction, whirled, and again fell. His legs threshed and he lay with upraised head.

I forgot my fright. Anyway, the swamp was growing strangely still. Shouting to Cottar, I ran to him, then he and I and the bearer sped to the fallen leader. Snorting bloody foam, he tried once more to rise; failing that, he gave us a last green glare of implacable hatred. Then his head slowly lowered, the great blunt flaring horns thrusting deep into the ground.

Six

IF now I could get a massive lion with a heavy mane, a fair rhinoceros bull, and any sort of mature leopard, my bag would be full enough, and so would my cup of triumph. Even if I had to skip the leopard—the taking of which was almost always a fluke of chance—if I could get the other two in good style and acquittal, I would still be content. The lion I could not spare. If not the king of beasts, he is still the symbol and the soul of the veld, and his Swahili name is *simba*, and a great pharaoh had recorded hunting him in imperishable stone. That great hunter, Stewart Edward White, had proclaimed him the most dangerous of African animals, and I believed that Cottar feared him more than elephants, despite the elephant's longer list of slain—as much indeed as his proud, wild heart could fear anything on earth.

Nor could I forego a rhino without deep defeat and loss. If, after these wonderful days had passed, I must leave Africa without his grotesque head, my expedition would fall far short of success. I had read a great deal about rhinos and mulled over it. They had excited my imagination more than I had realized, until I caught a glimpse of an old cow rhino and her gargantuan calf. A mature male weighs two tons. Sometimes his front horn stands three feet high, and often he carries it point foremost, like a lance. No other big-game animal is so likely to make an unprovoked attack, and this holds true all over the world. In Asia he has a counterpart, with overlapping skin like a vast armadillo, but he is protected from hunters. Unless I bagged an African rhino, I would never again have dealings with the monsters.

This was as far as I could reason with the passion, but it passed beyond this. As the lion was king of the brown and endless grass, the rhino was lord of the thorn. I had seen his stamping grounds and his great piles of dung. More than any other beast, he was a relic of the antediluvian age. To fancy him, with his huge bulk, prodigious head with its two horns, and incorrigible temper, existing in the same times with the airplane and the golf green and the night club pleasantly jarred the imagination. I wanted to hang him like a roc's egg in the whole front of my trophy room. He would be an ugly sight, but how he would kindle the eyes and thrill the heart! In the final counting, what a magnificent reward of the chase!

We have moved camp twice without seeing a good bull. Although we found much old sign, fresh sign was curiously rare. Three days after our third move, the luck was amenable to change, if I could back it. Driving a leopard from his tommy kill, and following him into thorn, we did not again catch sight of his spotted hide. But suddenly we heard a resounding snort that electrified us all, and then, out of nowhere it seemed, there loomed a rhino.

I think he had been lying down and had leaped to his feet on catching our hated smell. He was a big bull, bigger than I had ever imagined the brutes grew, and his front horn was fine and tall; he was a trophy of a tenderfoot's dream. All this I saw in one sharp view of him; then, before I could aim, he whirled and began to run straight away from us, with a rocking motion something like a buffalo's but with a longer swing. There was still plenty of time to speed a .405 bullet into his great rump, and it would rip through the soft tissue into the chest cavity, and then he would not go far. Cottar knew this perfectly well. He could count ten, if he pleased, and still shoot to kill, and it would mean nothing to him—a feat forgotten by this time next year. But I did not know it. It seemed I had been given only this one brief chance, reducing every instant, and unless I shot like lightning he would escape.

I fired and the bull ran on. Before I could throw in another shell, he vanished in a cloud of dust behind thickets. But maybe I had shot better than I knew, for had not a bull buffalo hardly half his weight run and stampeded and lived mightily for more than five minutes, more likely ten, with the heavy bullet in his chest cavity? Still I was faint in the stomach, and knew that my face had paled.

Very courteously, Cottar walked with me to look for blood sign. When the men seemed laggard in joining the search, he yelled at them. Meanwhile, though, I had seen their faces, and although they were hard to read—the face of an African native is almost as inscrutable as the face of the land he inhabits—I knew they had passed judgment. For some reason they did not understand, the old, great *bwana* sometimes put on a show for the young, little *bwana*. Now they ran about, gazing solemnly at the ground—one of them scratched at it with his bare foot— and they looked neither me nor Cottar in the face.

After about ten minutes that had lagged more and more in passing, Cottar shouldered his gun and spoke in an earnest tone.

"Look here, Mr. Marshall. No one can hit all the time, even the best, let alone a man who don't make a business of hunting. You missed that rhino. I knew it when I didn't hear the whack of the bullet, and we've whipped a dead horse long enough. Let's go look for a warthog. I saw where they'd been rooting, a few minutes ago. The tusks of a big boar are a fine trophy."

II

We flushed an old boar, unspeakably ugly and quarrelsome, and I bagged him in good style. In fact I made a shot considerably harder than the one I had missed, but after it was over, any kind of hit hog was cold comfort for a missed rhino. Moreover, my chances to recoup were sadly lessened the following afternoon, when Cottar was "hit by the bamboo"—the stout male bamboo is used as a cudgel in that half the world—a graphic native expression for the sudden flare-up of malarial fever.

For twenty years it had lain in ambush in the marrow of his bones. It had made innumerable onslaughts; sometimes he had stayed up and hunted "through" them as long-distance runners run through their ghastly retching. Often, though, they had put him down with rigor and delirium, and half a dozen times it had tried to kill him with blackwater fever. One day it *would* kill him, the doctors told him. His hickory-tough body and his indomitable will would avail him no more.

"But the doctors are wrong," Cottar told me, his face flushed and his eyes glittering with fever, and a half-hysterical ring in his voice. "I'll tell you what's going to kill me, if you want to know. A lion."

"Do you think so?" I asked, not humoring him, but caught up in amazement and suspense, because I sensed that the old hunter was about to tell me something he would have never told me, except for waves of delirium passing over his fevered brain.

"It may be a lioness," he went on in a dark, fatalistic tone. "Smaller and lighter, standing much less lead, yet they've done a right good share of mauling and killing. They're smarter than the males, meaner, and more prone to attack without warning. That may be the end of me. Still I hope it will be an old male, with knots all over his body where the muscles bunch, and a heavy mane. Since I've got to get it, what a difference between him and a cursed bug!"

I started to say, "Why can't you die peacefully in bed?" But it would be an outrageous thing to say to this Long Hunter born half a century after his time. That would be the worst death of all to one of his tribe; it would be worse than a lion's dying in a pen. Still I must prod him, to find out his secret.

"Why not some other animal?" I asked. "An elephant with big tusks, a buffalo in his rage, a cantankerous old rhino, or even a leopard, faster than fire?"

"I'll tell you why. Because they've all tried it and failed. Once I was knocked down by a crazy buff, and lay on my back in front of him, my feet on either side of his neck, with my legs braced so he'd push me backward across the ground and give me time to shoot again. Old Lord De La Mere told me I'd better not try *that* again." Cottar stopped and laughed harshly. "Once a bull elephant drove his tusks into the ground on each side of me, and I crawled out between 'em, and got my gun, and killed him. And once a cow, looking for me everywhere when I was hid in the bush, stepped clean over me. Rhinos? Old *Kifaru's* ugly enough—in looks and nature—but he's stupid, and he hasn't got the hellish quickness of those other brutes, for even an elephant can swing his trunk like lightning. Leopards are the quickest of all. Three times I've had 'em on me, and three times been mauled. Once I had a knife in my belt, and hadn't time to draw it; I could only throw that screaming beast off my shoulders and have him bounce back like a rubber ball."

He paused, and an echo of some passion I could not identify came into his face.

"None of those will kill me," he went on in a rumbling voice. "You mark my words. But lions have never yet put claw on me. I've killed fifty and more, way past the allowance for hunters. I mean the odds were with me for my first ten, but now they've climbed and climbed against me—and some day a lion will get hold of me, and that'll be the end of old Cottar, and the land will know him no more."

It was not the first time I had heard him speak like a prophet of old. Of all the things that had happened to me on this trip, or would happen yet, knowing Charles Cottar was the luckiest. That was my thought as he drifted into fevered sleep, and it was a true thought, because my hunt was for something more than game. Perhaps this is true of many big-game hunts, especially ambitious and dangerous ones made by fiercely ambitious men—men who do not know quite where they stand between courage and cowardice, good and evil, wisdom and folly. And the same is true of climbing mountains or flying across wide seas.

III

Cottar was better on the following day, almost well on the next, and down again on the third. And on that day our camp cook, on an errand to cut a quarter from a young topi I had shot and hidden under boughs from the patient sky-watch of vultures, came back on the run with an intense animation in his pleasant black face. Reporting first to the big *bwana* as a matter of course, he called out a name that brought on a great excitement in me.

The name was *kifaru*, and I heard it perfectly plainly, and as sure as the sun burned down and the distant herds of game drifted through the heat waves, it meant rhinoceros.

"Fundi saw a big rhino in a thorn patch about a mile from here," Cottar reported. "He's got a fine horn, and a lot of fight in him by the way he snorted and stamped, and tried to get Fundi's scent. Tomorrow I may be better, but tomorrow—he may be gone."

"Why can't K'nini go with me?"

"The game board says that a white hunter must be present every time a license holder shoots at dangerous game. If they knew I let you go only with a bearer, they'd make trouble for me. They hate me anyway. They know that I know this country and its game better than their whole pack put together. If you'd get killed, the trouble would be bad. But I've got to make up to you for these days you've missed on account of my cursed fever."

It was as good an excuse as any, I thought, for him to grant my plea—and to yield to some lawless but generous, perhaps noble, wishes of his heart. He did not believe in a grown man, who had come ten thousand miles to shoot great, fighting animals, being backed in every crisis by a guide's gun. He had seen that I shot quite well at times. There were other times that I muffed badly. Still, it was my *shauri* to decide.

"Just remember this," he told me. "Don't try to outrun a rhino. He looks as though he can't run very fast, but that's a snare and a delusion. If you can't stop his charge, dodge it. Wait till he drops his head with his horn sticking straight out, for then he runs blind. And don't shoot till you're ready."

I had listened as patiently as possible. Now the fever was on me to be gone, for a rhino's staying until tomorrow was hardly a worse gamble than his lingering a single hour. Big game is almost constantly on the move. That is the nature of the beasts. Need of food, water, and mating, sociability of a wild-beast sort, and pure energy and restlessness drive them ever on.

I shook off a light, thorn-catching sweater I had put on in the chill morning, and replaced it with a leather jacket I had kept, unworn so far on this safari, in my camp trunk. Seeing that both my .30 U.S. and Cottar's .405 were fully loaded, I dropped ten extra cartridges for the latter piece in my jacket pocket. The cook did not offer to go with us, loving his pots and pans more than adventure in the open veld, although he gave K'nini careful directions that required a long jabbering. Finally we were on our way in the small truck. In easy sight of the thorn thicket, we stopped and took to our legs.

The thicket was much larger than I expected—I thought it contained forty acres of close-grown scrub. We gazed in vain across its expanse for a dark, distant, grotesque shape, and then walked up a kind of avenue toward its center. Already my hopes were falling. There was only sun-baked ground and lean thorn and naked sky, and the rhino had gone his way—or if he was still here, I could not find him. . . . Then the weather in my heart made a sudden change. We came on a pile of dung as big as a bushel, and both of us touched it, and it was hot.

It might be that we could have tracked the monster in the close-growing thorn. When I considered it, thinking of the beast's discovering us on his trail, seeing us from his waiting-place long before we saw him, I did not have the nerve to go in. I looked for that nerve in a kind of aimless way, but could not find it. I tried to force it, only to fail.

Meanwhile I had caught sight of a mimosa tree not far from his spoor. I pointed to it, went through the motions of climbing, then, with my hand on my forehead in time-honored sign of spying, gestured for K'nini to do the job. Rather to my surprise, he appeared to understand, nodding and smiling in agreement and perhaps in pleasure at his own perspicacity. Actually, as time continued to prove, K'nini was a perspicacious man. There was quite a lift about him, always the sign of alert intelligence, that made his company pleasant.

He trotted away, cut off from my sight by the thickets, and

the next I saw of him he was shinnying up the tree almost as fast as a squirrel. But soon my attention was diverted from him by a sound in the thorn.

I read it as a big bush being broken off and smashed down. After some long seconds of silence, there came a great swishing and cracking and snapping along with the clump of heavy hooves on sun-baked ground, as some ponderous beast broke into a run. That beast was the rhino. Other than he, only an elephant would make so much noise. And he was not more than fifty yards away, and headed in my general direction.

The thought struck me that he might have scented me and charged. Rhinos usually threaten and snort a minute or two before they launch a formal charge—more often still they express ire, then go their way—but frequently they attack at their first scent of man and without the slightest warning. If so, I would not see him until he was almost on me; and such a situation called for a cooler head and an older hand than mine. I stood gripping the rifle in extreme nervous tension as the sound neared. When it paused briefly and resumed without getting louder, several seconds passed before I recognized the change and felt reassured.

The rhino had veered from his course. He had only been investigating a smell he did not like. I had hardly got it through my head when he burst into the avenue in which I stood about a hundred feet from me. I had a quartering and clear view of him, turned slightly away from me, and he gave me one of the great starts of my life. Seeing a mother and calf, and later a rear view of a running bull, had not prepared me for his monstrosity. He looked very dark and seemed to be framed by the gray thickets on either side of the opening. And even in the wild excitement of shooting at him, I did not quite lose the wonder of being alone with him here, in the whole of my present world. Fright was tempered and changed by awe.

I could not tell whether I hit or missed. He appeared to turn a little more, follow the avenue a distance, then again plunge into the thorn. By now I was almost ready to fire again, taking aggressive and close aim, but was a second or two too late. And then again I had to fight the goblins of losing a great chance.

But the sound of his rush continued only a few seconds, then ominously stopped. No doubt he was standing now within a hundred yards of me, sniffing for the scent he hated, waiting developments.

Automatically I reached into my jacket pocket for a cartridge to replace the one I had fired. My hand fumbled there in vain. At first I could not believe it: I started to grope in the opposite pocket only to recall beyond a shadow of doubt that I had put them in the right side where I could get at them handily and quickly, because a hunter holds the upper stock of his rifle with his left hand. Diving in again, I found a hole in the cloth, and remembered it well enough too late. I felt in the lining, only to find that the hole went all the way through, and the cartridges were hopelessly lost.

Four remained in my gun. It stood to reason they would be enough for any need that might come my way—if I had not stopped a charging rhino with these, I would not have time, anyway, to shoot again. Still my first intelligent impulse was to get to K'nini as soon as possible, take my stand at the foot of the tree where he had no doubt leaned the .30 U.S., and have him keep watch until the danger—or perhaps only the sport—had passed. I turned quickly for a reassuring sight of him, just in time to see him springing down. Instantly he vanished in the thickets.

No doubt he had seen the rhino's various maneuvers, knew his present location, and was hurrying to me to serve me in his place as a gunbearer. That was his job and his pride.

I thought to call to him, hesitated lest I provoke the rhino into charging me, then called anyway. "Be careful!" I shouted, a perfectly useless outcry, because K'nini knew hardly a word of English. And although I did not know it yet, at that very second a storm was gathering, the kind inherent in hunting the dangerous wild beasts of Africa, and which always breaks, if it does not pass over, with nerve-jolting fury.

K'nini was running toward me up the open avenue. He came in sight at about a hundred yards' distance, and ran toward me for thirty yards more and I thought that all was well, and in a few seconds we would have the comfort of each other's company. It is strange how quickly the frightened hunter feels reassured: there is a deep-seated belief that the quarry will not attack—a belief that is frequently shaken, but which begins to operate again in the briefest truce. My fool's heaven fell when there came a resounding snort in the thorn behind and to one side of the swift runner. "We're in for it," I said to myself, in that low, almost calm voice men use when great danger breaks upon them.

The rhino came forth in full attack. He was making for K'nini, and he gained on him at an appalling rate. I had not much room to shoot without danger of hitting my companion, but there was room enough, and my aim was hard and tight. By the time I pressed the trigger the rhino had dropped his head and his horn thrust almost straight forward, as Cottar had described. There showed not the least sign that I had hit.

My hands raced to pump in another shell from the magazine. I might have time to fire it, for the charge did not seem as swift as I expected it, judging, I suppose, by the rush of buffaloes and the flight of the rhino I had seen from the rear. Then the whole scene changed; and instead of terrifying it became thrilling. It arose through the pickup and prowess of a black man. Perhaps he had dealt with rhinos before; anyway, he knew what to do.

He whirled to face the charge, paused a brief second, then leaped out of its way. The rhino thundered on as though he did not know he had missed his target.

Apparently he had not seen me yet. He might see me, and then it would be my turn to face and balk the charge. If so, there were resources within me unfelt, perhaps unwaked before; still badly frightened, I had become more belligerent. It seemed to me he was headed for the brush. I had three bullets and could spare one more before we came to close and final quarters, and I refixed my aim and, with a leap of my will, fired.

Again there was no sign of a hit; he only continued on his course, and once more plunged into the thorn.

But he ran only a sort distance before he stopped, and a great silence fell, pregnant with the vision of him charging again, or never charging anyone again. K'nini's eyes met mine in a swift questioning glance. I could not answer.

Yet I knew I must make some kind of an answer soon. I let the matter slide awhile, as I listened with utmost intentness, only to have it insistently press upon me. Besides my great desire to reach hunt's end, either to possess the trophy or to forego it, I felt a social pressure which not even this lonely waste of thorn, this solitude with one black man, could quite abrogate. I had two cartridges in my gun, and the fully loaded .30 U.S. to fall back on—for what it was worth. What big-game hunter or aspirant thereto would yield to blue funk, leaving the field without ascertaining victory or defeat? Under these conditions, Cottar would walk straight into the thorn with the light rifle alone.

K'nini knew my trouble, and to help me resolve it, he found a stone and threw it where we had last heard the rhino. There came no sound but that of its light fall, and a stick that he broke and hurled had no more consequence. I began to feel oddly happy. Even if I had missed the rhino, and he was half a mile away by now, we were going to come out all right.

So I started into the thickets, K'nini close behind me and my gun ready. They were easier to enter than I had thought. Still I had to turn and get him to point the way, because I soon lost it. The way seemed very long, and I was beginning to despair when K'nini poked me between the shoulder blades with an eager hand, then pointed excitedly. I looked to where something enormous and almost black lay among the little thorn trees.

Kifaru had died in his rush, while he still believed there was a foe before him to impale on his great lance; and for the lord of the thorn, dim-witted and dim-eyed though he might be, and a hold-over from old time, an anachronism, dwelling in a changed world with which his brute force was at odds, it was a splendid way to die.

Seven

MY cup running over, I devoted my next ten days to gathering material of more direct use to my profession than hunting experience. The venture I undertook at the end of that time was in line with this. Although it involved big game, I did not expect to shoot, and only intended to observe. It began in a most casual way. If I were a good enough heathen—animist, I should say, for in my secret soul I had been a demon-appeaser all my days—I would have taken warning. If ever the old gods listened to our table and camp talk, to find inspiration for their practical jokes, it was when Cottar first broached the plan.

I have always had a hard time, even at the fireside, recounting the outcome, for it invariably strained the credulity of my hearers. Since I passionately and blunderingly hunted big game, numerous exciting *shauris* and some brushes with danger lay in the cards; but on this occasion it was as though I had been dealt a royal flush while my opponents had straight flushes and full houses. At least, though, I was given no large heroic part to play, either in triumph or failure. I was called upon for not much more than my usual performance, that of some brilliance mixed with bumbling.

It began by Cottar saying that, if I did not mind a little discomfort, I should sit up one night with Africa.

"I mean on the veld without fire. There's a good moon now, and you'd see a lot that would help you sell your books. The best way is to sit in a *boma*—that's a little shelter made of thorn brush, with a hole left to see through. I can't say it's completely safe, but what is? Lions and leopards avoid thorns. They know, although I don't know how they know, that a thorn in the foot often leads to a quick death by blood poisoning or a slow one by lameness. Every critter has to be in robust health to survive on the veld." Cottar, pleased with this last bit of understatement, stopped to give me a grin.

"How about man-eaters?" I asked.

"Man-eaters have been known to dive straight through the strongest *bomas*. For instance, those two devils up Tsoa way. If there was a Shenzi village near here, where they chuck out their dead for the beasts and birds, I wouldn't chance it; but these lions around here don't know any more what a man tastes like than I know patty-de-fraw-graw." Feeling very gay, Cottar grinned again.

"I think the chances of seeing very much would be pretty thin."

"Oh, I forgot to tell you. You'll shoot a zebra and I'll drag the carcass with the truck and make a long blood trail that the varmints will cross and follow. That'll attract 'em, no fear. And there's no loss of meat," he went on rather impatiently, because he had little sympathy with my conservation urge, the first letter of sportsmanship in America. "You'll only furnish the brutes with a free dinner that otherwise they'd serve themselves."

"What brutes?"

"Hyenas for sure. They pull down fawns and small bucks. You won't waste cartridges on them, but they make a pretty picture in the shine of your light. Lions very possibly. I wouldn't shoot them, not just because it's against the law to shoot lions at night, but because we can get 'em in the grass. They're not subtle devils like leopards, and there you and them too have more scope. If a leopard should come up, take him. It may be your only chance for a beautiful skin for the Missus. Elephants?—well, there's hardly any in this neighborhood. If you'd happen to see one barge by, he'll be tending to his own business—heaven, not me, knows what—and if you don't meddle with him, I reckon he'll mosey on." Cottar started to say something more, only to change his mind.

"Are you going to be with me?"

"I can't do that, Mr. Marshall. One night sitting up would wake the fever again. But K'nini will go. K'nini considers himself no end of a fellow since he dodged that rhino. And if you don't like the sound of it—and I wouldn't blame you—the boys will build you a platform in a tree, called a *machon*, and you'll be lord of all you survey. But you won't get the thrill you'll get on the ground, and that's a fact."

I decided to take it on the ground, as many animal-watchers had done before me. For long-seeing or shooting, we had a powerful flashlight with spare batteries. K'nini could turn it on and off when I elbowed him in the ribs. If I raised my rifle, that was a signal to cast the beam along the barrel, illuminating not only the target but my sight.

With very little other instruction, and with blankets to keep us warm and a flask of coffee, K'nini and I rode in a small truck to a big piece of veld, with scattered thorn thickets and mimosa groves, about five miles from camp. We left late in the afternoon, and my first care was to shoot a zebra, for Cottar and some of the hands were already on the scene—the theater, I might say, of tonight's play—building the *boma*. What I thought would be a five-minute chore took a full hour, for no reason other than the nervous wariness of the zebra herds in the lengthening shadows that presaged the perilous night. I had never before chanced to notice their alertness increasing with the failing day, and it caused me to reflect, in a close and imaginative way, on what they were in for, every night of their lives. Moreover, the scarred old male that I shot fell wounded and rose to fight, baring his teeth and whitening his eyes and screaming like a range stallion, before I hit, missed, and hit again to finish him off.

K'nini danced a step or two of a *n'goma,* then spoke two of the half-dozen English words he knew. "Good luck," he cried in an utterly foreign accent, pointing first at me and himself, then gesturing toward the dead pony. Perhaps I sensed something forced about the performance, causing me to wonder whether K'nini was making a little *dawa* of the kind that we call whistling in the dark, and the sign had been bad.

He chained the carcass to our axle and dragged it in a two-mile loop over the grass. When we reached the *boma,* Cottar and his men were just leaving in the big truck, and they waited to see the bait stoutly pegged down, so that the first lion who came by could not drag it away. I did not believe any lion would come. That was the direction my mind took—one of pessimism about any excitement developing to relieve a long, cold watch.

The big truck rolled off and its sound died away. I felt rather odd to be left alone here with K'nini, and slightly embarrassed. Here we were, two human beings with no means of human communication except signs. He, on the contrary, relaxed. Business would not pick up for a while yet, was what his eased muscles and glazed glance told me. Even so, I soon found something to interest me. At first it was a herd of zebras, dashing up into the middle distance, every neck arched and head alert as in Roman sculpture, and looking bright and splendid in spite of the paleness of the final sunlight. They ran on, pressed close to one another; and in a minute or two a high-watching vulture spied the carcass, volplaned down, and lighted in the grass about ten yards from it. When he had hopped toward it with revolting motions I expected him to attack it. Instead he spread his wings and hissed.

I shouted at him, and since he was only thirty measured feet away, he took flight to a treetop. Other vultures began to soar down, taking nearby perches. Why did none of them light by the bait? They did not look at me or care about me; it was the grass that they searched with their beady, demonic eyes. I remembered Cottar's telling me that any kill made after sundown was safe from these birds of death; they were afraid of what might be lying in wait beside the kill.

Today's sun had not quite set. There remained a red wink through the distant thickets. It disappeared, and it seemed that the air felt instantly colder. A big maribou stork flew in with great boldness and started to land, only to take off with a frantic flutter to a treetop. He had a long bill and was as great a ruffian as the buzzards, and his only boast was he had lighted a little nearer than the rest.

African twilights are exceedingly short. This one seemed longer than most only because it was like a watched pot that never seems to boil; and the light failed so smoothly and evenly that nearby objects began to look quite far. The scanty colors of the foliage—for the whole scene was of pale shades—faded almost imperceptibly, yet soon I looked for a little green and could not find it. All this was objective perception, for I think I made some sort of unconscious effort not to look inward. I realized no fright, but it was against nature for me to be sitting with one black man far and away on the veld, without a camp, without fire, with carrion pegged down at thirty feet to attract big, dangerous animals, a low brush wall around us, and no other refuge.

All at once the vultures took flight, flapping heavily and sorrowfully away, to some hell gate they guarded in the night. The stork lingered a few seconds, as though to prove to himself he was of different station, of higher standing in the eyes of God, then he too winged off.

The moon had risen about three hours before, big without being full-faced. I thought I would have her company throughout the watch, cold but still welcome comfort, until a haze spread through the sky and here and there formed solid cloud. For the present she was no help. The falling night now lay dark gray, in which I could barely make out the shape of the zebra carcass. When I thought a shadow moved, I could not tell whether it was a trick of the eyes. One had moved, though, for presently I heard a soft snipping sound, many times repeated. Only little teeth had made it; the visitor was a serval cat, a jackal, or a fox.

Then a worse gang than the vultures rushed upon the bait. It had come running through the dark in silence, assured of its waiting feast, and suddenly broke into wild and frantic clamor. The long hush of the night, like a close mantle, was torn to shreds. There was no dignity and no majesty in the outcries, as in those we had heard from the great lords. There was only hate of one's own kind and of life itself, hunger that never eased, cruelty and cowardice and treachery. So there was only one name to fit the beasts, and that was hyena.

If I lay wounded and helpless, I could hardly imagine a more horrible visitation. As it was, I felt no fear at all, only repulsion. Signaling K'nini to turn on his light, I saw the night give them forth, in all their ugliness. Their backs slanted from their high front quarters to their half-squatted rears. Their eyes were green in the glare, and their fangs white. Each one stood in an ugly graceless attitude facing the lamp, many of their heads turned on their porcine necks. Even their fur was coarse and ugly, and some were bloodstained from fighting or feasting. They could not face the glare; snarling or whining, they began to back off.

They disappeared, but they had not gone far. When K'nini obeyed my signal to turn off the light, they came rushing back as frenzied as before. From then on, we were never again able to disperse the whole pack; if we forced back the main body, one or more beasts at its edge would take advantage of a passing shadow to rush in, sink his teeth, snatch, and run. They wrestled and fought, the leaders gorging while the followers stole morsels, the weak harried by the strong until we were sick of the sight of them. An hour passed, with us no nearer to getting rid of them. When we turned off the light to save the battery, their detestable clamor still wracked our ears. Then the moon emerged from a big bank of clouds into a wide clearing in the sky, and we saw them strange and gray, like hideously animated phantoms.

Then something happened in which I found a great degree of wonder and a kind of perverse pleasure. There rose in the dark a tremendous growl, drowning out the running clamor of the pack, and every member raised his head and gazed in that direction. As the ominous voice came nearer they scattered in all directions. I waited for a lion to burst upon the scene—and waited in vain. It was not the big-maned *simba* that routed the cowards—it was another hyena. He snatched a big piece of meat and instantly loped away into the darkness.

K'nini's laughter helped me to guess what happened. The thief was not a member of the pack, but an outlyer, and he had imitated the lion's kingly voice to get a share of the meat. It was hard to believe that a wild beast would be capable of such cunning, and it would be almost unthinkable outside of the canine tribes, which often are too near-human for our comfort. However, there is no readily acceptable explanation of the

beast's behavior. I was glad for his success, applauded his courage and intelligence, and felt a little odd relief that such an ugly,
low-lived, accursed caste of scavengers as the hyenas could have
a star performer, with a gift for something akin to low comedy.

II

I had sat a long time with my head in the window of the *boma*,
my gaze out of focus, only half seeing the shadow shapes, and
put half to sleep by the tiring discord of the hyenas' clamor. The
moon had been sliding in and out of pale patches of cloud, and
the frequently changing visibility, stimulating at first, had no
doubt tired my eyes. Suddenly the noise ceased.

I became sharply aroused. Staring, I saw every animal standing still, and every head was turned in the same direction. I followed their gaze. I could not be sure that I saw anything, although far off at the edge of vision, perhaps nearly a hundred
yards away—a range barely discernible on a moonlit night in
such dry, clear air as this—I had a perception of movement. My
eyes have always been strong, and I had the feeling that while
K'nini experienced it also, he knew no more than I did, yet was
as profoundly startled. The position of his body and the set of
his head and the planes of his face indicated increasing strain.

The same showed up in the hyenas. There came a little movement among them and they bunched on one side of the bait—
the opposite side from the mystery out in the dark. One of
them uttered a low growl. In a moment all were growling, a
deep throaty sound, too subdued and uneasy-sounding to have
any real force. Their eyes had been fashioned to see in the dark,
and they saw what we could only guess at and half imagine.
Then a few more seconds passed, and a living shape, appearing
a little darker than the moonlit grass, became visible to K'nini

and me. At a leisurely, steady pace it was approaching the bait. I began to have a sense of awesome grace.

The growling grew louder, but no more ominous than before. The plain truth was, the whole pack was being intimidated by that nearing form. Suddenly one of them cried out like a kicked dog and bounded away. An instant later their whole rank dissolved as they fled in panic.

I could see the shape quite clearly now. It was that of a long, low-built animal.

"*Simba?*" I whispered.

"*Tui.*"

Tui means leopard. Instantly I was disoriented, because I could not believe K'nini, even though there was something slightly unlike a lion in the visitor's shape and movement. It was too big to be a leopard. Perhaps it was a lioness. But the main turmoil in my mind as I tried to make a sure identification—a man's first instinct when confronted by a half-seen object of danger—was caused by the behavior of the hyenas. Every hunter on the veld soon hears how leopards fear the big rending teeth of hyenas—how two or three of the ugly beasts, sometimes only one, will put the spotted beauty up a tree. In this case a hyena pack had fled its feast at a leopard's bold approach.

For I knew now, within brief seconds after he had spoken, that K'nini was right. The animal's lines spelled leopard, and he was twice as large as any I had seen in a zoo or had imagined.

The suspense grew; the drama intensified. Leopards have especially keen vision. Indeed they hunt by sight instead of by smell, and that meant he had seen my head in the window and knew perfectly well that some living creature lurked behind the thorn, and probably he had identified me as a man. That ought to give him pause. Instead he continued his resolute graceful advance that had terrified the hyenas and now badly frightened me.

He walked up, his head in the air, a magnificent figure even in gray moonlight, and came to the bait and appeared to be looking at it. And almost at that second the moon took another dip behind the clouds. Although the darkness that fell was not deep, it reduced the leopard to a dim shape.

I signaled to K'nini. At once the flashlight beam cut a big golden wedge in the thickest shadows, and there was a sight to remember all my days. An immense leopard stood there in all his beauty. I could see every perfect spot, the long, low-hung tail with its lifted end, the paler belly, the flat head, and his litheness and symmetry. And it must be that he was king of the leopards in a way of speaking, the acme of his kind, for he did not even look up at the blazing lamp, and instead set his white teeth in the meat.

I felt a deep yearning and need to kill him, partly out of fear. He stood thirty feet away. If he felt inclined, nothing but my quick bullet would stop him from clawing in the window or leaping lightly over the thorn wall—and I believe the inclination could strike him as readily as that of driving a pack of hyenas from a carcass. Ordinary rules of animal conduct did not apply to him. He had somehow got the impression that he was invincible—perhaps in some bloody shauri in the bush—and the thought flashed across my brain that it was man that he had met there, and killed. And my lust for his golden pelt with its black spots was worthy of any adventurer seeking the ancient pride and glory of the chase.

I knew all this by perception, immeasurably swifter than thought. My gun had not been slow in coming up. I felt it wedge my shoulder, only a second before K'nini leveled the flashlight, casting its beam along the barrel. I looked quick and hard at the target filling my sights.

As the gun roared, the leopard took a vicious bite at the carcass. It was a wonderfully quick movement and an unforgettable one, there in the blaze of light, because it told me that the wonderful integration of his being was already shattered, or he would have made a better answer to the bullet's blow! I shot again. The beautiful beast fell on his side. His legs threshed a few seconds; his tail and his neck stretched; then he died.

Is death the fixed price of all great defiance? I sat in revery.

III

K'nini and I were now faced by a hard choice. It was to go out of the shelter of the *boma*, into the open danger-haunted grass, and bring in the trophy, or to see it torn to pieces by the returning hyenas. I had the odd feeling of having foreseen some such challenge throughout our preparations for the watch; and perhaps that accounted for some of the tricky paths my mind had taken. I did not want to go. I dreaded going with a dread out of proportion to the estimable danger. We should be gone only half a minute; the fact remained that for that period we would be immobilized and largely defenseless against surprise attack.

My nerves were already shaken and my imagination began to bound. I imagined that we had seen only part of the animals that had collected about the bait, and that many more peopled the farther shadows, and all would be aroused and hair-triggered by the smell of the meat, the conflict, and the now fresh blood. Cottar had told me that lions, looking well at a man, become oppressed by the unknown and almost always go their way; but, taken by surprise, or seeing him suddenly when their great dynamos of life were already purring, they often attack by instinct. Everyone knew that a lion at night, in his own element and medium, was an Indian of another skin from a lion lolling and yawning in the torrid day.

Well, I had better get shed of these fancies, because I was fated to go. That fate had been written by my mere maleness, long conditioned by fear of shame. The errant coward would do the same, if there is such a thing as an errant coward—and I had never seen one of pure quill, and doubted if he existed. K'nini knew what I had been thinking, and had calmly awaited the upshot. When I gestured for him to remove the thornbush that served as a rear gate to the *boma*, he made a little sighing sound that no doubt expressed relief, for he hadn't been sure what a strange *bwana* would do, *bwanas* being unpredictable, unless they were completely mad, like Bwana Cottar. For me to yield my leopard skin to the filthy hyenas would have shamed us both. Moreover, I did not doubt that K'nini's concept of "face" was much clearer and stronger than my own.

We crawled out, he with the light and I with the rifle. As we ran forth, he swung the beam in all directions to try to blind or baffle anybody lying in wait. Each of us caught a pair of legs in our free hands, and began to drag the heavy body toward the *boma*. These were the seconds of our greatest disability, when a lion or a leopard could give us short shrift. We knew it, and were scared, but all we could do was hurry.

For one instant, the slicing beam of K'nini's light picked up eyes. These two showed fiery green but they looked bigger and less slanted than a hyena's eyes, and I wondered if they blazed in the flat head of the leopard's mate. In a few seconds more we reached the *boma* gate. There we dropped the trophy, closed the gate again, and resumed our watch.

It grew rather cold. The pack of hyenas had returned, and their monotonous broiling and sharp-edged outcries began again; I did not need coffee to keep awake. Indeed I felt an intense and pleasurable alertness, a quickening of all my senses and strengthening of my life force, and it could stem from nothing but the strong inkling that the big doings of the night were not nearly over. Something had happened on our veld tonight. Perhaps we had drawn our bait and laid a blood trail through a neighborhood alive with game. Perhaps by luck or lore old Cottar had erected our *boma* in the animals' crossroads. And now I awaited the next chapter with a tingling confidence. Half-drunk on excitement, I felt equal to all that the gods of this half-moonlit enchanted night might have in store.

Still its overture took me by surprise. The hyena uproar ceased, as it often did for a few seconds; then did not resume. I had never listened to a deeper silence, and the moon was hid, and I could not guess what caused it. Then the moon looked through a hole in a cloud, and I saw that the whole pack had vanished. Not a wail, not a sob, not a laugh rose from the grass. What had silenced them so completely that their natures seemed changed? They had quit their feast without complaint. Once more they were the outcasts of the veld, and I felt they had gone for good.

It did not come as a surprise to me when K'nini murmured, "*Simba!*" This was a wonderful word, and he pronounced it wonderfully, with a sibilant "s" and a deep-throated "a." Yet I felt that he saw no more than I; and his inkling that lions stood close by in the dark, surveying the scene before they entered it, resolved from the behavior of the hyenas. I was gazing over the bait, into the gray deceptive distances beyond. Then a shadow passed the corner of my eye.

From the brushwood behind us paced three splendid shapes, that of a heavy lion and two lean lionesses. The lion and one of his mates moved straight on to the bait, but the rear lioness turned and, startling me almost out of my wits, came up to our *boma*. She stopped and gazed into the window hardly six feet away. I saw her big tabby-cat face with its odd-set eyes. She gave no sign of rancor; I believe now, and I think it came to me then, that she was moved by intense curiosity, a common enough trait in animals. Her stillness let me be still. I did not fling up my rifle or move at all or make any sound. I do not think she would have leaped over the *boma* wall, although it would be a perfectly simple feat for one of her agility; I do believe she might have tried clawing me through the window. I have not heard of it happening to photographers and other *boma*-sitters in late years. In old days, when travelers and work crews used *bomas* for protection, a number of Hindu and Negro laborers and some Europeans as well were attacked and killed by lions leaping or bursting through thorn walls.

The lioness got her fill of looking at me and turned away. I breathed again, and in a moment all three beasts were gorging. The moon showed the big male, wonderfully vivid in this dim light as by the stepping-up of my powers of vision, as he sank his teeth in the carcass, braced his foot against it, and pulled till the tough flesh gave. It seems inconceivable that they could forget K'nini and me in our just-at-hand hides, or that they did not recognize our existence as living beings, but they certainly ignored us.

There they were, and here I was—this being that I called myself, the same person that had been given a .22 rifle at age eleven and who dreamed childish dreams on the quiet Indiana plains—sitting with a black man in the little pen of thorns thirty feet from three wild lions, watching and listening to their feasting, able to believe it and still not greatly afraid. I found myself thrilled with the litheness and grace of the two lionesses. In the lion I sensed a dignity, a kind of royalty, that breathed a wonder and a half-glimpsed divinity over all my world. I felt the consummate mystery and miracle of being alive.

I V

It was time for the show to end. It had been a kind of passion play, and an inchoate sense of its application to all life had come to me, and I felt at once tranquil and triumphant. Now I had enough; my wits and my nerves were tired, and my sensibilities would soon dull. All the guests I had invited to the feast had come and gorged—those that Cottar had promised and those that he had mentioned as fair prospects. True, he had spoken of the remote possibility of an elephant's wandering by on other business. Happily, I felt certain that I need not contend with this.

So any more would be repetition, and that was bad showmanship. And what I meant, really—the hidden truth—was that I had stayed on guard too long, and if a new crisis rose I might not be able to meet it.

I wished the lions would finish their meal and go. I wanted them to vanish in the night, then K'nini and I would lie in our blankets and sleep. I had no more than thought it than they did vanish, in an abrupt and impolite fashion. One moment they were eating noisily and greedily as ever, and the next they were gone.

This was not the answer to my wish. It only seemed to be. Something had gone wrong. To try to put a stop to the mumbo-jumbo in my brain, I glanced at K'nini, expecting to find him calm and happy and thinking of his light-o'-love in some elegant sheet-iron hut in Nairobi and of the bright silver shillings he would jingle in her ear. Then the back of my neck prickled fiercely.

His crouching position only *seemed* the same. Actually he was poised as a coiled snake. His head was a little cocked; the lines of his face showed very deep; his eyes were big and empty; and he was either smelling or listening to something very faint. I ached to reach him with words. But he told me a good deal when he picked up my rifle that I had leaned for comfort's sake against the *boma* wall and put it in my hands.

I listened with him, as though leaning out into the night, and presently heard a very soft swish, as from someone passing slowly through long grass. But it came from too far to be a light body; only one very heavy would be audible at this distance. All at once the noise grew louder and became mixed and then drowned out by the crackle of brush.

"Buff?" I asked, for most of the camp men knew this white hunter's word for the great Cape buffalo.

He shook his head and instead asked a question, not of me, perhaps, but rather of his own perceptivity, and the night and his gods. "*Kifaru?*"

"Yes, it's a rhino," I told myself with dark fatalism.

In a moment we heard him declare himself with his resounding snort. And now I knew what it was that Cottar had started to say when, talking of my night watch, he had fallen silent. These were good rhino grounds.

Had this rhino merely blundered in our way? I could not be sure, when I remembered the direction of the breeze which long ago I had learned to mark. Quite possibly he had winded us and his usual sulkiness had turned into evil temper and he was coming up to quarrel, perhaps to fight. Certainly he would smell us soon, if he continued in this direction.

I had thought I was done with rhinos and their everlasting belligerence. Now K'nini and I were up against another of the brutes and rapidly approaching the most critical situation, perhaps the only truly ugly one of our night on the veld.

I made the quick decision to get on my feet. The rhino would see me no better there—anyway, he wasn't an eye-minded animal, and interpreted his world through scent and sound—and I would be able to see him immeasurably better. At my signal K'nini got behind me, ready to throw his light. I could shoot now if I had to, and there was a hard core of resolution in my mind, which neither fatigue nor fear could shake, to shoot my level best. We had no room for maneuverability. I had no battery to fall back on, only a single piece. I did not have old Cottar, with his gun that was part of his body, to get me out of a fix. My responsibility for K'nini might be giving me a little lift, especially when I saw in his face that he felt responsible for a good performance of his job.

In a few seconds the moon showed the brute—black, vast, grotesque—trotting surlily toward us. Thank the stars above me he was in the open, and thank the moon for letting me see him plain, because plain seeing is the better half of straight shooting. He stopped about fifty yards away. Again he snorted, lowering his head and pawing the ground. But his steam was not up yet; he was willing to fight not spoiling for it and not committed to it. So he raised his lance again and walked belligerently nearer. Only forty yards from us he again stopped.

Long ago, when the white man was new in the land, he was so bedeviled by ill-natured rhinos that he made a practice of shooting them on sight. I decided not to wait any longer. The full-dress charge of a rhino, horn lowered, quarters rocking, is harder to stop than a lion's, a leopard's, or even a buffalo's; the elephant's alone being more irresistible. The beast made a clear target and could become a perfect one in the glare of the flashlight. I meant to place the heavy bullet in the base of his neck.

He pushed on a few feet more. When he lowered his horn, his tail jerking, I signaled for K'nini to throw his light. Meanwhile the rhino moved, causing me to change my aim a little, and I think my shoulder knocked the black man's arm. In any case, the sleeve of his cotton shirt caught on a thorn and the burst of light fell not on a rhino but on a young tree, some twenty yards to one side of the blind.

Before he could free his arm, there came an utterly astonishing development. The rhino saw the trunk of the tree light up—the brightest, most conspicuous object of the scene—and in the great stupidity of his mind, he picked it as the object of his rage. Down he thundered upon it, missing it with his horn and striking it with his shoulder. Then he stood there as though dumbfounded.

What followed was even more dramatic. It was, when I thought about it later, perhaps the most thrilling example of human wit and resource I had ever seen.

As the brute turned his huge head, seeking another target, K'nini provided it for him. Many wild-animal charges have been stopped by accident, many more by the beast's vacillation—the greatest number were only bluffs to start with—but a black man stopped the one now threatened, and with a joke. With a truly remarkable grasp of the situation, he threw the light's beam on a low bush about fifty feet from the enemy. The rhino caught sight of it and lunged toward it. In a few seconds he rode it down and stopped, wondering no doubt, where it had gone.

Both Cottar and I had observed the gaiety of K'nini's spirits since he had dodged the rhino in the thorn. He thought himself a devil of a fellow, Cottar had said. That lift, that *élan*, was no doubt a factor now, in K'nini's playing the joke through, instead of having me turn this comedy into an affair of shooting and bloodshed. When he threw his light on the trunk of a stout tree fully fifty yards away, the rhino started for it at a full gallop. I noticed, though, that he did not lower his horn, and that his pace slacked a little as he neared it. I thought he was seeing it with his dim eyes, and although he could not make sense of it, he could no longer accept it as an enemy. He ran up to it, gave it a little butt with his nose, and came to a dead stop.

Then, as though in shame and ignominy, as if he knew someone had made a fool of him, taking advantage of his stupidity which he could not help, he turned a little and galloped off in another direction. This time he did not stop. K'nini and I heard him enter some thickets and crash through them. For many seconds more his heavy feet clumped the hard ground, the sound dying away at last.

I took K'nini's hand and shook it hard.

"*Bwana Kifaru*," I told him. The way he showed his teeth in a big smile told me that he understood that I called him the Rhinoceros Master. So ended our magnificent adventure. I produced some biscuits and dried meat from my packsack, and my companion and I chomped on them together. Then we drank some hot coffee and settled in our blankets.

The old moon, that had seen so many sights and was hard to amuse or startle, shone serenely and with great beauty overhead.

Eight

ONCE in the early dusk, when the first big stars began to gleam in the shadowing sky, I came into camp with K'nini to find old Cottar sitting on a grub box, quietly weeping.

I paid it no attention and sat down to enjoy my evening toddy. One of Cottar's sons had told me, before our outfit left Nairobi, that the old hunter had crying spells, almost always following harrowing experiences. During the event he was never known to weaken. Nobody in East Africa could remember when he could not outhunt and outshoot all comers, although some game officials in whose flesh he was a thorn and a few jealous white hunters admitted it grudgingly if at all. The fact remained that his nervous system had been gravely damaged by malaria, great exertion and exposure, and a hundred men's share of narrow escapes.

K'nini and I had been looking for lions in the dongas over the hill, without finding any. It turned out that Cottar had found too many at the edge of camp.

"I walked out in the grass to see what the game was doing," he told me, when he had wiped his eyes. "All of a sudden I saw a lion stick up his head. Before I could shoot I saw two more, and then they were all around me, getting fixed to gang me. It was what we call a mob of lions, and they were rough customers, too. I counted seven of 'em, and maybe more. I had only my buck rifle, but I shot into 'em, and I heard more than one of them growl. They'll be some dead in the morning, mark my words. Next time they'll know better than to sneak up on old Cottar."

Like many lone wolves, he often spoke of himself in the third person. And thinking of that, thinking of him, great renegade that he was as far as civilized society was concerned—although no more than Boone and Crockett, Jim Bridger and Kit Carson—I could not tell him that I wished he had held his fire until he was a little more sure of the animals' intentions. I could have fairly and decently done so, in my belief that his risk was far greater in attacking a mob of lions with a light buck rifle than if he had quietly withdrawn. Indeed I thought he had imagined the lions' "sneaking up on him"; from what I had read of their behavior, they were more likely just waking up from their afternoon nap.

Fearing lions as he did, convinced in his heart and soul he was fated to die in the fangs and claws of a lion, he was always believing the worst of them and seizing every excuse to fire on them. And this evening's brush with them had been bad luck for me. Probably he had dispersed the mob or put them to flight, and my chance of putting one of them in my bag—the one great African prize that I coveted and still lacked—had likely gone by the boards.

In the morning we found only spilled blood at the scene of the shooting. Then my hopes rebounded when one of the trackers brought word that five lions were "on" my three-day-old rhino carcass in the thorn. Vultures had feared to light in the thickets, so the meat was intact except for some hundredweight consumed in last night's feasts. He thought there were two lionesses, two cubs, and a big-pugged male.

These were too many lions for K'nini and me to face alone, Cottar said, and I was inclined to believe him. *Simba* became especially irritable if disturbed on a carcass, and a good many serious accidents had happened to lion hunters in such situations. So it came about that I had to speak to Cottar about his lion-shooting propensity, and could only hope the old Afrikander would not be offended.

"*Bwana*, you don't like lions."

"I don't hate 'em, like I hate wild dogs, for instance. I admit Africa wouldn't be Africa without 'em. But I don't like to have 'em pressing me."

"Will you promise me you won't shoot at any of these lions except to save somebody's life? Will you take your time about it, and not fly off the handle? It would be a great blow to me to leave here without a lion, and I don't want one you've shot."

Somewhat to my surprise, he changed color.

"Yes, Mr. Marshall, I'll try to do what you say."

A grassy hill rose beside the thorn, with a few patches of underbrush and groves of mimosa, only about a quarter of a mile from my kill. As we were skirting this in the truck, K'nini's quick eye caught a glimpse of tawny-brown moving and disappearing on the hillside. His cry of *simba* gave us all a great thrill. It was a magic word when spoken on these sunburned plains; it came to me that it meant more to the black men than to Cottar and me. They had breathed it in their secret rites and wondered at it in their hero tales and folklore. A fierce look came into Cottar's face but he appeared to remember something, and his big hands dropped in his lap, and he did not speak.

He and all the others gazed higher on the hill. My eyes slipped to an open place around and slightly lower, just in time to see the whole pride—that rare, apt word which describes a group of lions, more than a family but short of a mob—cross in file. Besides the mature male, even at this distance looming far larger than the others, and the two cubs that the tracker had reckoned on, there were three, not two, middle-sized beasts that might be either lionesses or young males.

There were, indeed, a good many. A shiver of fear came over me when I remembered that so far on this trip only K'nini had drawn a charge—by that rhino in the thorn. Other quarry had theatened us, but had turned away or stopped, or had never got started, in the case of the lioness by the dry watercourse. Several full charges were common to many African safari, even when the white hunter tried conscientiously to avoid bad ground and situations, not at all like this old trailbreaker whose eyes lighted up at the bare prospect of a shoot-for-your-life shauri. Seeing all those lions, I wondered if I had picked the wrong day to ask Cottar to hold his fire.

II

A tracker had seen the pack and pointed. The driver stopped his truck, and Cottar and K'nini and I leaped down. The tracker asked to come with us, and Cottar nodded; the more the merrier was his doctrine. We ran around the hillside and soon came into clear sight of the band, halted in short grass, at about three hundred yards. I did not like to shoot a hard-kicking rifle at this distance, at least without a dead rest, from lack of confidence in hitting a vital spot. From a different motive, Cottar too wanted closer quarters. He thought they would offer more excitement.

We drew back a short distance, and began to encircle a thorn thicket. As we walked swiftly but lightly, Cottar told me the relationships of the group. The animal next in size to the big male was a young male. Of the two lionesses, the smaller was the mother of the two cubs; the other was a barren female. Some stress in his voice implied a deeper significance to this term than I could catch, and although the time was short, I thought I had better get it straight now.

"Do you mean barren this season?"

"I mean she's an old maid. Her build and her faded color look like it. If so, she's taken up with that mother with the cubs as a kind of self-appointed guardian. It's not very common, but not rare. They pour their love out on 'em and turn into she-devils when it comes to watching over 'em. Even a maneless male is hardly as wicked, and I think—though I can't prove it—that most of them are sterile too."

He fell silent as we drew close to the lions. Coming in view of the patch of low grass where we had seen them last, we found they had moved on to waist-high grass farther down the slope. The head of the big male showed a brief second, his luxuriant dark mane a splendid thing to see, but gave me no time for a shot.

"We better follow 'em," Cottar said. "They're not alarmed, just drifting off, making for the donga at the foot of the draw. If they get into it, we've lost them."

So we too entered the grass—Cottar and I flanking each other at a distance of thirty yards, K'nini close behind me, the unarmed tracker ten yards behind our leader, and the driver bringing up the rear. Although I had followed buffalo into a swamp with blind patches of reeds, I had never before shared the high, lion-colored grass with dangerous quarry. They were not far ahead of us—often we saw the grass move and bend at no more than fifty paces. Cottar had spoken too mildly when he said they were not alarmed. More than that, I knew full well that they were annoyed and that the heat was growing in their beast-brains and mighty breasts and that heat might soon explode into the great rage of lions. They saw us following them. How could they help it when our chests and heads rose above the grass? They could have fled, for although the walking pace that Cottar set was fast, they could have run out of rifle range in a few seconds. But out of ill temper and perhaps great pride, they kept to the same distance.

What if one of them charged me? Could he lunge through the thick grass without giving me sight of him, and all I could see until he sprang would be a wild threshing approaching at stunning speed? The possibility was not remote; only a little trigger in his brain or heart needed to be tripped. The lions were beginning to give voice to their growing anger. Twice we heard short low growls, then a long snarl. Cottar's piercing eyes were darting ahead and to both sides. Did that mean he thought that a lion might crouch down and wait until we fell into his ambush?

I felt cold in my belly and along my backbone and a sick lack of confidence in my nerve. These symptoms eased a little when I came on the open bank of a deep-cut, dry, rock-bottomed watercourse leading toward the donga. Because of its angle Cottar had not come up to it yet, and I thought to wait here a few seconds until he did so. A second after that, he uttered a low, tense shout.

"Look out!"

Beyond the donga branch the grass went into violent motion. A great snarling went up, from different places, as several lions scattered in front of us snarled in unison. Up out of the grass bounded a long, tawny form. I saw it silhouetted as it all but cleared the tassels. It rushed on in a series of powerful, wonderfully graceful bounds, almost as light as the 'mpalla's, and I knew without stopping to think that this was the barren female. She had lived up to the reputation of her kind, fiercely loving and fiercely hating because of her dry teats, and become the first of the band to turn to fight.

It was a magnificent turning. The charge was not aimed at me; it would come on Cottar's side, and that gave me a little time, a breath of confidence. Almost instantly I saw that its target was our tracker. He had been too proud to retreat and afraid to hang back, and the two guns that K'nini and I carried had drawn him a little way, like an opposing magnet, from his original position directly behind Cottar's one gun. But why didn't Cottar shoot?

For a split second—then a whole second—the silence held, great lapses of time in which the lioness bounded nearer and a man's thoughts flew far. Tearing my gaze from that terrific tawny form, I shot a glance at him. He stood with his gun down, waiting. He had not shot and could not shoot until the lioness burst through some low thorn on the opposite bank of the branch. As yet he could not see her.

As the lioness reached some low grass on the farther side of the thorn, she dropped down and almost disappeared. I caught only a dim sight of her, and thought she was crouching for a long bound to clear the thickets and the watercourse as well. I flung up my rifle and shot. It was not the time to shoot—no old hunter would have done it—it was my business to wait till she showed clear, never to trust to a bullet to win any kind of gamble. Even so, I believe the ball "creased" her hide, because she uttered a short growl and, forgetting her goal, sprang rather awkwardly into the bed of the watercourse and dashed down it toward the donga. Many a hunter's life has been saved on the veld because lions and rhinos are less steadfast in their anger than is man. Leopards are more persistent; buffaloes are often single-minded in their maniacal fury; and once an elephant has declared war he is as implacable as an Arab seeking revenge on the desert.

In her dash down the donga branch the lioness passed within ten feet of me. I could not shoot, and in fact could not see her because of its steep wall. When I viewed her again she was only a tawny glimpse spurting around a bend. And now, swinging my piece, I stared wildly about in dread of seeing some other of the band launch an attack. I saw grass moving at a distance and to one side, and then Cottar came to me on the run.

"Follow this down to the donga as fast as you can," he ordered, a note of exultation in his voice. "I think we're going to get in a sure-enough fight."

The source of the inkling Cottar could not tell me, and I never guessed. Perhaps it was a real presentiment.

We had no more than reached the brush-grown rivulet when the fray began. The ground was more open here, the small patches of high grass broken by thickets and nearly naked ground, and Cottar and I, standing almost back to back, could command a good distance and guard against surprise attack at close range. The young male and the barren female burst from the thicket together, running shoulder to shoulder. It seemed that I saw what happened out of the side of my eye, because I had caught a glimpse of the old male in high grass farther down the bank, and his swift walk toward us told me that he too was about to charge.

Cottar's head and shoulder and arm moved very rapidly and the barrel of his big double express rifle came up and blazed. As the yellow lioness toppled headfirst, the nerve of the young male broke, for he was not yet great *Simba*, lord of the veld. He had killed many zebra, including stallions that fight savagely at the last, and antelope with rapier-sharp horns, but perhaps he had never yet sprung on the back of a bull buffalo, and it was not at all likely that he had ever attacked man. When he saw his companion topple, the dauntless one, he checked his attack, half turned, and loped away in another direction.

The old hunter was not yet in the clear. The fallen lioness got her feet under her and bounded on. I got the impression that she was greatly weakened, that her life was ebbing fast—certainly her gait was no longer an incredibly fast scuttle, low to the ground. But her fury remained unabated. She came on, her face one great snarl, her muscles bunching, and if she lived long enough, she would kill. Her dugs were dry and her belly had never squirmed with child, but for this frustration she had found relief in jealous and ferocious guarding over a mother lion and her cubs. Now she went into battle for them for the last time. To weakness she would not yield; death she held at bay; and she dreamed she was going to press home her charge and tear down this defiant ominous tall form.

She did not win her last fight. Man with his mind and his tools —especially this man, this old and gray Achilles of the veld—was too much for her. The tried hand moved, the fierce eyes blazed, and the rifle leveled on its deadly track and roared again.

She pitched down, a great heroine in her poor beast way, coughed once, and died.

I wished it could be the end of this lion shauri. I felt too unnerved to meet a crisis. But Africa seems a peculiarly treacherous land. Old dwellers in it like Cottar seem to sense a malevolence there, perhaps a hate of mankind abiding in its unthinkable spirit; or a humor sometimes grim, sometimes ribald.

At the instant the lioness died, the big lion charged. One bound had carried him into the open; then the dirt flew up from behind his feet as his legs threshed so violently he could not at once get traction. His tail rammed stiff as a board and his huge head dropped. Both eyes fixed on me; I saw them and knew what it meant. His gait was smooth as the flight of canvasback duck. It was not a bounding as in tall grass but a prodigiously fast run, his legs well under him and driving. Cottar had told me that he could stalk, flush, and overtake in a short dash the swiftest bucks in Africa, including some of the desert gazelles; it might be that in this distance he covered ground like the famed cheetah, the hunting-leopard.

There would be only a few seconds—three or four or five—in which he could be shot and stopped. And my only thought was that I must act alone. Cottar had fired both cartridges in his double-barreled express rifle. Even though he was reloading with great swiftness, I could not believe or hardly hope he could shoot in time to help me.

To shoot into the low head and from thence into the breast would be an easy shot of itself. Even under these conditions—the fury of the beast, his size, the speed of his rush, the primal terror inherent in the situation, and its stark scene—still a man of steady nerves, at all handy with a rifle, could have placed his bullet well. I was not that man. If I were, I need not have come here. And I knew about lions. I had told what they did, the terrible dark secret, in my first childish composition. *They ate folks.*

Still I think that Cottar's standing by me, his lame hands racing to ready his gun, became a little added thrust to my resolution. With a great effort of will I held my fire until I saw the dropped jaw under the pale-colored eyes in the center of the big mane, then squeezed hard on the trigger. The big lion, weighing a fourth of a ton, dropped in the middle of a stride. Not one muscle stirred thereafter.

That less than an ounce of lead could have broken the lock of his life, could have found and smashed a hidden vial that held his life's force, I could hardly believe. That strength, fleetness, ferocity, royalty, and a great part of that beauty had gone where a leaping flame goes in the dark. Still my sense of awe at this convulsion of nature became lost in exultation.

III

It has always seemed to me that just before I fired I heard a soft metallic sound as Cottar's opened gun barrels shot home to their fit with the stock. If so, he had been ready to back my bullet with his, and could have saved my life if I had missed. Still I could never lose the satisfaction of stopping the great charge without his help.

Now our hunt was nearly over. With four wonderful trophies in my bag, all taken fairly by my own aim and fire, I had reason to believe that a quest which I could hardly put in words, its goal expressible only in general and inadequate terms, was approaching a successful end. I was wrong about that. It must go on for many years more, throughout many long miles of wandering and search, and bring many thrilling adventures. The omen and inkling of it was given me in my last days in Africa. And this was a shauri in which Africa revealed herself more clearly to my inexperienced eyes than any of the safari.

It was one which we had not sought, only blundered into. Making for camp in the small truck after a morning spent in vainly hunting kudu, Cottar and I were talking of matters ten thousand miles away. K'nini was listening to us, wondering no doubt at the alien speech—silly-sounding and so different from Swahili, the rich universal language in which all men, white and black, could sensibly converse—and only the driver was tending to business. Suddenly he gave an excited shout. Crossing low grass, he had driven up on a leopard kill. The killer had finished his feast long before, but had gone only a little way into a thorn thicket for his midday sleep, intending to guard the 'mpalla meat from vultures. The noise of the truck had flushed him, and there he went, his long spotted body fully extended as he ran in a bounding gallop toward a patch of high grass about three hundred yards beyond.

He was not nearly as big as the great leopard I had killed from the *boma*, yet was a full-grown male, weighing about a hundred and fifty pounds, and Cottar remembered three of his ilk who had bitten and clawed him and left him indelibly scarred. Cottar had told me that if leopards were as big as lions, and could stand up to as much gunfire, they would be the most dangerous animal in Africa, barring not even the mighty *Tembu* of the white tusks. Indeed, the great Martin Johnson gave them the palm straight-forth, without restriction. So it was no wonder, I need not feel the least surprise, that he yelled to the driver to give chase.

Driving forty miles an hour, we still could not overtake the fleet and graceful runner. After the wild and reckless ride, we gained the open ground beside the grass patch where he disappeared; and here the truck was stopped, and Cottar, K'nini, and I sprang out. Cottar's big rifle swung in long arms, and in his face was a glory. I did not know what was in my face. I had been badly frightened by a giant leopard that had cowed a whole pack of hyenas not many nights ago. In K'nini's face I thought I saw signs of intense anxiety and perhaps dismay. He had been greatly impressed by the king leopard's actions, had spoken of them frequently to Cottar, and now he saw what I did not—that this ground was not favorable for a brush with *Tui*.

Our actions remained haphazard and unstudied. Cottar began walking along the abrupt edge of the shoulder-high grass, his rifle ready in his arms. Feeling little confidence in my own aim to stop a sudden attack, I felt a boundless amount in Cottar. Meanwhile a strange thing was happening that neither of us observed. K'nini, carrying my .30 U.S., was slowly dropping behind us.

No one knows to this day why he did not keep his place. K'nini himself did not know, if I guess right; if he was obeying intuitions they were ill-sent. It was certainly not logical behavior, because the safest place for him as well as for me was close under Cottar's gun.

We heard a terrifying noise. It was a wild-beast cry—a feline outburst, half snarl, half growl, so loud that it shattered the quiet of this sunny noonday scene—and instantly continuous with it, a human yell. Already alerted by inchoate fears, I whirled in time to see a yellow missile, with black spots, light from a soaring spring on K'nini's shoulders.

The leopard's attack with fang and claw was immediate and indescribably savage. Yet, after the first outcry, it was a man, not a terror-driven animal, in his clutch; it was a man's mind functioning to preserve the life that actuated it. I could not possibly realize this at the time; Cottar did, because he knew the ways of leopards. Demonic in battle, filled with a raving fury differing from the rages of all other animals, leopards cling with their front claws to the shoulders of tall prey, while they bite at the throat and scoop with their rear claws, their hind legs threshing, at the entrails. Somehow K'nini knew this. While almost any powerful white man, Cottar included, would have hurled the beast off, only to have him come lashing back, K'nini adopted defensive tactics. Dropping to his knees, he covered his face and throat with his arms. Thus the leopard had to stand upright on the ground, biting and clawing naked flesh and scalp, but not yet reaching the vitals of his prey.

This was happening before Cottar's and my eyes. There was not the least shadowing of the scene; nothing was hid from us. Nothing I had ever seen was as vivid, as knife-edged and glaring bright, and it could not help but be stamped on my memory forever. In this sunlight the leopard's pelt was bright-gold with coalblack spots. K'nini had not worn his cotton shirt since its sleeve had caught in the thorn of the *boma*, even though the outcome of that accident had been happy; and his naked back, burnished with sweat, became instantly streaked with blood. About them stretched the pale-gold grass and overhead arched the burning sky of African midday.

Still the essence of this scene was movement, all the more telling because it swirled around the still, crouched form of K'nini. The leopard's front legs threshed in a circular motion, the claws sinking and tearing out at every pass; he bit cleanly and sharply like the cat he was, not worrying like a dog. Meanwhile he snarled continuously and loudly. And only a second or two after the beast's spring, Cottar and I were in rapid movement too. Not I, or even Cottar, could fire without danger of killing K'nini, so we both ran toward the fray.

We had only about sixty feet to go. We had covered half the distance when the leopard saw us, and bounded clear of his inert prey to rush at us. We fired simultaneously, the roar appearing to drown out the beast's screaming snarl. Actually it had ended before then, with the ending of his life as the bullet struck.

There was only one bullet—the hide showed where it had entered and left when I had time to look—but since it was Cottar's—and this I never questioned—it was enough.

What if Cottar had not been with me? When we had rushed K'nini to camp, poured raw iodine into his many wounds, and sped him on his way to the hospital in the small truck with the rest of the outfit breaking camp to follow soon, I found time to think of that. Missing the leopard with my first shot, I would not have had time for another. Nor would I have had the sense to cover up under the beast's attack. Even had I done so, my chance of survival would have been unlikely, since K'nini was too badly hurt and shocked to save me with the .30 U.S. So I had better recast my thinking and feeling about my qualifications as a big-game hunter. I was still only another tenderfoot visiting the lonely veld, and trusting to cooler heads and greater prowess to keep me safe.

Still, when Cottar had sheepishly suggested that it might be my bullet that had laid the leopard low—that he had been shaky that day and might have missed—and I had given him a great horse-laugh in reply, I knew I was making headway.

IV

K'nini lived. But he was never again to gain face and silver shillings by carrying a *bwana's* gun, or even by going on safari as a camp tender. He had become too proud, he told Cottar—when he dodged the rhino in the thorn, and then multiplied that pride by beguiling another rhino into charging bushes and tree trunks about my *boma*—and therefore jealous gods, who cannot abide the sight of men's glory, played him this dirty trick. On the other hand, he had won some striking-looking scars. They would be of help to him in the other great pursuit that men must make, for the most cunning and most dangerous game of all.

As for me, I had acquired a picture. It would live on, ever fresh, when the pretty pelt I had put with my trophies had become moth-eaten and frazzled. The background was all sunlight, and its central figures, appearing at once still and wildly animated, were a study in gold, black, and red.

A more momentous picture was the one I had of Cottar. It was not complete as yet; it had not been filled in. Actually it was a sketch, for I had seen him in only a few of his manifestations. This was my regret, for I knew I would never again behold his like. Even so, I took another interesting snapshot of him before we left camp.

It so happened that engine trouble, which our *fundi* could not correct short of several hours' work, prevented our departure hard on the heels of the small truck. Cottar did not worry greatly about the delay, because K'nini was in good hands, especially those of one of the trackers who knew first aid. And the little truck was sturdy, well-tired, and perfectly adequate, short of accident, to take the injured man to the hospital. To pass the time, Cottar and I visited some mimosa groves in late afternoon. His excuse was to have another look for a family of kudu, very rare in this section, that a skinner had seen a few days before. Actually he wanted to give me a good last look at the veld.

It turned out that I saw its monarch. Not under, but among the trees, stood a bull elephant. He was a lone bull, it seemed; his immediate business here Cottar did not know. He appeared to be loafing, rhythmically swinging his trunk and switching his tail. Nor was this a dinky, a second-rate bull. He stood a good twelve feet, and Cottar guessed his tusks at ninety pounds apiece. To me he became something more than even a great bull, indeed the king of all the immense, mysterious sunburned land, its avatar, and its living link with the long, long past.

He gave me a good view of himself, as though extending royal favor. Filling the lens of my binoculars at two hundred yards I saw the leanness of his skull, the great sounding board of his ears, the marvel that was his trunk, the shifting of his mighty feet. More wonderful than these, I sensed the boundless vitality super-charging his vast and seemingly sluggish form, plainly visible only in his rages, his furious matings, and his wild stampedes. This is the greatest wonder of the elephant.

"Take him!" Cottar muttered; and I had never seen him so eager, young, and brilliant-eyed.

"I can't. I haven't a license."

"To hell with the license. I'll have the boys chop out his tusks, and I'll ditch 'em until I can come back for 'em from Nairobi. If we've got a traitor in camp—a low-lived spy from the game office —he'll know better than to report it. I'll cut him to ribbons with the *kiboko*. I tell you you've no business leaving Africa without an elephant."

"I've got to do it, just the same."

"Then I'll take him myself."

I waited a few seconds until I could get some sort of hold on this. Cottar was dropping extra shells in his coat pocket.

"No, sir, don't do it," I said. "It's not a fair deal with me."

He looked at me, and his face changed; a great sadness came into it, a kind of sadness that only the giants know. For he knew, I think, or else he became more fully aware, that this Africa was not his any more; that tame people had come and taken it, and that the greenhorns, backed by paid guides, could kill the ele-phants that he had once lived by and felt were his own, and he was a remnant of a bygone age, and his day was done.

"All right, Mr. Marshall," he answered at last. "I won't bother him."

This was my unforgettable good-by to the veld. We went into Nairobi, and after I had listened to and smelled the town, I wished that old Cottar could live where he would be better appreciated and understood, say in one of the raw, made-over gold-camps of the American West. Here was the typical fawning worship of position found in English colonial towns all over the earth; anybody with an office, or a membership in the country club, was a bigger man than old Cottar, a true pioneer and probably the greatest hunter on the earth. I witnessed a bad instance of this attitude in the chief game warden's office.

This self-inflated official accused us of breaking the game law by shooting our rhino. Although the schedule printed on my license permitted me a rhino plain as day, he said that the game board had recently closed off the area in which we had shot him, and he had forgotten to warn us! However, he would not fine me; he would only confiscate the head, with its horn worth about two hundred dollars, and sell me a foot, which I had saved for making a humidor, for the nominal sum of a shilling!

Cottar, of course, protested, politely and mildly, saying that the rule was unfair in the face of the printed schedule. Then in an insulting voice the warden demanded, "Who are you to criticize the game board?" I wondered what would have happened if he had said this away from his desk, out on the veld, when Cottar was not belittled and bewildered—like a lion blinded by auto lights on the Nakaru road—by the fences of a civilization he could not cope with or understand. I think he would have thrown him down and given him the *kiboko*.

When I spoke in Cottar's defense, the game warden informed me that if he had his way, "we"—meaning British colonials—"would keep our game for ourselves," whereby Americans such as Cottar and I would be shut out. When I asked him if he cared to be quoted in America to that effect, he told me I could "quote him in hell." I could not very well make a proper answer in an office of the British government in Africa. But at least I have quoted him.

I heard of another instance of some of his town's people's attitude toward brave, rebellious, unconquerable Cottar. A law firm there hung and made mock of one of his savage, ill-spelled letters. I cannot help feeling a deep, enduring anger at such conduct, partly perhaps because Cottar represents America and America represents Cottar. He is of the spirit and genius that made America.

One comfort to me, of a queer and creepy sort, was that Cottar would not have to stand such abuse for very long. There could be no doubt of his nervous impairment. Soon would come the day when he could not shoot so fast and so straight. I could be sure he would not stop shooting unless he could no longer swing a piece. Then he would come to the end that was fit for the Long Hunter. My greatest fear was that fate would play an ignoble trick upon him and cause him to die in bed.

On the night of the arrival of a certain report I wrote the following paragraph, first published in *Field and Stream:*

> Now, at last, the news from Africa has arrived. It is the stuff of legend, to be told and retold, as that scene when Wild Bill Hickok sat at cards, or when Yellow Hair faced the foe on the Little Big Horn.

A more detailed report, arriving later, told that Cottar and his son Bud had been in Masai country. On a jaunt into the veld, the two had become separated when Bud heard a single shot. He stopped and listened, and then, reassured, walked on. Then came other shots. Bud turned back and hurried to the scene.

He soon came upon it—one of the great scenes in East African history. A rhinoceros had attacked the old hunter; and although he had wounded it mortally, it pressed home its attack and gored him in the thigh. They lay a few yards apart, both of them dying, but still gazing at each other across the bloody grass.

So it was not a lion that gave the old man the *coup de grâce.* He had lived and died their victor. Neither was it a leopard by whom he had been attacked three times, nor a bull elephant who had been his mightiest adversary, nor a buffalo such as had once knocked him down and hooked at him in vain. In its being a rhino, it seems to me that fate did well by him, a stroke of such poetic fitness that all his friends could rejoice. The rhino too has lived beyond his time. He too is an anachronism; he too remains untractable and tameless. Both were overwhelmed by civilization, but they fought it to the last, and in the end killed each other as in a Greek tragedy.

I wish that a great park in the East African highlands could be named for Charles Cottar. Surely there are many thousand colonists in Kenya and millions of British citizens elsewhere who would bow to his great prowess and his indomitable spirit the same as we, his native countrymen. There he could come back, and see the game thriving, spreading out to other hunting grounds, *Tembu* and *Kifaru* and *Tui* and the rest; and there no rails would be laid, or land put to plow, but the tall black men of the pastoral tribes could herd their cattle as of old. It would be a monument not only to Cottar but to a vanishing age. And there the old man could build his camp fires, and hear *Fisi* wailing and sobbing in the twilight, and listen with fierce eyes to *Simba's* rhythmic grunts, as he paced the distant plain.

3. Big Jungles

Nine

TWO years after my return from Africa I felt able to under-
take another big trip. My choice of grounds lay between India
and French Indo-China, both deep in the far-flung jungle of southeastern Asia. Having devoured Kipling as well as many heavy
tomes dealing with *shikar*, I had much stronger feelings about
India and knew far more about that great country than French
Indo-China, that far corner of Asia rarely visited by Americans
and almost not at all by American sportsmen. In fact I had
written two short stories, "The Elephant Remembers" and "The
Heart of Little Shikara." They were so charged with enthusiasm
for India and rich with its lore that both were honored by the

American Society of Arts and Sciences, and one of them won the O. Henry Memorial First Prize.

Thus it seemed that India would be the logical choice. However, there were two—perhaps three—opposing factors. One, probably the most important, was that I had not yet been able to locate any sort of outfitter for hunting parties in India, let alone a guide. I was told that I could rent a reserve forest—I did not quite know what this meant—and hire interpreters and assemble my own outfit and that I would be given advice and other assistance by the District Commissioner. As it happened, I felt a little shy about approaching district commissioners or any kind of English officials above the rank of London bobbies. Anyway, I did not feel equal to going forth into the jungles without some kind of a bear leader. Perhaps I would gain such self-confidence in time, but I did not have it yet.

However I heard of and wrote to a Saigon Frenchman, Francis De Fosse, who with his Eurasian son Louis made his living taking French and a few American sports into what was called, rather excitingly, Moi country. The letter I received in reply was literate and enthusiastic. With any good luck at all, I could take tigers and banteng—the large, red wild ox of Indo-China—and have better than a sporting chance at elephant, leopard, wild water buffalo, and the great saladang. And behind the cold type I could hear this last great name roll grandly off his tongue.

Although they were supposed not to run as large as Bengal tigers, the tigers of Indo-China were very fine. If the elephants had been picked over and shot up by ivory seekers, so that not many big tuskers were left, the wild water buffalo did not suffer in comparison with the savage African buffalo. Larger, with an imposing back sweep of heavy horn, he was regarded by some English sportsmen as the most dangerous Asiatic game. And it happened that I had heard about saladang. Reading about him had caused a pleasant tingling sensation throughout my skin. Kermit Roosevelt had declared him the greatest big-game trophy in the world, the only head of his taking that he valued more being his Marco Polo sheep, so rare in America that it was a museum piece.

The first flush of an infatuation with saladang was my second reason for veering toward Indo-China. The third was a hard-bitten conviction that despite the country's many attractions, including saladang, its jungles could never quite come up to the jungles that Kipling had described, that Mowgli had ranged, that Tomaii of the Elephants had smelled on dewy mornings. And, as a kind of dessert topping off my feast, I would save great India to the last.

When Agnes heard the news, she asked me, with some acerbity, "Where in the hell is Indo-China?" I showed her on the map —one door east of Siam and west of the South China Sea. Being on the 106th parallel east of Greenwich while Augusta, our Georgia home, lay 82d west, Saigon was 188 degrees away, roughly halfway around the world. It was also very far south, and by far the longest way I had ever set out in quest of my special kind of Golden Fleece. She sighed, regretting that she had not married a stamp collector, but in the end gave me a good-luck piece for my journey.

It was a Mauser .404 bolt-action rifle, shooting sixty grains of cordite and a four-hundred-grain bullet—much more powerful than Cottar's lever-action .405, well-balanced, stoutly fashioned, and one of the most positive if not foolproof arms I had ever put to my shoulder.

II

The most striking feature of Francis De Fosse was the difference between him and his son Louis.

Some Americans, not I, would be surprised in the first place by a French "white hunter." Frenchmen have become so widely known as *boulevardiers* and dudes that we forget the *voyageurs* of the North and the history of the fur trade. Actually I know of no temperament, unless it is the American, that so lends itself to a life of adventure as the French.

The words chauffeur and aviator came into our language from the French in the early days of automobile racing and flying. The argot of many a perilous sport is at once rich and exact because of French terms. In the case of swordsmanship, none other exists. Being a Latin—and a Frenchman is a Gaul, a heady mixture of Latin and Teutonic—does not militate against love of danger and the hair-triggered nervous mechanisms that make for competence in a crisis and superb timing, muscular coordination, and hardihood. Though we should not speak of it now, for the British won, the French penetrated our Middle West long before any other white people except a few hairy American renegades, strangely resembling Cottar. We must remember the Foreign Legion and the Three Musketeers!

Francis De Fosse was a man of the world as well as a great *cheval de chasse*. In early middle age, tall, erect, soldierly, notably handsome, neat as a pin, he *did* know the taste of *pâté de foie gras* and at the same time what it meant to be tossed by a buffalo. His son was also tall and neat, as well as handsome in a striking and unfamiliar way, but he had never seen the boulevards and the wild looked out of his eyes. His mother was Annamese, and his sweetheart—at least when he was not in town—was a Moi girl.

I did not know about the Mois as yet. I began the fascinating study only when we had ridden several hours in a jerky little train reminiscent of the French provinces and landed in one of Francis De Fosse's base camps near a Moi village. Compared to these people, the Bantu Negroes we had seen in Africa had been like Oxford dons, and even the lean, tall spear-wetting Masai, cattle- and wife-stealers since the days of the pharaohs, had a rich and ancient culture.

The Mois lived in long community houses, perched on stilts.

They farmed by burning out the jungle, planting their crops of rice and opium for two or three years, then moving on. They practiced polyandry, worshiped stones, and hunted with bows and arrows, the latter's points often being smeared with a fast-acting poison. Ethnologists thought them a mixture of Caucasian (from India) and Mongolian from the North. The fact remained that the tribesmen were pleasant little fellows, always ready to grin, and the tracks of their oxcarts were the only semblance of roads in all these spacious jungles.

Most of the villagers, men and women, came with us when we started on the Indo-Chinese equivalent of safari. They would drive the oxcarts, take care of camp, track, and skin. None were gunbearers in the African sense, not knowing how to fire a piece, but they took a great comfort in having such a mysterious magical killer in their hands. At the same time they were practical enough—and it was perfectly good primitive thinking—to believe that the power of a gun could be judged by the sound of the hammer snapping on an empty chamber. It turned out that Francis could speak enough Moi to make his wants known. Louis, however, had mastered the bewildering jabber, having been raised amid the small brown people. In six weeks in their country I learned one word—*nee yah*—which, if pronounced with exactly the right inflection, meant "camp." On the other hand, an engaging Moi youth with whom I experimented could not learn to say "horse." His vocal chords and tongue could not shape the sound—the nearest he could come was "oss-su."

The outfit contained three small stallions, for Francis, Louis, and me to ride. We started forth on these nippy, shaggy little beasts, our stirrups almost touching the ground, while the Mois followed in oxcarts or on foot. With the latter was our kitchen staff—an agreeable Chinese and his son. This boy, about ten, would have stunned a society of ethnologists. His skin was four or five shades darker than his father's, while his features looked emphatically Caucasian. This pleasant, skilled man liked to be called Cookie, although his talents were not confined to preparing delicious meals. Francis told me that he was also a top-hole soothsayer and seer. As a rational Frenchman he did not believe in that sort of thing. But the fact remained that if Cookie predicted something, no matter how unlikely, it had a perfectly irrational way of coming to pass.

I had spoken only a few words to Louis—modest, he stood back while his father talked—but my curiosity in regard to him was buzzing, and my hunch was that he would prove one of the oddest and most fascinating personalities I had ever met.

For the present I was happy to be taking in the jungle, smelling, seeing, listening to it, tasting it in the air, and feeling—at least reaching toward—its obscurities. It had closed around us as swiftly and completely as the North Woods around our pack train when Dean Cochran and I had set forth into the Caribou. In our own South and in the Northern rain forest I had seen rank growth, and the African dongas had often been hidden in rich verdure. But here were the first true jungles I had ever seen. I had always loved the word, and soon I found myself limiting its use to a certain kind of tropical forest, without the least authorization from the dictionary. Second growth and scrub did not deserve to be called jungle. Even the fastnesses of the Congo and the wild, flamboyant greenery in tropical America did not seem the real jungle of my heart's desire. The real jungle was Asiatic, where the trees stood tall with intertwining limbs, and between the towering trunks the ground lay cool and damp and almost open. Tigers dwelt in the dim coverts. Without tigers it could not fill the bill. Tigers were the incarnation, the titulary godhead, of the jungle.

We had not gone half a mile before Francis got down from his horse and showed me the footprint of a young tiger in the rain-wet cart rut. It was four-toed and its palm was the size of a man's.

To my eyes the jungle is incomparably beautiful. The inter-meshing foliage overhead becomes a true canopy, cutting off the blazing sunlight, but letting its gold sift through—softened, tinted, it seems, by green, falling in spots and splashes. Creepers hang from the boughs and often intertwine the trunks, and some-times flowering vines form curtains that must be drawn aside in order to pass. There are many more birds to be seen than on the veld, and greatly more to be heard, as they croak or cry or sometimes sing in the unseen treetops. They were not very musical, these jungle birds; I did not hear one that could come up to our mockingbirds, or hardly a meadowlark, but their feathers were very fine. A great number wore a brilliant green that became invisible the instant they darted among the foliage. Others with the harshest cries wore the gaudiest colors, black and red and yellow and blue, and you felt they were touts and mountebanks and rough customers at heart. In a little while we began to see incomparably splendid pheasants. Their fine dress appeared to be useless except for vain display, and in fact their tassels and plumes were a drag on their flight. Still I would not trade the sight of them for ten times their number garbed quietly, sensibly, and in good taste.

The greatest of the pheasants were the peacock and his hen, and the Mois looked at them with brightening eyes, perhaps be-cause of their place in ancient demonology, or, just as likely, be-cause they wished that they too could dress as gaudily, strut, and as successfully make love.

Besides these exotic fowl there were flocks of pigeons, some of a large variety, and innumerable parrots that jabbered a little among themselves, but not nearly as noisily as some of the birds lacking the gift of tongues. The most heart-warming to an alien in these distant shores, and arousing real nostalgia in the dweller of our South, were the jungle cocks and hens. They appeared the spittin' image of the small-sized red and brown and burnished chickens so common in the South. They clucked and scratched for worms and the roosters crowed and chased the hens exactly as in barnyards at home.

There were nowhere near—not even by an appreciable fraction—as many animals to be seen here as on the veld. In spite of the openness of the forest with only occasional thickets and young trees, we could not see far; a hundred yards seemed about the limit except in occasional lush, surprising parks. The light appeared to fail beyond that, rather than undergrowth intervene. In these ranges we saw ferretlike animals, squirrels, mongoose, jackals, and the small, reddish-colored barking deer with its loud raucous cry. These last we kept seeing, every few hundred yards; and they would provide most of our venison. The first big game worthy of the name was a herd of sambur, that splendid stag that I knew from Kipling's writings.

> As the dawn was breaking, the sambur belled,
> Once, twice, and again.

These sambur did not bell, but they made a dramatic and quite beautiful picture—being about the size of the Scotch red deer, the bucks having massive branched antlers and the does shapely bodies and a singular grace—as the little herd stood poised as though about to take wing instead of run away. Then they darted off and the jungle that was both their protection and peril shielded them from our sight.

A few minutes later I was startled by a loud rushing sound in a knee-high thicket. So much noise indicated a big animal, and it was a queer sensation to stare and see nothing. Then out of one end of it ran a creature as ugly as the sambur was beautiful. It was a lizard the size of big 'gator, running high on his legs instead of crawling, with a sinuous neck, reptilian head, geometric designs on his hide, and a long, revolting-looking tail. Francis told me quickly that it was of the varanus family, and a first cousin to the huge dragon lizards of Komodo.

We gained the first outlying camp before the rain broke. It was due to arrive about two in the afternoon, and was rarely as late as a local train in the States. Broke was the right word— I had come in the rainy season—and when the somber clouds had rolled and rushed over every blue inch of the sky, and the light dimmed swiftly to a kind of purplish dusk, and a deep silence held for long seconds of suspense, then a rattling roar ushered in the storm. I sat in a dry palmwood hut with a thatched roof, deep eaves, and opened ends, but the rain did not beat in, because there was no wind. I heard it lashing straight downward through the trees, shouting in the distance, beating and then gurgling on the ground.

I listened to its symphonies, and a keen pleasure came upon me. It was a wonderful thing to be sitting here in the cool, deep in the jungle, soon with good luck to meet and engage tigers and the great saladang, so far from both the joys and trials of my life at home, halfway around the world. I listened to the thunder's raving and crashing. Every few seconds the gloom of the rain was shattered by the white glare of lightning. But I did not feel afraid—the green forest giants raised their heads on every side, defiant of the bolts, and they would keep me safe.

Wearing a yellow mackintosh and looking unexplainably comic, Francis popped in my door and stood dripping.

"Mr. Mar*shall!*" he began, in correct English and with military aplomb, "if you are agreeable, we will devote the first half of our hunt to the great saladang. Of course we will take other game as we encounter it: a good boar, a big sambur, a barasingh if you want one—and they are very fine—and if we are lucky, a bull buffalo. We'll by no means rule out the hope of an elephant —although big ivories are very scarce—and there's better than an even chance we'll walk up on a tiger or a leopard. However, our declared goal will be the saladang. We'll spare no pains to put him in the bag, and not digress short of success throughout this period. If, toward the end, we feel that he has escaped us, we will find what solace we can in a big head of banteng."

"That suits me very well," I said, when Francis paused.

"The remaining half of the hunt we will give to tigers, a waiting, watching game for the most beautiful prize in Asia."

With a wave of his arm suggestive of a salute, he turned smartly and marched out. He left me marveling over him, such a handsome and virile figure, the true Gaul, so far from Saint-Cyr or the little cafés. Suddenly I felt quite sure of the success of the hunt, although it would be gained by good strategy and tactics, not by barging about the bushes as with old Cottar. Then, like a shadow, Louis slipped in the door. He was naked except for a sarong, which was wringing wet.

"My fat'er is a very fine hunter," he remarked, after a long and comfortable silence.

"I'm sure of it."

"Also he is a European while I am Eurasian," he went on. "He uses his brain in the business, and I follow my nose. And together—Europe and Asia—we're going to show you a good time."

I answered politely, sure that something more was coming.

"None of the saladang have names," he went on, drawing deeply at a cigarette. "They live in the deepest jungles and are rarely seen by the Mois, who don't know one from another. But there is an extra-big tiger that has a name, and I know his hunting grounds. He goes away for a few days, but always comes back. The Mois call him some jabber that means the Old Man. He's a cunning old devil, staying clear of other hunters that came here. And I want you to be the one to get him."

I thought of a question, decided not to ask it, then asked it anyway. What the answer might be defeated my imagination.

"Why have you picked me?"

"So you will put my fat'er—me, too, if I deserve it—in a book."

Life was one great fabulous book, I thought, in which wonders never ceased.

III

The advantage in coming to Indo-China in the rainy season was the escape from the broiling heat of the dry season. However, the danger of malaria became much greater, and the warm damp brought a large increase in insect pests. Once red ants invaded my bed; once I stepped on a nest of black ants; and twice I was ambushed and bitten by scorpions, which are not insects, I suppose, but fiendish fellow creatures called arachnids, which is no balm for their excruciating sting. A nuisance, but with such odd behavior that we did not complain, was a kind of wasp, obsessed with a passion for packing the muzzles of our rifles with dirt. Since the cementlike deposit would cause a shattering explosion, we had no choice but to keep them covered.

Snakes increased somewhat, Francis told me; at least they became ubiquitous. I never dared reach for my boots in the dark dawns without first throwing a beam from my flashlight, lest a little harmless-looking krait should be coiled there. The krait is a small cobra, which kills almost as surely, although a good deal slower, than the great king cobra, the hamadryad. Once Francis heard a call of distress from across a river, and he reached the caller in something under five minutes, probably about three. He found a fine, strapping Moi girl already in shock from the bite of the king cobra, and before he could pick her up and put her in his boat, she died.

The common cobra is too well-named, being common to all southeastern Asia. Russell's viper kills his thousands every year, and in the dark wood ranges the huge python, never known to kill anyone.

On one occasion Francis and I were resting under a rather rare jungle tree always in the process of growing and shedding stiff, flat, pale-yellow leaves, considerably larger than a man's palms. Seeing one of these move of itself, I picked it up to find it not a leaf, but the back of a toad, fashioned by nature to imitate the leaf with incredible fidelity, even to its appearance of veins. The body of the toad was red-colored like the ground; and all in all it was the most stunning example of protective coloration and configuration I had ever seen. When I turned the toad loose he immediately disappeared among the litter.

"Are these toads common?" I asked Francis, when we were walking away.

"That's the first I've ever seen in twenty-five years in the jungle," this keen observer answered. Since then I have wondered if I missed a chance of having a rare Indo-Chinese batrachian named after me.

I began to realize Francis' abilities as a naturalist soon after I became aware of his prowess as a hunter. Under his guidance I put in the bag a very large and beautiful civet cat, also the fine sambur he had promised. And to judge by the amount of energy he and I were expending, the military thoroughness of our efforts, it would not be long before I became one of the few Americans to take the great saladang. Cookie called me at half-past four. After a hasty breakfast, Francis and I tramped about five miles to an immense spread of elephant grass, like a deep-green lake. Stealing along behind us came two Mois. They never spoke, and we never heard their footsteps—they could have been a couple of their own wood sprites. Into the grass we went in search of saladang.

The jungle cooled and dampened us with dew, and in the broiling hellhole of the six-foot grass our clothes were soon drenched with sweat. Almost always we found fresh sign of the huge beasts, tracks, and dung, but day after day went by without affording me a shot. Then, one signal morning, we heard the drum of hooves and a great tearing and swish of the grass as we flushed a big herd. At top speed we ran after them, and then Francis stopped, and laid his hand on my shoulder to quiet me. A few feet farther on I saw the whole herd, stopped dead still in broken-down grass, and all at once I knew the splendor of the saladang, and why, having come to his stamping grounds, I must take one of the bulls for my trophy room; knew that he was as essential as a tiger, a great tiger; and if I failed to bear away his huge head my trip would have come amiss, and I would fall short of victory.

There were many cows and calves and one colossal bull. I had heard how the saladang bull is the largest ruminant in the world, that he often stands six and a half feet, sometimes seven, to the top of his high arched shoulders; but I had not realized what this meant. He was far larger than the largest African buffalo. He was black as Satan and he had black, upcurved horns and all over him was written majesty and might.

He had started to turn, so I took a quick aim and shot. He made a great bound, and he and all his followers dashed into high grass beyond. In spite of their weight they appeared to dash— wonderfully quick in the eyes of a nature lover, but woefully quick in mine, as I caught a last glimpse of the fleeing bull. Protected by our guns—for the saladang often flees, only to steal back to attack the foe—the Mois looked for spilled blood. The search was brisk and positive; it was not drawn out to save my feelings. In about five minutes both men ceased making animated movements and became listless.

"Where did you hold?" Francis asked.

"About a foot under the high shoulders."

"That was too high. I should have warned you. The saladang has big plates of bone above the shoulder that a bullet can penetrate without fazing him. We'll have to look for another."

"Maybe I missed him." I controlled my voice well.

"No, I heard the bullet whack. But it comes to the same thing."

Not quite, I thought, for the target had been easy and I had taken intent aim. If I had patently missed I would have lost my new-gained confidence, and received a severe setback in the pursuit of my goal. . . . At the same time I remembered that Francis knew this, that he was an understanding man, and perhaps he had told a white lie about hearing the bullet whack. I ended up not knowing the truth or having any solid evidence either way. I could not ask the Mois.

Ten

THE saladang grew upon me in my thoughts and dreams. His name was notable, and these jungles where he slept and loafed and the elephant grass where he grazed made a dramatic background for the king of the wild cattle, coal-black with white lower legs. Louis told me tales of his rages, his raving and bawling, and his studied hate when he circled back on his own track to ambush his pursuer.

"He's got a Roman nose," Louis told me. "They often go with aristocrats. And the saladang is the highest in these jungles."

I looked at Louis' nose and it too was Roman. Sometimes it gave his face a fierceness, sometimes a great distinction. And when I stopped to think of it, Louis, also, was an aristocrat. In that respect I thought he differed from his father, who seemed to me a middle-class Frenchman, of officer capability, and with the level head and staunchness of his kind. Aristocracy is not a matter of high lineage but a state of mind, an attitude toward life. Louis, for instance, did not know he was a half-caste—I mean by that, he was like a mule who did not know his strength or a white crow in a flock who did not know he differed from his fellows. I had met a good many half-castes on the ship, most of them from India, and almost all of them were tragically conscious of the fact, either with forced pride or defiant shame. When Louis thought about it at all, he was amused by great Asia and little Europe meeting in him. It was only a sign of his composure that he went to bathe in the heat of the day in the company of his Moi sweetheart, she carrying a big towel to dry his back, and in the sight of the whole village. He had heard of Paris and would like to see it, but he made no religion out of it; he would rather see the birth of the Mekong in Sikang.

When I became a little weary with repeated disappointments on the saladang grounds, he recommended, for a change, a deer hunt at night with headlights. If we killed a big sambur, we would peg him down for tiger bait, for Indo-Chinese tigers, largely unlike the Bengal variety, would readily come to a carcass of other than their own killing. There would be no loss of meat—he explained this as carefully as might old Cottar—for Louis, also, was dealing with an alien. We would simply feed a tiger meat which, except for this free meal, he would get himself. Several tigers had come into this jungle lately. He had seen their spoor, smelled one of them rank in the grass, and he would like to give me a chance at one of them before they moved on.

I was not sure I would like night hunting. What I meant was that I remembered a night with K'nini in a *boma*, and how my panting heart and popping eyes had drawn, with the gods' collusion, the kings of the veld; and perhaps I shouldn't risk it. This was superstitious folly of the most patent sort. I had not the slightest reason to believe that such wild luck would follow me to Asia.

11

Soon after supper Louis and I boarded the oxcart, with one Moi to drive, another to help us hunt, and a third who just wanted to go. Somewhat to my amazement, Louis did not bring a gun. Nor was the omission a compliment to me. He knew I had shot at a saladang without bringing him to bag, and I had regaled Louis and Francis too with the tale of some African bumbling, not for modesty's sake but to prepare them against more of the same.

Then there recurred to me an inkling I had felt from the first, that Louis was not in any sense the hunter that Francis was. He loved the jungle just as much and possibly more—he knew it as well and perhaps strangely and immeasurably better—but he did not care very much about shooting its inmates. Rather he wanted to roam its vastness with little brown Mois. Betweentimes he relished big meals and sleep laced with vivid dreams; and he liked never being under pressure, and taking his own time about everything.

Still I had not got to the bottom of why he had brought no gun on our jaunt tonight. Maybe he was making *puja*—the Indian word for the unwritable Moi equivalent of magic or medicine —to bring much game into our flashlight beams. More likely he did it in the way of a joke—for the hell of it. It made me feel very odd to have the only gun on a jungle jaunt in pitch dark. Certainly it would entertain the Mois, who as yet had no convictions about me and my gun, and Louis most of all would enjoy the potentialities of the situation. He did not know what would happen, and for a jungle brat like him, that was most amusing.

As soon as we had cleared the camp, Louis and I turned on

our headlights powered by pocket batteries. The brilliant beam from his light searched one side of the pair of ruts that we called the road, and mine swept the other side. Meanwhile it was hard to stand without hanging on to the cart side, so violently were we jounced and jolted over this rocky rain-washed ground, and the riding grew worse when we turned into a cart path so old and little used that the ruts had grown to grass. Even so, the experience became immediately worth any discomfort we would undergo, a hundred times over, even if we did not fire a piece.

In daylight in the high jungle there is very little sharp perspective. Beyond fifty yards a sense of distance sets in—a dimming and a merging of the various shades of green—so that it is hard to distinguish a nearer tree from a farther one. At night in the lamplight the visual range was shortened still more; but what was seen stood forth as in a stereopticon slide, a little like the various wings of a well-devised stage: vines hanging, creepers coiling, little trees standing almost in silhouette against great trees, large white blossoms hanging as though freshly dead. And all beyond this, and sharp and stark on each side of the sword-like beam, lay black night. The night leaped as the shafts moved. The effect was indescribably entrancing, poetic, and somehow weird.

The sense of the jungle's life—not now its feverish growth but its teaming inmates—became clearer and stronger than in daylight. Everywhere we looked were small, shining eyes. A great number of these were birds, so far away or so obscured by foliage that we could not make out their shapes; many were small mammals; squirrels, ferrets, mongoose, and jungle cats; some were frogs and snakes. Speaking in a low, blithe undertone Louis identified jackals, mouse deer no bigger than an African dik-dik whose hoof could rest on a dime, and before long, so far off that the beams diffused and spread, a whole troop of monkeys whose eyes lighted up some big-limbed forest giants as though they were Christmas trees. The strange twin lamps burned true only for a few seconds. Then the monkeys quit their dazzled stare, broke the spell as few deer have wit to do, and immediately got into motion. The first sign of it was the lights shining and winking out as the animals were caught on the move. Many instances of this occurred simultaneously, as we cast our lights a long way, and the effect was spectacular, as of some strange kind of fireworks.

Presently the whole troop got under way in flight, once more organized according to monkey law and functioning intelligently. The trees stood deserted, and we followed the story through sound, not sight. There was a great swishing of foliage, for one monkey makes only a good fuss as he swings through the leafy branches, but five hundred cause a prodigious uproar. Limbs rattled and knocked against each other, twigs crackled and broke, boughs creaked and shook violently in recoil as a little furry acrobat took off on a long leap. Hearing the racket, a newcomer could easily believe it was an elephant stampede.

It slowly receded, and at last the silence of the jungle swallowed it up. Louis spoke in an odd and almost priestlike tone.

"Every leopard in hearing will follow that rumpus. He'll try to catch up with it or intercept it somewhere in the jungle. And every python will run like hell through the dark to get to a tree where he thinks they'll land in passage. Their idea is to get their hooks on one or more of them. Monkeys flushed at night are easy killing."

I thought that sambur would be the same, when dazzled by the lamp. A little later, when a pair of eyes, slightly higher off the ground than any we had seen, identified the owner as a barking deer, I felt a waning of my enthusiasm for the deer-hunting part of this jaunt. The fact remained that we needed a heavy buck to put out as bait for a tiger, to draw him out of his green shadows and get a shot at him, the striped killer, the most beautiful big animal in the world except the human animal, and the most terrible except him—the soul and spirit of the jungle, in

whose existence outside of the cage, running wild and free, subject to being hunted like a common beast, I could hardly believe.

So when two eyes looked larger and much higher than any
we had seen, of a beautiful sapphire color, I got ready to shoot.

"I think it's a big sambur stag, very close to us," Louis told
me in a hushed tone. "Bring your gun up slowly until the eyes
go dark behind your sight, then fire."

I had been instructed in this last. When the front sight lights
up, brushed by the beam falling in a long slant to the target, the
twin circles reflecting the glare become invisible. So it happened
as I slowly raised my barrel. As I fired, I thought I heard a sound
under the roar of the explosion, and it seemed that of a body
striking the ground.

One of the Mois grunted in satisfaction. Louis and I jumped
out of the cart, and guided by our headlights, made our way to
the kill. But it was not a sambur stag, but instead a cow-creature
of some kind, a long way off. It looked like a yearling calf of
some very large reddish variety of beef cattle.

"It's a young banteng heifer," Louis told me. "She weighs a
good six hundred and will make a fine bait."

"Is this good tiger country?"

"I haven't been here for some time, but I have a notion it is.
The amount of grass and undergrowth is just right to attract
deer and wild cattle. Finding young banteng here means tigers
are not far away. You'd better lay down another bait while
you're about it."

So we rode on, and the lights continued their merciless quest.
It was not the right thing, at least not a good-mannered thing,
to be exposing the jungle's secrets in this bald way. The tender
deer hid from the light of day. They crouched down in the
coverts, and did not move about a great deal, to avoid attracting
the attention of their enemies, and they looked forward to the
dusk that set them free. At night there was only the moon and
the distant twinkling stars to show their shapes. They trusted to

this, and lived their lives accordingly. Our lights were as arrogant and cruel as would be, to us, a newly invented demonic camera that exposed our secret thoughts.

I decided not to shoot, on tonight's jaunt, another big animal for bait. I thought the resolve might be hard to keep if we saw a big sambur's eyes shining in the dark, or at least it would be hard to explain to Louis. I was wrong about both of these things, as was proven when we came on a herd of sambur—a dozen pair of eyes, some high, some medium high, and some of them low, shining away with a wonderful brightness and blueness on both sides of the road. Between and among the shadowy greenery in mid-distance, they made a picture I would never forget.

"Sambur?" I asked.

"Yes. Pick a big bull."

"Can't we buy worn-out buffalo from Moi villages to use as bait? Francis said they usually came to a pretty cruel death."

"That's right." Louis spoke with a new ring in his voice. "But the little devils will charge you about five American dollars apiece."

"I'll pay it. Then we can shoot them and put them in the most favorable spots."

"Well, in that case, there's a certain jungle god that our Mois won't have to placate tomorrow. He's the god of the deer, especially of the sambur deer with big horns—the horns enter into it through some connection with fertility—and if we feed any to the tigers they'd have to cough up some copper coins and rice, not getting off with free flowers and fruit as in most sacrifice."

"How do you feel about it?" I asked boldly, for he and I were in a deep and secret place, our Moi companions unable to understand us, and the offense of probing his secrets was thus half mitigated.

"As long as the jungle lasts, there will be plenty of deer," he said gravely. "They'll furnish food for tigers and leopards, baits for hunters like you, venison for our parties and for the Mois, pretty sights for me. When the jungle's gone, they'll be glad to be gone too, and so will I. Meanwhile they have to take their chance like all of us."

It was by no means a complete answer. There was no language in which Louis and I could communicate fully. I wondered what kind of a faun I had got a hand on.

Before long we came to where the two ruts forked into four ruts.

"One of these roads would take us to camp fairly straight," Louis told me. "The other's round about through this same kind of jungle. Which shall we take?"

My legs and back were somewhat tired from the jolting. My head ached slightly from our close watch, and the interplay of brilliant light and black dark. But I was not in the least incapacitated, and answered, "I'm in no hurry to get to camp, if you think we might see something."

In spite of my knowing only one word of Moi, I would bet my nightcap toddy that he had repeated my remark, and beyond a doubt he spoke in a tone of pride. Could it mean other than that I had not shamed his own white-man blood before the jungle men?

They too appeared childishly pleased. They stood a little different, slightly taller and squarer, and one of them, bolder than the rest, gave me a big grin in the side-shine of my lamp.

So we took the longer road; and only a minute later we heard a crash and saw another herd of sambur, already in wild flight. When they had rushed out of the glare and vanished in the darkness, Louis made an odd remark in a low voice.

"You'd be surprised, Mr. Mar*shall*, how many animals use this road."

"So?"

"You see it was once a deer and wild-cattle path. They always take the quickest and best route from the grazing grounds to the ponds, from highland to lowland, from opens to thickets, and such as that. That's why the Mois used it for their carts. And now some other animals use it for hunting or from pure laziness."

"For instance, what?"

"Well, elephants. They mosey along here. And there's no animal as lazy as a tiger. He's as self-indulgent as a house cat."

There was nothing pertinent about it, I told myself. The fact remained that the mood of our company had changed. The brown men stood hushed and tense. Louis probed his beam farther than before, and with greater care. I saw his face in the aura about the lamp, and it looked like an eagle's.

III

Ten minutes went by quickly, with nothing happening to explain time's swift passage. I knew only that I was aroused and tense. Then a momentary gleam, what might be Louis' beam striking a bright leaf, passed over before he could stop its swing, made him reverse its course to find the glimmering object. At once out of the blackness blazed twin circles of green fire.

I have since wondered if any real difference existed between these eyes, as reflected by our lamps, and others we had seen. Although they were no larger I have the distinct impression of their being far more brilliant—incandescent, it seemed—and more like incredible emeralds than sapphires. I flung my light in the same direction. Now both beams focused on the eyes. My heart bounded as Louis spoke hardly above a whisper.

"It's a tiger. Take good aim."

I knew the necessity of this last, perfectly well, but it did me good to hear it. It brought a sense of fellowship between me and him and the Mois that gave me that much more to stand by. There was only one gun and it lay in my hands. Out in the dark stood the tiger, briefly blinded, but with his great potential set for instantaneous use in a blaze of action. I raised my rifle until the front sight started to eclipse the twin green lamps, then pulled the trigger.

The piece roared, and the answer was truly tiger. Through the reechoing blast came his growling roar as the bullet hit. Then we heard the brush crash as he ran off a distance, and the sound lasted what might have been four or five seconds, then we heard it stop.

It is the common way of a tiger to fly when first hit, then quickly come to bay. And in coming to bay he becomes what many men believe is the most formidable quarry in the world, and certainly the most likely to attack. Not even a raging elephant or a gone-mad leopard or a green-eyed buffalo will charge as many times in a hundred provocations as a wounded tiger resolutely pressed. Unless he is downed too soon, it becomes almost a foregone conclusion.

That was why I heard what Louis said in a kind of incredulous dream.

"Let's go look for him with the lights. That's the best way to find him."

In his voice was high repressed excitement, even fright, but nothing to make me doubt his deep, essential sanity. He meant for us to walk, with only one gun, out into the thick and blinding dark, broken only by the beams of our flashlights.

"I refuse," I answered. Men often express themselves in an odd precise way in moments of great conflict. It seems that the brain, working at extreme intensity, comes out with the best language that it knows.

"Listen, Mr. Mar*shall*," Louis urged quietly and quickly. "It's safer now than in the daylight. Then he could very likely ambush us—you can't see the devil in the daylight, in places like this, until he's on top of you. But if he's got his head up, our lights will pick up his eyes if he's anywhere in range. My fat'er and I found it out years ago. It's just the idea of it that makes cold shivers. Wherever he is, the light can find him, and we've got two lights."

"I'll try it a little way," I answered, bleak and cold.

"We'll be all right. Remember, he can't see us behind the light. A tiger never charges till he can see good."

The argument was utterly reasonable. All I could raise against it was my deeply ingrained instincts against looking for a deadly enemy on his own ground at night. As the man with the rifle, I took the foremost place, moving toward where I had last heard the tiger.

"A little more to the right," Louis murmured. "He crept on a little distance after he stopped running. I'll cast my light over your left shoulder to guide you."

Happily the forest was open. Even so there were great spaces of blackness between the golden shafts, and I did not know, and greatly feared, what they might bring forth. We walked very slowly about a hundred feet. I was about to stop and turn back —I could not go it any more—I was at the end of my rope when Louis's beam held still.

"There he is. He's turned his eyes from the light. Take your time."

In a few seconds more our great quarry, lord of the dark but now betrayed in his own medium, faced the light again. Maybe his boundless ferocity, by which he hunted and lived and killed, made him do so; perhaps he was dazzled. Again I saw the eyes blaze forth. He uttered a low growl, and it was a sound no brain could ever forget, in the silence of the deep, black forest.

My rifle came up smoothly in spite of my fright, and since we were so near that I could make out the tiger's shape, I found his big head in my glimmering lights. By a last forcing of nervous energy into a split second of great stillness, an extreme effort that riflemen know, I touched trigger.

The intense twin moons stopped shining; the eyes turned dark.

The outline of the tiger that I thought I had seen before had disappeared; and it might be—I could hardly believe it yet—that he had sunk down into a low thicket. I could not go and see. Not for a long, long time—I judge a minute or more—could I bring myself to draw any nearer. I waited, gripped my rifle, fixing the spot with my beam, while Louis cast his beam back and forth, patiently and with extreme care.

A Moi came up from behind us and spoke to Louis. He nodded, and turned to me.

"He said the tiger is dead."

"I don't believe it."

"I swear to you, he is. I knew it as soon as you shot. And now the Mois say so—that stops all possibility of a mistake."

"You can't see his body."

"I think I can, in the thicket. I can make out his stripes. I'll go up and see, if you like. But it's against my fat'er's rules to go up without a gun."

"I'll go with you."

So we walked together a little way, and at every step the truth became more plain. The tiger was lying on one side, his head thrown back, as though with a last effort to see his foe. I looked at his gorgeous hide and his black stripes and at the beauty and wonder of him, even in death, and I knew that this was the greatest trophy of all my hunting until now. From now on, although I would hunt the other great beasts of the chase, I would make tigers my main quarry and goal, for the promise of intense adventure, exultation, and danger that lay in their pursuit.

The tiger was an average-sized male in the prime of life, weighing close to four hundred pounds. One of the Mois drove the cart close by, the oxen not in the least troubled by the smell of a dead tiger, and with a good deal of grunting and heaving, lugged him in. Then, half out of our heads with excitement, we started home.

There was a quite wonderful impromptu celebration when we arrived with our gorgeous trophy. The Mois came screeching from their huts, and rice wine flowed freely, and Cookie solemnly burned a whisker in the campfire while he pronounced an ancient charm, and there were other delights and excesses. But it was a quiet affair, Louis told me, compared to the one that would follow the killing of a notorious tiger, one well known to the Mois, who preyed on their plow beasts, such as the Old Man. But it was Francis who made the most unforgettable statement.

"Louis told me how you and he once stalked a wounded tiger with flashlights," I said, when I had recounted the episode. "Except for that, I couldn't have forced myself to go."

"When Louis' blood is up, he's not always careful with the truth," was the cryptic, dignified answer.

Eleven

FRANCIS and I continued to beat through the elephant grass in search of the great saladang. All we found were stale tracks, cold dung, and abandoned stamping grounds. And as passing time raised my esteem and deepened my feelings for this huge, black, embattled wild ox—not only through Francis' factual accounts of his doings but Louis' imaginative concepts of his relationships with the jungle gods—it brought nearer the day I must forsake the chase to round out my bag of tigers.

The thought of going home without the most famous and distinctive trophy obtainable in the Indo-Chinese jungles was a bleak and miserable thought. Hating to confront it, still I was forced to do so. A big bull banteng, easily obtainable on nearby grounds, was frequently taken as a substitute. There is no such thing as a substitute for a blue ribbon, for winning instead of losing by a nose, and for the prize on which man has set his heart. He can persuade his own brain, perhaps, but not his soul.

The day came when Francis trekked to some grassy dales to look for fresh sign. On the day before, Louis had taken off for the Moi villages to buy four or five superannuated buffalo, cases of "long labor urged on aged breath." I thought to lay late abed that morning, but wide awake at the usual hour of half-past four, I rose and dressed in the still-black dark. Then, as Cookie gave me my usual breakfast, the two Moi trackers who usually accompanied Francis and me came up grinning. When I put an imaginary gun to my shoulder, wiggling my fore-finger, one of them ran light and swift as a deer and brought the Mauser.

So we made for the same grounds that Francis and I had been hunting for the past three weeks. It was a chilly trek of five miles, and today a lonesome one, for I could not speak a word to the Mois; I did not know their thoughts; and all I could do was admire their light, graceful gait so in contrast with mine. We ventured a short distance into the elephant grass, but it was already steaming from the feverish early sun, and I swiftly re-treated to the cool of the jungle. I was thinking of giving the order to head for camp—indeed the word was almost on my tongue—when one of the boys stopped and gazed at a big, deep footprint in the moist dirt of the cart road.

It seemed to me the largest track I had seen in Indo-China. However, I had not measured the others, and could not be sure. It had been made by one of the great wild oxen, certainly a full-grown bull; whether the saladang or the banteng I could not tell. I tried to ask the Mois. I raised my hand high to indicate the saladang's towering shoulder, then lowered it to mean a smaller beast. The men smiled and nodded in both instances. But when I gestured to them to follow the tracks, they started off happy as beagles.

Happily the spoor led not into the high grass, but deeper into the jungle. This could mean that the bull had finished his early-morning meal and was going into the cool shade, the dimness and stillness of the forest, to lie down. The latter belief found encouragement when the tracks no longer kept to a straight course, as though the bull knew exactly where he wanted to go, and instead wound back and forth and around. The Mois thought we were getting close to his bed. All other communication cut off, their increased alertness and piercing glances told me plainly.

My nerves grew taut and I was not in my best form to shoot well. As the tension increased, I tried to cool my brain by various tricks and artifices I had employed before. I derided myself as a big-game hunter, pretending a fatalistic attitude, thinking of women and lust. I even tried to make light of the object of our search, as being only the Malayan phase of *Bilbos gaurus*, wild cattle whose greatness as big game was no doubt wildly exaggerated by the small exclusive club of sportsmen who had taken them. None of this worked very well. My heart beat wildly; I was sensitive to every sight and sound and smell; my blood pressure stood no doubt at a frightful height. I thought I had started to calm down a little—the bull was probably a mile away—when a loud crash of brush gave warning that he was just at hand.

He gave me a glimpse of himself between two tree trunks, and he was black as the devil and he had wide bow-shaped horns and he looked as big as a rhino. Then as he dashed on I heard his hoof-drum in a rather open glade running off toward the thicker jungle. But I could not see down it from this height, so I sprang up on a three-foot anthill which luck or the gods caused to be just at hand. Away, at stunning speed, dashed the saladang, the only one I would ever see. He was a bull as vast as Europa's lover, lord of the forest, to whom the ruffed and bearded tiger might yield the trail.

I flung up and shot. Then I remembered, too late, a rhino that likewise had run straight away from me, at whom I had shot and missed. As in that case, I had thought the quarry was almost out of my reach, that I must shoot instantly on the chance of a lucky shot. I forgot that luck is a smaller factor in rifle shooting than in almost any game, even scientific billiards. I failed to remember that a rifle ball is not a charge of birdshot and can travel far at lightning speed. Now I had made the common mistake, a bleak and shaming mistake in an experienced hunter, of shooting too quick.

The saladang thundered out of sight. I would never lay eyes on him again, I thought. Sick at heart, I walked behind the two Mois as they went up to look for blood signs. . . . You are wasting your time, you chaps. . . . I would have said it aloud, losing face now to save some a little later, when the truth came out, if it were not waste of breath. They looked diligently. They did not know about the rhino or about me; another saladang had run off but a tiger had fallen dead and maybe the strong magic was still on me or in my gun. Yes, they would very likely attribute the miss to some inimical spirit or god. I wished I were a savage who could do the same. But for all the mumbling of the shamans, the Neanderthal hunter knew perfectly well when he had cast his spear, whether his eye and brain and nerve had been dedicated in agony to its flying true. To shoot too quick shows loss of self-control, which is a faltering of inward strength, which is a lapse of the essential dignity to which men aspire.

Then, without much sign of surprise, one of the Mois called to the other. He pointed to the ground; both of them gazed. I hurried there, and there was a splotch of blood.

It spread about six inches, dark red, not bright red. It could come from a scratch or from a mortal wound. But it changed the whole face of the scene and of the future. Instead of turning back to camp, we would follow the spoor.

I I

My pocket watch showed eight o'clock when we set out. The two boys walked in front, so lightly and swiftly at first that I could scarcely keep up with them, which I must do—I must not let distance or thickets sever our close contact—in case the saladang had come to bay and would make his charge. The tracks were easy to follow in the soft, moist dirt of the jungle. The shade was deep and cool.

But I looked in vain for other blood signs, and if the boys found any, they did not tell me so.

For the first mile I remained sharply on guard. Any thicket we came upon might burst open and the huge black form rush forth. But I could not maintain it after the first hour had passed, knowing full well by now that the bull had not received a quickly mortal wound, that he was able to travel and travel far, and the likelihood was far greater that he had only a flesh wound. If so, he would escape me. The issue might be already settled, its upshot certain. This labor and deep mental distress might be in vain.

At the hour's end I determined to seek evidence of the severity of his wound. If he were still running or even trotting at this distance from the shooting-place he would escape and survive. If he were walking, the chase would be justified, no matter how long and hard. But I was such a poor tracker, indeed no sort of one, that I could not read this simple fact in his footprints. It was only the ABC of tracking, and I did not know it. I called the boys—an American "Hey!" because I knew no better word —and when they came to me, I put on for them a little show. In its first part I acted out the animal running; in the second part I showed him walking with a limping gait.

They smiled and nodded. Still, they did not appear to think that the white man had gone crazy—they did not look frightened, or embarrassed, or exchange knowing glances. Apparently they thought this was characteristic white-man behavior, although they had never seen it before; and quite likely it had a good sensible motive, such, perhaps, as winning the favor of his gods, and for all they knew, it worked.

We walked on, one, two, three hours more. Added to these were two hours of hiking and one of hunting before we had flushed the bull. A man of my age should be able to leg it seven hours without weakening, hardly feeling it. However, there had been a good deal of other change, not striking, hardly noticeable, but which affected all three of us. The bull's footprints no longer kept to the jungle where it was easy to follow. Often they led out into the grass, and there the Mois must almost feel their way along, smell it, it seemed, looking between the stalks, noticing broken blades, and often losing the trail, only to quest for it like bird dogs. On one of these occasions they would not find it, I thought, they would give up, and then we would go to camp.

Sometimes it led into deeper jungles, the wildest, the most beautiful and enchanted I had ever seen. There we saw many of its people. They did not appear to hide from us today; they seemed to know we were bound by a great quest and would not harm them. I felt eerily that they would not harm us, either. The tiger, the leopard, even the bull elephant, in heat and raging, would let us pass. The boys showed me a python, coiled and sleeping away a gargantuan meal, and his black hide was wondrously marked and had a strange luster in the shadows where he lay. They showed not the slightest fear of him, and seemed pleased that I could see him too, one of the wonders of their jungle. We met herd after herd of sambur, so beautifully poised, their heads up and alert but unafraid; and their feet looked so light, and mine felt so heavy. Of barking deer, which we saw in every thicket about camp, we counted but one head.

And then what I thought was a dark shadow, close to the ground, grew blacker and blacker, and I dreamed it might be the body of the saladang mostly hidden by herbage. But it was even more raven than he, and far smaller, and alive with such life that no raging bull could dream. He stood up and stretched, and he was beautiful beyond description, and I knew the gods must be with me, for I was seeing a black panther.

I did not shoot at him, although the skin of a black panther is a trophy of trophies, because the roar of the gun might frighten a wounded saladang, almost ready to lie down.

Another hour passed. Soon my watch said two, and I had been tramping since five. My feet and legs ached, my body was under duress; it seemed I did not think as fast as before, and was more and more inclined to drop behind. Presently the younger of the two boys took his post behind me, leaving it to the older tracker to find the trail. But long before then, both had ceased to take precautions against surprise attack. They no longer looked carefully where we were going or approached thick grass clumps and heavy bush warily. I did not think that their lean bodies had tired, rather they were suffering from mental fatigue caused by their long concentration on the spoor. Now it was almost time for the rains to break. When they did, the tracks would be washed out and the hunt, the sport, would be over.

A few drops fell, and both boys came up to me and looked into my face. Unlike some dark-skinned people who have been indoctrinated in inferiority by the conquering whites, these savages felt no self-consciousness when our eyes met. The older man said, "Nee-yah?" in a questioning voice. I shook my head and gestured for him to continue. Then the younger man touched me nervously on the shoulder and began to employ sign language. He opened his hands and moved them up and down in front of his chest. I thought he meant to indicate the saladang walking or running; there was a rhythm in his movements some-how suggestive of a traveling animal. Then he made a big sweep-ing gesture to tell me that the beast had got away.

I shook my head firmly. Both Mois understood this most ancient universal sign language; and half-crazy with fatigue, I wondered how it happened that a head moved horizontally meant no, verti-cally meant yes, and not vice versa. Their faces fell a little, it seemed, but they uttered no word of complaint and calmly went back to their posts.

I made up my mind to persist another hour, then, luck or loss, to hit for camp. Even now it was doubtful if we could get there by dark, although I hoped fervently we were not as far as all our tramping might put us. Surely the trail had wound and rewound in jungle and grass. Just now we trudged through the latter, broiling hot under this close, cloudy sky, and I could not stand it much longer, come what may. In about twenty minutes the trail turned sharply out of the grass into the big tree jungle. It went through an opening between dusky thickets oddly like an archway. I had a dizzy, dreamy feeling as I fol-lowed the tracker. I have since wondered if it was connected with a repulsed and discredited presentiment. Something was about to happen, but I did not believe it.

In the next second, the very next perhaps, so sudden and swift was the onrush of events, I heard a low-pitched bellow, inde-scribably ominous. Even before I had fully recognized it, the older tracker, walking ahead of me about thirty feet, got into action. He sprang to one side with terrific energy that plainly told he was leaping for his life. He disappeared behind the thick-ets, there was an interval—not of waiting but of all-pervading expectation—a second or two long, then a great black shape burst by the opening. We had come up on the saladang and he was in full attack.

I too was now in action, instinctive and unconscious. I must have been so since I saw the Moi's leap. I ran and entered the opening and came upon a scene of magnificence and terror, as though some great tale of old had come to life, such as the oldest and most tried big-game hunters behold but few times in their lives.

The stage was a glade, almost free of underbrush, about sixty feet long, in which stood several tall trees mainly with naked trunks. All around it hung big verdant boughs, so that it seemed to have deep-green walls as well as a pale-green canopy overhead, as the soft light from the shrouded sun poured through the leaves. It was the place that the saladang had chosen for his last stand. He had fled as far as he could, and perhaps he knew that the sickness sapping his strength was a fatal one, and his last move and motive was revenge. Even so, he had made a tragic mistake. Wanting a clear view of his dogged pursuer, he had waited at the end of this open place, instead of lying in ambush in the blind grass. Otherwise he could hardly have failed to catch one of us on his horns.

Still the issue remained undecided. The present action showed the finish of a deadly race between the saladang and the Moi tracker. The latter must have evaded his pursuer until now, a matter of two or three seconds dodging around trees. Now he had come up to a tree with low boughs, easily climbed if he lived that long. Behind him, with lowered head, rushed the attacker in that rocking run of the bulls. He was already beginning a furious sweep of his horns.

As I came upon the scene the bull was broadside to me, not more than fifteen feet away. I shot, and whether the butt of the gun was against my shoulder I never knew. I presume I had got it there, somehow, or the recoil would have put me off balance and perhaps prevented a quick second shot. The ball struck him in the side and almost knocked him down. His feet scrabbled, he got his balance, and with a snort he swung his forequarters toward me, with his head still lowered.

The picture now was completely changed, although perhaps

more magnificent than ever. The Moi had got a hand on a limb, his almost prehensile feet ran up the trunk and he now hung safe overhead. The bull stood in line with me, his muzzle close to the ground and bent down a little to give full sweep to his horns, and he was already beginning the lunge which, if completed, would give him victory and vengeance.

But I was an old duck hunter. I was quick in reloading, used to shooting fast. I saw the broad forehead between and under the horns perhaps six feet away, certainly no more than ten. Without thinking, instinctively to save my life, I shot into it. The saladang fell dead.

III

Often I have told fellow sportsmen how, when the saladang lay still, I fell into a revery that arrested my full perception of immediately ensuing events. Probably I yelled as the beast fell, and I must have considered firing again to make sure that his fight was over, only to refrain from the sure knowledge of its needlessness. I do not remember the Moi descending the tree. His companion too had no doubt sought the safety of the boughs in some tree behind the arena, honorable as well as intelligent behavior, since a Moi cannot fight with a saladang, and he could not help me in the least. When I began to emerge from the strangely dreamlike spell, both boys stood beside me, smiling, perfectly composed now that the peril had passed, patting me and my gun.

I came to, and began to realize the sweep and splendor of the event. I was not its hero; the saladang was. While we had shown persistence in the pursuit, he, severely wounded, had shown heroic endurance in the flight. The time had come when he would retreat no more, then he had given mighty battle; and only a two-ton blow, administered by my gun, had prevented his paying his debt of blood. The fact remained I had earned the trophy almost as fully as any man could. I had had no white hunter to help or back me, and I had shot straight in the instant of need.

The fact had already begun to dawn on me that this saladang was not, by the usual standards, an extra-fine specimen. His horns were not blunt and craggy; instead they were smooth, sharp-pointed, and of slate-blue color with white tips, indicating he was no old king of the jungle, but a bull just come to his prime. True, he was a lone bull. In the counting of sportsmen this made him a better trophy than a herd bull, in fact in a category of the elite. They believe that lone bulls are more wary and more pugnacious. However, almost always lone bulls are superannuated, driven from the herd by younger rivals. My bull lived alone because the leaders would not permit his presence in the herds, and he was not yet so mighty, so schooled in battle, that he could dethrone one of them and take his place.

I measured the horns. The two were forty inches across the outside curve, each seventeen inches in circumference at the base. I had the boys cover the carcass with cut boughs to hide it from the vultures until we could arrive tomorrow to take the head, and now the time had come to start for camp. So I said, "Nee-yah," and the boys looked greatly pleased at these linguistics, and straightway began to smell out the right direction home.

I call it smelling, although actually there is no word in the English language to express, let alone explain, their way of orientation. They walked about with their heads up, not looking at the sky, it seemed, but rather at the top of the jungle. Presently one of them uttered a pleased cry. The other hastened to him; both were overjoyed, and happily beckoned to me. At once we started on a straight course through the forest.

Thus began the most striking exhibition of a sense of direction I had ever seen or imagined. In a little while the rains broke, dimming every vista; still they never hesitated, never turned, always kept their true and certain way. We trekked for miles through the jungle. Those miles were terribly long, but one of the boys eased them a little bit by carrying my gun; still I would hardly have covered them, utterly weary as I was, if I had not had complete trust in my guides and if we were not returning victorious rather than defeated.

At best it was a bitter test. We managed to reach a Moi road that my leaders knew, before the dark came down. Then it pressed down and about and around us, singing and roaring with rain. When I was walking like a mechanical man, all my pain gone, I saw a glow among the trees that soon proved unmistakably lamplight under eaves. Someday, sooner now than before, I would come to such a light, and not have to trade it for the wills-o'-the wisp of the jungle. My bag and my heart would be full.

But just now, in that jungle, lay the cooling carcass of the great saladang. He had died at my hands, his course run, and I did not know the truth of it, just what it meant, or why it had happened so. All that I knew was, a strange thing, that this game was a great game, and that his death was as well-warranted and as noble as the death of a splendid bull in a Spanish ring; and neither shamed the race of man, because he is only a little more than the bulls, sometimes a little less; and because he is a greatly troubled creature who must prove his hardihood and prowess, lest his heart fail.

Twelve

LOUIS returned from the village with five decrepit buffaloes limping to our camp. Lame and hard-driven, covered with harness sores and in pain, they would be given a merciful death in order that some of their natural enemies would follow them, and many cows, and calves, and young bulls in their prime might be spared. . . . No, that was the excuse, not the cause. The cause was an alien's covetous passion. The Mois mistreated their old folk too, by necessity rather than design; still I could not buy them, shoot them, and use them as bait for tigers. Follow the idea far enough, and both practices would seem to be cut from the same cloth. While civilizations may sanction euthanasia, the saints never can.

We could not put out all five animals at once, because the

meat lasts only seven or eight days in the jungle heat; after it had melted away, our tiger hunt would be over. So we tied up three in camp, led two to likely places, shot them, fastened the carcasses to tree trunks with heavy chains to prevent tigers from dragging them off, and built *bomas* thirty feet away. And these *bomas* were a different kettle of fish from the low, rude thorn hut K'nini and I had sat in on a memorable night. With Louis bossing the job, first the Mois built a frame, like a cage, made of green sticks about an inch in diameter, and inside was a seat with a backrest. The roof was laid overhead, dressed with rain-shedding palms, and the whole covered with greenery. The men also erected a leafy screen farther back, in easy rifle range of the bait, on an incoming trail.

The trick was for me to come up to the screen in early morning, peer through it, see if a tiger was on the bait, and if so, make a careful shot. If there was no sign of him, and the bait had not been disturbed, I must return to camp and loaf or piddle time away till tomorrow morning. But if he had come and gone, if the carcass had been dragged the length of the chain, or if a big meal had been eaten, it stood to reason that even now the tiger hung about, lying in the thickets perhaps not a hundred paces away, wondering about our foolish actions but giving hardly a damn about them, waiting for us to leave and let him sleep. Sometime during the day, and especially at day's end, when twilight lowered, he would come creeping back. By waiting silent and motionless all day in the *boma*, I bid fair to get a chance to fire at him.

I would wait alone. I would see no more of my fellow men until they came for me in an oxcart, their lamps flashing in the thick dusk. I would hear the creak and rumble on the road; and if I fired a single shot, it was a sign that I had wounded a tiger, and they must approach me only under the strictest guard. If I fired two shots, it meant a tiger lying dead. If I did not shoot at all, it meant that my watch had been in vain.

"But maybe it might mean that I, not the tiger, am lying dead," I suggested to Louis with a wry grin.

"It's not happened yet, with any of *our* parties," he answered with professional pride.

"Could it happen?"

"Mr. Mar*shall*, there's hardly anything that can't happen in our jungles. Suppose you wound a tiger; suppose he smells you —but tigers are not good smellers, and some people think they don't smell good, either, but that's what my fat'er calls *double entendre*. The truth is, an old male does get pretty rank—"

"Go on with what you were saying about me."

"Suppose a tiger smells you and knows you are somewhere nearby. Honestly, I don't see how he can help but know this, if he can smell worth a sou; yet if so, it doesn't stop him from coming in. Suppose you wound him and he comes up to fight and he knows you're in that *boma*. Still he can't see you well enough to attack you. I admit a tiger could tear that *boma* into kindling in a few seconds, but—such things don't happen."

"Then it looks to me that this is not a very sporting way to shoot tigers."

"Wait two or three days, the whole livelong day, sitting here alone and not even stretching your legs, and you'll know you've earned that tiger. Besides, if the chance comes—and often it doesn't come—you'll quite possibly miss."

"At thirty feet?"

"It's easier than you know. Take the greatest precautions against it, or you'll do it. The nerves get frazzled when—after that long wait—a tiger comes on the scene. It's even worse just before he comes, when you know he's there and can't see his yellow hide. But you'll find all this out for yourself before these days are done. That's much better than my telling it. Believe me, Mr. Mar*shall*, this kind of hunting is noble hunting. If you live, and lose, you'll never be sorry. If you live, and win, you'll be in heaven!"

11

While we were waiting for tigers or perhaps leopards to find the baits, the meat meanwhile getting riper and malodorous, I did not wholly fritter away my time. I had long talks with Francis and Louis, I shot small game for the pot, and I put in the bag one of the finest boars that either of them had ever seen. One of the Mois had spied him rooting in the jungle. At the first shot, not very well placed, he had turned to fight; and the second had ended what I could not doubt was a notable life. For the swine are not second-rate animals—they range and are increasing all over the world except on the desert and in the polar regions where they are too smart to go—and this boar was king of the swine. He was very much larger than my African warthog, although not as ugly. He stood about forty inches at the shoulder and we guessed his weight at five hundred pounds. His tusks, as long as my hand, were extremely heavy; he was fine as the wild boar of the Ardennes, Francis said. Not knowing the story then, I compared him favorably with

> The great wild boar that had his den
> Amidst the reeds of Cosa's fen,
> And wasted fields and slaughtered men,
> Along Albinia's shore.

More than outweighing this good luck, tigers and leopards had become scarce on our grounds. The good number Louis had reckoned on had drifted away to distant jungles out of our reach, to be safe, the Mois said, from the stubbed-thumbed white man's strong gun. Actually they had been greatly impressed by its knocking sideways and then down a bull saladang almost in the act—only a twinkling of an eye beforehand—of hooking my great tracker. This was heart-warming enough, but it could not atone for the strange lack of four-toed tracks in the rain-wet paths.

On the seventh morning after our laying the baits, when the carrion was almost eaten up by larvae, luck gave me a fleeting smile. That was one way to put it. Another way would be to say, that my *nat*, a guardian spirit which all men possess, according to animist notions, was able to chase away the bad spirits dodging my footsteps. True, its name in the Moi language was not *nat*. This is the Tibeto-Burman word; the other I could not learn. The Mois thought that the less name calling they did in regard to supernatural beings, the better they would fare.

Louis came down the trail with me to his usual waiting place. He asked me to be especially careful in creeping up to the screen, because there was evidence of a tiger being now on the bait. All signs fail in dry weather—and I wondered if this saying, which I had heard as a boy in the Middle West, had come down to us from the *voyageurs*. Still, when jungle chickens quit picking up larvae and fly to the treetops to cackle and cluck and complain with great vehemence, the omens are very good indeed. Would he come with me? No, he would not, because he did not wish to double the sound of my approach. This was specious in the extreme, for the only sound would be made by me; Louis could drift along as inaudibly as a *nat*. Since he wore a priestly expression, meaning that I must continue my solitary progress into the mysteries and through the ordeals of the jungle, I did not protest.

I crept down the path, my heart alternately fluttering and bounding. These disturbances could easily affect my shooting, but they were what I was buying—perhaps they were the best bargain in my basket—and thinking of this and trying to grin at it made me a little more capable. As I drew near the screen, I was taken at my word—for the excitement became almost unbearably high. I soon knew why, for there came to my cocked ears a very soft, odd, rhythmic sound that could mean only one thing—a big animal chewing meat.

I gained the screen and gazed through. There stood no great yellow tiger with black stripes; but I could almost excuse him from my heart's desire for the sake of a golden leopard with black rosettes. He did not look burning-bright like the leopards I had seen in the sunlight or the lamp glare in Africa. He stood in the deep shade, and in one little move he could have disappeared entirely and no man could tell where he had gone. Just now, though, he had come on to open ground, and the jungle had exposed him. He had a round head and a perfect sinuous form, and his tail was long and upturned. In southeastern Asia he was commonly called the panther, and the black panther was his brother, often of the same litter. Although he looked a little more splendid, with larger and more perfect spots than most African leopards, he was essentially the same beast.

Presently he stopped chewing. Something had attracted his attention, or, I can fairly say, and perhaps more truly, a thought had passed through his brain. Things seemed to him a little different from before; he had not the same content. Still he could not guess he was face to face with death. If he did so guess, he would fly or fight. He only stood there, watching, listening, wondering.

In the middle of his thought, the bullet crashed through his miraculous heart chamber. Yet, as I saw him lying dead, impotent, although still of surpassing beauty, I could not help but rejoice.

III

When the two baits had melted away, we put out two more, saving only one very old and heavy bull buffalo for the last. While waiting for tigers to find them, Francis and I searched some swampy lowlands where lately we had seen wild water buffalo. We rode in buffalo carts over the drowned Moi roads until we came to good ground. Our draught beasts were identically of the same blood and species as our quarry, but because for hundreds of generations they had toiled in the fields beneath the whip they grew stunted and puny of horn, instead of tall and great-horned like their far-distant cousins who had never bowed to the yoke.

In habits and disposition, the wild water buffalo could be readily compared to the far more numerous African buffalo. However, he was a size bigger, only a size smaller than the saladang, and his massive three-cornered horns, flaring out behind his head, suggested a unique crown. Only an animal of monstrous strength could wear and toss them. Even today, on the roads and in the rice fields, the strength of the long-suffering domestic buffalo remains the wonder of man.

A full-grown lion will readily attack and kill a bull buffalo of the African species. On the other hand only the greatest of tigers, the royal tigers considerably larger and more powerful than any lion, dare challenge wild water buffalo, and then only at desperate risk of defeat, goring, and death.

Francis and I saw several young bulls, cows, and calves. I was given a brief glimpse, between thickets, of a mighty bull. Francis guessed his horn at four feet, and the same measurement between their outer curves. I knew nothing of that. All that I knew was his grand aspect—his stature, magnificence, and immeasurable power, the black glory of the brute in the rank greenery. I knew I must sometime take the time and the care, and go after him, and put him in my bag, and keep him by me until I grew old and could hunt no more.

We returned to the high jungle, for at present our business was tigers. At first it seemed to promise brighter than before. Two sets of four-toed tracks, one of them fairly large and the other small, surrounded the baits, and a thigh had been half eaten. The Mois at once foresaw the pelt of a good-sized male and his undersized mate soon to be on the drying racks. In the morning Louis and I set forth with a feeling of excitement and elation which, alas, began to evaporate when we reached the scene. The Mois who had made the discovery could not see that the visitors had fed again. Only on close inspection did we find a few mouthfuls taken from the throat, and this looked more like leopard than tiger sign, for tigers almost always start on the hind limbs or the belly. Then Louis himself found the tracks of the larger of the two beasts wending steadily and purposefully down the road. Without much doubt he had quit the feast for good.

Any tiger bigger than a cub is a trophy worth taking—the skin of a yearling being as large as a full-grown leopard, and such a tiger can kill a man or a sambur stag. So I got in the blind with a light rifle, a .35-caliber pump gun which a manufacturer in America had asked me to try. I had not dared use it against full-grown tigers, saladang, or buffalo, but I thought it would be a sound, efficient arm against small tigers and leopards. Louis handed me in a tea flask, warning me not to drink from it on account of the gurgle, if I thought a tiger was near, a stock of native cigars—as I have said, there is not a scrap of evidence that tobacco smoke frightens game—and a box of French chocolates I had bought in Saigon which had melted to a dark-gray cake.

There are three rather interesting reasons why cold tea is the standard drink of Americans visiting Indo-Chinese jungles. In the first place, they cannot drink wine with a Frenchman's relish without getting tipsy. In the second place, the camp hands consider that boiling water for drinking is the height of white-man folly, since the boiling does not appear to change it in the least degree, and will dodge the chore. But they will, without looking silly, boil tea. In the third place the taste of tea conceals the remarkable medley of flavors that plain water acquires in a few hours in the heat.

Smiling over this, mainly to exorcise a bleakness of spirit over being left alone on what I felt sure would be a long profitless watch, I took my seat and listened to the noisy departure of Louis and the Mois. They talked and laughed all the way up the road, to persuade any tiger lying in the thickets and listening that the scene was deserted. A deep stillness settled in that I felt sure would not break until after a weary wait. Actually, although I did not know it yet, stillness is a temporary condition here, usually caused by man's invasion. When he comes into the green courts, many birds fly, numerous little animals run away without his seeing them, but many more stay perfectly still and thus disappear, and the scene seems without life. Still, if he listens closely, he will soon become aware of faint sounds, some of which he can barely hear, and many he cannot quite hear. And when he walks on, the jungle symphony resumes.

On the present occasion I did not get to hear it. The staged noise of Louis and the Mois had died away, a few birds had begun to hop and cry, and I had hardly finished a close survey of all visible approaches to my blind when I noticed a big-leafed shrub, in underbrush about sixty feet beyond the bait, bend very slowly, then as slowly straighten. It looked about three feet high, and no wind or lighting bird had caused it to incline, and I knew that some animal was approaching me from that direction. Then I watched a wonderful thing. It was the passage of a perfect stalker through low, thick cover. I caught no glimpse of him, no hint of a golden hide with black rosettes or stripes, and I heard not the slightest sound. It was as though the stubborn shrubbery parted in magic silence to let him through.

In a few seconds he walked into the open space. I could see only his head and neck and the top of his back over the buffalo carcass, so I was not yet initiated in one of the great sights in all the jungle, truly in all the world—that of a tiger standing clear in the open and the wild and in pure light. Maybe he would have shown himself to me in a few seconds, if I had had the will power or the heart—perhaps guts is the best word—to wait. As it was, I must level, sight, and shoot with swift deadliness, lest he turn and break and the jungle that had given him forth instantly swallow him up.

I leveled the rifle through the loophole, took a hard aim at the tiger's head, and pulled the trigger.

He proved to be a yearling male, weighing about a hundred and fifty pounds, well furred, and brilliantly and fantastically marked. Indeed, he was one of the most beautiful tigers Francis had ever seen. If he had lived to be old and great, he would have won a name for himself through many leagues of jungle— and the Mois would have been loath to speak it, lest it call him and he come, and only the wizards would have dared sound it aloud, after ceremonies of propitiation. By then he would know better than to come to a carcass less than an hour after mysterious interlopers had gone away. Likely he would know well the blast of the gun, the cold breath of a grazing bullet. If he had grown stiff, or too heavy and slow to catch many deer and pigs, and perhaps even feared the horns of the fierce wild oxen, he would know well the smells and ways of man, from having lurked about the byres and grazing grounds of the plow beasts, and having torn down many of these—perhaps hundreds. And if he had lived that long, perhaps once, or more than once, a living form like a monkey's, much larger although not nearly large enough to explain its mysterious and awful powers, had screamed and died in his talons.

But he did not live to reign long. As he thought to begin his feast he had seen a spurt of fire come out of an odd-looking bush, but he had never heard the roar of the piece, or felt the thud of the bullet, and he never knew of the silence and nothingness that had possessed him. At best the barking deer that had learned to fear him missed his fearsome scent about their pools and grazing grounds, and strangely knew him no more.

I V

No other tigers came to the two baits we had laid out. I spent the time studying natural history with Francis, who I learned was a correspondent with several scientific societies in Europe, and in being grounded in anthropology by roving about the Moi villages with Louis. Indeed, a visit to the long house was almost as enlightening as opening the *Golden Bough*, and in a somewhat more pleasant fashion.

The day came when Louis killed and laid out our last bait. He put it beside a Moi road where lately he had found a very large tiger track, with one toe of the right front foot slightly askew, the sign of the Old Man.

For five days no tigers visited the kill, and it became an offense to the fresh, fragrant jungle. On the sixth morning, as I was having breakfast, Cookie consulted some chicken bones he had thrown on the ground, and came up with the augury that today I would have good luck. So he said; I did not believe it. But Louis believed, and was not at all surprised to find the bait dragged to the end of the chain, one leg almost eaten off, and tracks of a good-sized tiger—about as big as our night prize— all about the bait.

"It's our last chance to end the trip in glory," he told me, his dark eyes glowing. "So don't muff it."

He and the Mois went away singing and talking. I settled in my blind, the Mauser .404 leaning in the corner. I knew better than to expect a mature tiger to return this soon; still the memory of a small tiger coming silent as a puff of smoke kept me alert. In the second hour the jungle life, paralyzed for a while by the intrusion, began to revive, apparently quite unaware of an eavesdropper. The first visitors were birds, rodents, and small lizards. It seemed to me remarkable how loud and startling were their low utterances and nervous movements in the trees and undergrowth, against the brooding silence of the forest.

Quite a flock of jungle chickens came running up like hens to corn to pick up larvae. Thereafter I almost never lacked their pleasant, bustling company. A barking deer strolled by, tested the wind, did not like it very well as shown by his rough-voiced cry, and quietly went his way. A gorgeous peacock lighted down and spread his tail and strutted—for whose benefit I could not guess, unless it was the modest little jungle hens and their pert cock. Green parrots clamored and quarreled in the treetops, wild pigeons uttered their soft, characteristic call, and a herd of elephants or a troop of monkeys—only an expert could tell which—went crashing through the jungle a mile or more away.

In the heat of the day, when the sun blazed through loops in my *boma* roof, there came toward my blind a creature bigger and more bold than any I had heard so far. Indeed, his approach was so noisy that I could not vision a tiger—which habitually moves in stealth, slithers rather than bursts through thickets, and usually observes silence except when fleeing, fighting, singing— I had been told of the Song of the Tiger, but had not heard it in the magic stillness of the night—or making love. Elephants, saladang, buffaloes, banteng, or heavy stags would not be drawn to a bait. So the only other animal I could picture as out there, coming nearer, was the Asiatic bear wearing the white chevron on his breast, to all intents and purposes the Himalayan bear common in north India.

From these speculations I was rudely wakened. Out of the shrubbery crawled a varanus lizard, of the same dragonlike kind that had crossed my path early in the trip. Now I was given a full, clear view of him, and truly he was the most repulsive living creature I had ever seen. This specimen was about eight feet long. Why should vultures, ugly enough at best, lift their wings and bend their heads in hideous postures? Why must hyenas, standing almost like respectable beasts on their front legs, half-squat on their rear? Both of these are habitual carrion eaters. Isn't this disgrace enough without their being an eyesore in the land? Why should a varanus lizard curl his tail, never letting it hang straight, and eternally twist his neck, meanwhile opening and shutting his mouth, deep-cut in his reptilian head? Moreover, his habits are more disgusting than his appearance.

My visitor went to the front end of the carcass and deliberately thrust his head into its mouth and down its neck. Then, bracing himself with his four dragon legs and stiffened tail, he pulled and tugged until he tore out a long, dangling piece of rotten meat. This—and to see him eat it, swallowing avidly and choking on it like a vulture upon no less dainty fare—was sickening enough. Now he crawled around to the rear and capped the climax. Even so, I could have felt pity on him, and conceded that God might have had a good reason for creating him, if for one single second he would stand still. As it was, his continuous movements—tail, neck, head, and feet twisting or turning or clawing in a slow frenzy—would prompt impious questions in a saint.

After my visitor had lingered about two hours, he suddenly and abjectly fled. This was one of the signs Louis had told me to watch for. It could easily mean that the tiger was coming back. That would be a thrilling outcome of my wait of many days, and my watch of many hours. Instead, as I learned soon enough, the newcomer was a larger and, if possible, ghastlier varanus lizard. He passed close to me on his run to the bait, and the breath of a hyena could hardly be as bad as this, although Cottar, who had smelled it as he lay helpless on the desert, said it was the worst of all. He plunged upon the meat and began to gorge.

In a few minutes the smaller reptile came creeping back. The larger ran at him and chased him away. And this became their constant, unvarying behavior, lasting until the rains broke, the smaller making innumerable witless sallies, only to be driven back before he could snatch a mouthful, but never punished enough to discourage his efforts. For some unknown reason confirmed carrion eaters are more frantic, gluttonous, and brazen-bold than any other carnivores, and when feasting convey an effect of grisly rapture.

I was glad of the rains, if only for the change. They lashed down through the leafy canopy, and the rattle and drum became a deep-toned roar everywhere under the sky. Still I sat warm and dry except for an occasional cool jet running off a misplaced palm. I could see only a little way and felt very lonely and I wondered if old age was like this—finding one's self all alone, still looking for something, the eyes dimmed.

The shower stopped at sundown. There was still time between now and dark for the tiger to come—indeed it was the likeliest time—and the creeping shadows excited me and I heard little rustlings that made my neck tingle, but the light continued to fail without showing the splendid golden form. And at its very last, when dusk had fallen and I could no longer be sure of my sight, I heard the rumble of a Moi cart. Louis and his comrades were coming to take me to camp. The long watch had failed.

The jolting ride tired my stiffened body. I did not work one of the headlights, leaving the job to one of the Mois, although it might cause me to miss a chance at the tiger. I ate supper late and alone, then slept heavily. Two hours before dawn Cookie brought me a hot breakfast, but no word of cheer for the day. If he had consulted his oracles they had nothing good to promise.

When I was riding back to the scene, I saw and felt the jungle so fresh and beautiful and green that my hopes of noble fortune were restored. However, I could see that Louis was troubled by the immense hole that had been made in the carcass in our absence. "I think he must have gorged all night, and if so, he'll sleep all day," Louis told me when I demanded the truth. "Either that, or he's got the biggest appetite of any middle-sized tiger I ever saw."

At this rate the bait would not last for another day. It seemed to mean that today could be the last day of my Indo-Chinese hunt, and I could not bring myself to face it. I was an old duck hunter, and I could sit all day and all night too for a last chance at a tiger. So I told myself on this dewy morning, with the sun not yet up and every prospect pleasing and fresh and hopeful. But I might sing a different tune, and well I knew it, when the long day was done.

What a long day it was! The minutes dragged away to make a stingy number of reluctant hours. I was fighting time, and more grievously, fighting myself. I could not believe in the jungle and its wonder; I had been victimized by my own imagination. What was there about tigers that I must go into banishment in a cage made of sticks in the hope of keeping some dubious rendezvous with one? Already I had spent too much of my life alone. At home I had an agreeable wife and two delightful brats, and self-fulfillment instead of self-escape. Here in this dark forest I spent my time and treasure among aliens, in quest of a pelt that had no intrinsic value, that was only a token of God knew what. After this trip I would hunt no more big game, alone and wandering. I would shoot ducks with my true friend Corning. We would laugh and find companionship; we would sit in cold blinds but the birds would come in flocks—we would not wait all day for one; canvasback and mallard could give quick, passing but sharp triumph; in the evening we could have toddy and talk. It would be so much more fun. It was far and away more human.

The jungle chickens came; the varanus lizards came; monkeys swung through the tree limbs almost overhead, performing the wildest acrobatics. A tender and beautiful sambur doe came up to my blind and actually stretched her neck to crop from its dressing when a backdraft of smell reached her. She leaped straight up for what seemed six feet, then darted away. And after a while the rains came. But the sun went down and the tiger did not come.

As the light began to fail, two varanus lizards feeding or fighting by the bait pressed their bellies close to the ground and crawled away. A second later I sniffed something. It grew stronger; and all at once it burst forth in full power—a great reek that could be nothing else than the tiger. Indeed I identified it instantly. It was like that of a tiger cage in a zoo but a hundred times stronger. But there was no sound but my heart's thud as I waited for him to move out of his green cover. He might be standing twenty feet away—surely he could not be more than fifty. Still I watched with strained and burning eyes and waited in vain. Then the air slowly freshened and I knew he had become suspicious and had made off.

One other thing I knew, a secret I would not tell Louis, perhaps to "surprise" him if I won, or, if I lost, to hide from him the measure of my loss. This was no middle-sized tiger. Francis had told me only the oldest males gave forth that rank smell, and that was natural enough, for aged goats, minks, and men smell strongest. Also his caution indicated a veteran tiger. I thought quite likely he was the Old Man.

V

After all these comings, dusk came, and then Louis. I rode back to the huts, for no quick arrangements could be made for me to spend the night in the blind. Anyway I doubted if I were equal to it. Long before dawn, Cookie lighted my lantern, and in his hand was a tin plate laden with eggs, meat, and toast.

"Velly good luck today, Melikan mas'," he told me.

Louis and I saw no sign of it when we reached the *boma*.

The bait had vanished except for a few bones and scraps of hide—a good part of it eaten but a large part rotted away. My spirits, so lately livened, fell, and I could hardly face the prospect of another all-day watch.

"He won't come back," I said. "I might as well go to camp."

"He may not come back," Louis answered, "but he certainly won't come to camp."

"I could read. I could hunt small game. I would see people. I wouldn't just sit."

A dreamy look came into his face that I had seen once or twice before. This was his Mowgli aspect; he became then a priest of the jungle.

"This is what I'd do if I were he," Louis told me, looking far away. "I'd come back, and a little earlier than usual, and clean up these scraps to stay my stomach for a night's hunt."

Of course tigers must sometimes stay their stomachs, the same as people. I must always remember that big animals were very like people—in fact, our fellow mammals. That would help me to become a big-game hunter—if I did not give up.

"I'll stay," I said. "But can't you come at three o'clock with all the mosquito repellent in camp and a night rig?"

"I'd hate to subject you to it, but we'll see."

They went off, cheerfully enough. Ahead of them lay many hours of talk and laughter and good eating. In the heat of the day Louis would go to bathe in the clear, cool stream with his Moi sweetheart, and I thought of them making love on the bank, and of their transports; and of the Mois knowing it and feeling proud of their kinswoman—for look what she received in food, and bangles, and even silver coins, for giving almost nothing! Like most savages they prized woman mostly for her capacity to labor. Louis was a savage by adoption only. On his mother's side he descended from the ancient sensuous Annamese, and his father was French. He had wakened the jungle daughter, and I could picture the pair as passionate as mating tigers.

The picture did not reconcile me to a patient wait in the blind. I had to stand it, though, and actually, although I did not know why, the time seemed to pass faster than on the previous days. Perhaps I expected no great developments at least until late afternoon; hence I was more interested, less bored, by what show there was—the commoner sounds and sights and parade of lesser creatures. Soon after I ate my lunch it got to be three o'clock. I listened for the Moi cart, but heard nothing of its distant rumble, and soon concluded that Louis had rejected my plan to sit all night, if indeed he had ever considered it. So I would stand or fall by what happened between now and the thick-pressing dark.

About six o'clock, a moment identical with hundreds of other moments that had passed, two varanus lizards were quarreling over scraps of the bait while a flock of about a dozen jungle chickens picked up larvae. The lizards stopped bickering and hissing and crawled rather hastily away. I had seen the same thing happen several times before, and the fowl were continuing scurrying and driving down their beaks, so my quickly rising tension passed off and my pulse went back to normal. During the reaction I must do something to fight my depression, so I eased a strained leg, awkwardly thumping the *boma* wall with my knee, and while about it, I took a long, gurgling swig from my tea flask. And at that instant, utterly the wrong one, all the chickens flushed at once, lighted on the tree boughs, and set up a frantic cackling.

And in the next second I smelled tiger in his full prodigious reek.

I thought he was standing within a few feet of my blind, debating whether to enter the clearing. I was quiet enough now, not even breathing, and only I could hear my heart. But in me was the awful feeling that the damage had been done, that he had heard the sounds I had made and would drift away and not return until after dark. In a few seconds the signs began to bear it out.

The half-stifling smell of ammonia and musk weakened slowly and the clack of the jungle fowl grew less. Even so, they did not want to risk lighting again, for the day was almost done, and presently they flew quietly away.

Although my heart was heavy, I resumed an intent watch. I would keep it until too late to shoot. That time would not be very long, I thought bitterly, and perhaps far shorter than I reckoned, for the tropic twilights were dramatically brief. Already dusk was setting in. The foliage no longer looked brilliant green; thickets appeared darker and thicker; shadows spread and massed. I watched the dismal change ten minutes more. Only the white bones showed sharp; perhaps the fading light would no longer limn my sights. I put my rifle to my shoulder, and discovered I could still find aim. Very carefully I put the gun in its place.

The jungle beyond the bait had become a black wall. As my gaze skirted it in passing, I saw in great astonishment that it had changed. An immense pale circle, suggesting yellow, had appeared in the middle of it. For a long second I could not identify it and was stunned. It could not be the head of the tiger because it was too large. . . .

Then I knew that it was, because it could be nothing else. Its seeming immensity was an optical illusion caused by the falling night. The jungle growth looked very far away, while actually it was hardly forty feet, and unconsciously I expected the out-thrust head to appear small in keeping with the feeling of distance, a common trick of the mind.

A second later the tiger pushed boldly into the open. The illusion of distance still endured, and he seemed to loom out of all proportion to my expectations. But although the light was dim, he did not appear so, and perhaps this confused and perturbed my mind. He was the first wild tiger I had ever seen alive in full view, in the open. And such was his beauty and symmetry and vitality, and his terribleness that had conjured my imagination ever since I was a child, that he appeared to blaze.

My gun was leaning in the corner of the *boma*, its trigger guard toward me. I felt for it blindly, my eyes riveted on the tiger, and thrust my finger against the safety button. Finding it locked, I assumed that I had unconsciously cocked the piece when I aimed it a few minutes before, and had forgotten to push over the safety when I had put it back. This was far from my habit, and ordinarily I would have investigated the lapse. In this moment of extreme tension I let it go, carefully raised the arm, thrust the end of the barrel through the loophole, and leveled on the tiger's head. Joy rushed through me as I could dimly see the front sight and, aiming with great force, I touched trigger. It was locked. The gun did not fire. The shock was inevitable and severe. How great I have never been able to remember, because I recovered from it so quickly in the necessity of doing something, the powerful mental drive to function intelligently. Fortunately, I was used to guns. Almost instantly I guessed what had happened; that when I had tried to take off the safety, I had failed to perceive that the bottom side of the piece was toward me, and I had pushed the safety button the wrong way. Instead of already cocked, it was still on safe.

Holding hard, I pressed the button and leveled again. The tiger still stood in the dim clearing, magnificent and immense, and I saw his big head along my barrel, full in my sights. With the utmost rallying of nerve, I steadily pressed the trigger.

The gun roared. The tiger made one great movement, and to this hour I am not quite sure what it was. It seemed to me he reared up on his hind legs, his forepaws spread, although this would be a strange action for a brain-shot beast; then he crashed down. Surely I had the strange and stunning feeling of his falling from a great height.

Swiftly I aimed and fired three more shots. I firmly believed that all were needless, but I could not *know* it—I was not seasoned enough—and many were the tales of tigers that had fallen stunned, only to rise, and fight or flee. The fact remained that I functioned well, considering my extreme excitement. When the time came that we could examine the prize, the first bullet hole was found just above the eyes, and the other three, close to the ear, could be enclosed in a three-inch circle.

For the present I dared not leave the *boma*. I was too shaken. The shadows lay too deep, the possibility of the tiger having a mate nearby was only too real. I decided to wait till Louis arrived with the cart and an extra gun, and this was a common-sense decision, under the circumstances. Almost at once I heard the well-known rumble on the road. When the sound drew near, I fired two signal shots. And a little after that, my nerves suddenly quieted and in hand, I found myself capable of coming out into a twilight that was hardly more gray than when the tiger had first appeared. That a good deal of time had passed was another illusion, caused by the rush of events.

As soon as he came in hearing, Louis shouted.

"Is the tiger dead?"

"Yes, he's dead."

"Is he a pretty big one?"

"He looks pretty big to me." I spoke as calmly as possible, imitating, I suppose, great *shikaris* of whom I had read, who could light a cigarette with a steady hand immediately after stopping a tiger charge. Truly it was one of the few understatements that I had ever managed to pull off.

Now that illusions caused by misjudgment of distance had passed away, and the tiger lay huddled, he still looked immense. That the middle-sized tracks had been his I could not believe. Obviously a larger tiger had come into the country and usurped the kill.

How much larger? Louis gaped a little at sight of him, then immediately set about removing him from this ground, so his skin would not be injured by larvae. The Mois lashed his feet, cut a stout pole, and slipped it between the hind and fore legs.

Not until they heaved on it did the wonderful truth begin to break.

The three wiry, muscular brown men could not lift this tiger. Only when Louis and I lent our shoulders were we able to move him to the cart and heave him in. It had an eight-foot body, which he filled snugly, with his tail hanging out. We counted him six hundred pounds of tiger, and if this was an overestimate, it was only by a narrow margin.

All the way to camp Louis looked at him and swore, and our companions were wondrously cheerful, and played tricks with the flashlight beams. When we reached the huts, two Mois, equipped with torches and armed with a rifle that they did not know how to shoot, set off down a Moi road to a nearby camp, where Francis had gone on a last-ditch scouting trip for fresh tiger signs. They returned with him in about three hours, where-upon the sound of revelry in our camp—raised by the rest of the Mois, the cook and his son, a half-caste, and, unquestionably, a visiting American—died quickly away.

Louis walked all around the tiger, viewing it from every angle. Then he made his pronouncement.

"Mr. Mar*shall*, I regard this as the largest tiger taken in this neighborhood in my twenty-five years in the jungle."

When this had been translated for the Mois, and they had grinned at one another and the Moi maidens had gone around sniffing all available cheeks in their tribal expression of happiness and friendship, Louis asked the question which hovered on my tongue.

"Is he the Old Man?"

"As to that I don't yet dare venture an opinion."

It came to pass that the gods of these jungles had given enough and did not want to spoil me. When Francis looked for the broken or crooked toe apparent in the Old Man's track he could not find it; nor was there any sign of an old bullet wound dealt by one of Francis' hunters several years before. Very obviously then, this was not the Old Man, although about as large, as well-ruffed, and as time-tried. Measured unskinned from peg to peg he beat nine and a half feet, which made him a royal tiger. His fur was not as thick as that of my yearling or as that habitually worn by many tigers in India; but he was nevertheless brightly painted, a beautiful delineator of sudden death.

The Mois thought he was the same tiger that had passed through their jungle about six months before, and that he was a wanderer with no fixed home. There were many such; old tigers who had outlived their fertility. Certainly he was very old, as shown by a missing tooth, the growth of his ruff, and certain configurations of his body. If so, the count of his slain was like David's—whole droves of wild swine, countless sambur and barking deer, buffalo, and wild cattle, and probably a hundred ponies and plow beasts from the villages he skirted on his travels. With one great blow he had smashed and killed. He had not come to his end in the way of nature—say, on the horn of a saladang whom he had assailed and who had proved his master; still I thought it had a certain magnificence. The picture that I brought away was of him rising to his full height, in a last gesture of kingship of the jungle, before he crashed to earth.

4. Jungle of Mowgli

Thirteen

TWO years after my return from Indo-China, I made another journey to that same far corner of the world, the most unusual journey and the nearest to real exploration of my travel-rich years. Approaching through the Gulf of Tonkin I crossed the highlands by pony and native boat from Vinh to Luang Prabang on the Mekong River in the beautiful kingdom of Laos. Quite a number of adventurous Americans had reached that fabled city by coming up the river, but only a handful, possibly only one, had preceded me overland. On this ambitious trip I touched the dead city of Chieng Khuang, explored an incredible cave which I named the Cave of the Million Buddhas, talked with the king, and made my way out via the Upper Mekong and the Siamese town of Chiang Rai, and from thence on down to Bangkok.

On this journey I was usually alone with natives and saw much of the hill people and was greatly smitten with the dashing Laotians, but kept my guns in their cases and a notebook in my hand. By and large I attended to my business as a writer. If now the so-called Bamboo Curtain has not closed down over that enchanting countryside, it is dangling ominously overhead.

But two years after that, an hour struck for which I had been listening ever since my boyhood. Assembling my outfit of guns, cameras, comforts, and medicines, and shucking off all cares and responsibilities with which I could possibly dispense, I took ship for India.

In my pocket was a letter from John MacDonald, who lived in Kalimpong, close to Darjeeling, whose name had been given me by someone I knew in Calcutta. He was an Eurasian, a linguist, and the interpreter for one of the main expeditions to attempt to climb Mount Everest, and he was prepared to outfit hunters in the malaria-ridden Tarai, the hills and lowland under the Himalayas, in the half-wild and jungly province of Assam. At first I had rather pined for the Central Provinces. In these lay, specifically, the Mowgli country—readers remember Mowgli's dealings with the Gonds, an aboriginal hill tribe of that region. The few Americans who, lacking truck or drag with maharajahs or the British government, had still tried to hunt big game in India had usually gone to those grounds. However, I had not been able to make satisfactory arrangements there, and now had great expectations of a great hunt in jungles greener, wilder, wider, and less known.

Did I have influence with native kings and British sahibs? It can be gathered that I did not, or I would not be making arrangements with a half-caste. Perhaps I felt a little jealous of the affluent and politically prominent Americans who were invited to the royal and viceregal shoots, because nothing could be more swell—pavilions, pennants, trained elephants to ride on, liveried servants, swarms of beaters, tea in the afternoon and banquets in the evening. Seated in your howdah, you waited for the tigers to be driven to the guns. You never had to walk on your two feet or sit over malodorous baits or associate on extremely intimate terms with common natives. Certainly you never sat by a campfire in the heart of the whispering jungle. Several exalted Englishmen I had met, and some not so exalted, had shot bally tigers in this style, and made it quite plain that they would not care for the style in which I intended to hunt them. Actually, I did not know my luck.

I did not suspect it, and in fact feared it might turn dismally bad, when I first met John MacDonald. In his early thirties, tall, athletic, rather handsome, he was an Indian of another skin from Louis De Fosse—indeed an Anglo-Indian, who appeared never to forget the fact and hence never let others forget it. As for me, I was interested in it only insofar as it enriched his personality, and did not want to have to walk warily and contend with it every day and night of our association. He leaned backward toward sahibism. His language was the latest London. Actually he succeeded, for a while, in almost completely concealing a truly rich personality and a very real charm. His father, who I believe belonged to one of the old Anglo-Indian families, had lived an exciting life in Tibet. John himself had roved and roamed, picked up an astonishing amount of fascinating lore, and could speak fluent English, Hindustani, Tibetan, Assamese, Sikkimese, Nepalese, Bengalese, and Bhutanese.

On the other hand, he was given to big, periodic sprees. I had been warned of this, and knew I must deal with it, and it did not take me long to know that the infirmity was closely connected with a complex of feelings arising from his acute and tragic consciousness of not being pukka English. I can say with pleasure that he performed, on the whole, very well. He gave me some trouble, but also a great deal of satisfaction. Instead of getting steadily worse, in the general way of bottle-ridden employees, he improved markedly throughout our trips. Together he and I had many a gay hour, many a triumph, and excitement beyond measure, and when all these were done, and I prepared to leave India, it was with the feeling that John was going to make it through, realizing his potentialities for a successful life. In all conscience I confess never to have written to inquire if the hunch was working out. Often we say we have neglected doing something; we mean we did not dare.

II

The town where John and I and our native followers detrained was named Rangiya. From there we rode in trucks into what was called officially the Duars of Bhutan, the jungle at the foot of that wild-and-woolly hill state, which is still terra incognita to all except a few official visitors. I have always suspected that *duars* meant nothing more or less than doors, as pronounced by some English geographer with an exaggerated Oxford accent. Anyway they are so written on the maps.

At the end of this road lay a tea plantation beside a wide, white, almost dry river bed. Here waited two elephants for our express use, one of them a very young tusker, caught only a few years before and with the smell of the jungle on him still, that could carry baggage, and a rather scrawny, temperamental old-maid elephant fit to ride upon. John told me that a big tusker, a trained *shikari* elephant, that had been known to slap down a charging tiger with his trunk, would be brought for my use shortly, but I could only keep him a few days unless I were willing to pay a shocking sum. The other two, however, I could keep throughout the trip.

I had dreamed of riding forth into the great and storied Indian jungle on the back of an elephant, but I had hardly believed in its coming true.

Great days and scenes lay before me. The most unusual member of the troop that was to accompany me was a small, lean, boyish-looking Nepalese who wore the kukri, the big curved knife fit for chopping trees down or men open from throat to pelvis, of the Ghurka soldiery. Whether he had ever been a soldier I never learned. If I ever knew his name, I could not pronounce it, and promptly christened him Bimbo, which delighted the whole camp and by which he is no doubt known— as a kind of honorary title—ever since that day. He had a boy's blue suit with short pants that he wore on important occasions; where he had obtained it defeated my imagination. He had come along as my personal servant, although I knew no Nepalese and he no English. Actually he did not pan out exactly that, but something much more.

The cook I named Cookie, after our fortuneteller in Indo-China. He was a middle-aged Nepalese with a doleful mustache. With the trackers and skinners came two native *shikaris* with cap-and-ball muskets which I guessed were army issue. The word *shikari* means hunter. It was the regulation, John told me solemnly, that one of them must accompany me everywhere I went in the jungle, to protect me from wild animals. If the rule were enforced, I would be seriously handicapped and my good times curtailed, but I hoped to dispense with it quickly. Anyway I did not relish the free-and-easy way these hunters handled their loaded pieces. I certainly did not want my hunting trip to be ended by a smoothbore slug.

One of the mahouts proved to be a kindhearted fellow who had grown up with his elephant, the small tusker. Instead of an iron ankus, a cruel goad, he used a little stick, and the elephant's attempts to hide from him after playing truant— his head in a bush and his rear extending forth like a snagged balloon—delighted the whole outfit. Even when he was being drubbed, we could not help but laugh at him, his moans and groans being out of proportion to the punishment. The other mahout struck me as a cruel fellow, and I asked to have him recalled. Happily he did not own the spinster elephant, and the native who took his place turned out a pleasant addition to our number.

Early in the morning we crossed the river on our way to our base camp. Almost at once the jungle closed in, and this was the jungle I had been waiting for all my days, its outer aspects almost identical with the high Indo-Chinese jungles, but the home of the tiger of tigers, the fabulous Bengal tiger, and the wild tusker. And besides these, it had far more numerous and exciting gods. Finding out on the journey that I was interested in such beings, and would never dream of laughing at them, John had stopped speaking of them in scoffing terms, shed some of his pukka sahib mannerisms, and told me a little about them. That he believed them in his heart I deduced from the glowing of his fine, black eyes.

Another great advance lay in seeing this jungle not from a footpath, or astride a pony, but from high on the back of an elephant. Then and there I concluded there is no such thrilling locomotion in the wide world. We did not ride in a howdah. Our she-elephant had never had such a contraption on her bony back; anyway, it would not pass under the tree limbs, quite a few of which had been plastered with mud. How had they become plastered with mud? By wild elephants, fresh from wallowing, passing under them. Several that we saw hung nine and a half feet off the ground, while our flighty and heart-winning spinster stood hardly eight.

The mahout sat on her neck, while John and Bimbo and I rode on what we called the elephant pad, a kind of stiff mattress like a little deck, cinched to her belly. On this we could move from side to side, face forward or rear, hang our feet over, and otherwise take our ease. Meanwhile she took us through heavy jungle, four clean miles an hour, and one mile of Indian jungle contains more sights than a hundred miles of common country. When a big sapling got in her way, she pushed it over. When a moderately sized limb hung too low, she would twine her trunk around it, give it a little jerk, and break it off. When we came to steep ascents, she panted her way to the top. On steep declines she would sit down on her ample bottom and half-slide.

Later, when we had traded off her surly and abusive mahout for one whom she could love, she performed even stranger feats —strange, that is, to the eyes of an alien, although the brown men thought nothing of them. Once, when I dropped my matches, I poked the mahout and pointed. He spoke at some length to the elephant; she whirled around, picked up the box in her trunk, and handed it to him. She was sometimes moody but never ill-tempered, always patient, and ready to travel at any hour. However, she did not like live tigers, and was altogether too enamored of big, wild, jungly-smelling tuskers.

On this brief jaunt I shot a hog deer in the grass to furnish camp meat. When we had had tiffin—a rather silly-sounding Anglo-Indian term for a lunch as heavy with meat as the one that I consumed—I prepared for my first penetration of the untrodden jungle. John would be busy arranging for tiger baits and improving camp, but I could make signs to Bimbo, who was wonderfully quick at guessing at their meaning; besides, he knew at least twenty words of English. For protection, I would have a native *shikari* and his muzzle-loader. Fortunately, I had no reason to expect any serious gunfire.

Of course the jungle is often utterly unreasonable. I knew that by now; one of the prime and rubbed-in lessons of the big-game-hunting school. The fact remained that even if we saw water buffalo or gaur—these last the Indian bison, of which the saladang is the Malayan form—I did not expect to shoot. Seeking a truly noble head, I would probably have to look over a good many. We might see sambur, boar, and the spotted cheetal deer, surpassed in beauty only by their great enemies, the tiger and the leopard. It would be quite possible to encounter some wild elephants.

The chance became more likely when we came upon and turned in the bed of a dry nullah. Here lay the huge tracks in almost frightening profusion. We had already heard elephants far off in the jungle, and now we listened to them at not more than a half mile. All last night we had heard the bells and gongs of the villagers, trying to frighten them from their ripening grain. Actually the concentration of elephants in this immediate neighborhood was one of the great wonders of all my trips. There seemed no possible explanation other than that they had gathered here to raid the fields lying at the very border of the jungle, in a kind of no-man's land, where the plowed land ended and the green sea washed, unlike most farms that were out of the raider's reach. All through the growing season the farmers had fought wild pig and deer, and now were all but overwhelmed by monsters.

I had no license and no desire to take a bull elephant, and the hearty wish to avoid a brush with one.

III

This nullah bed seemed a thoroughfare through the jungle. As we ventured on, away from the river and toward the hills, other tracks appeared—deer in great numbers, wild boar, big cloven imprints made by nothing less than the hooves of bison or buffalo, and, very soon, tiger and leopard tracks. Once there was such a maze of these that I got down from the pad to examine them. I could hardly imagine the spoor of at least five different tigers, all fresh, in ten square yards of moist sand, yet they were unmistakable. While looking at them, I became distinctly nervous about the jungle-grown bank only a few feet distant. The elephant was thrusting her trunk in all directions, frequently stopping it in a snaky dip and upward curve, as she caught a fearsome scent. The mahout had long since stopped prodding and abusing the good beast, only because he feared for his own skin. The native *shikari* swung his old musket back and forth, and only Bimbo maintained any sort of poise, for he could not forget he was a Ghurka and the only high-caste man in our out-fit. Still, even Bimbo's boyish face looked a little strained.

I was glad when, at the mahout's command, the elephant knelt and let me climb aboard. I had intended to order an immediate retreat from this uncaged zoo of wild beasts, to get out and stay out until John could back me with another rifle. But being hoisted eight and a half feet in the air reassured me somewhat, stopping the quiver and jump of my nerves, although the banks were now three feet high and starting to rise more steeply. We would go on a distance farther, I thought. It would be unseemly for a sahib—and whether or not I liked it very much, this was my title pro tem—to turn tail on the quarry. My followers and I must stand much sharper fright than this, before retreat could be countenanced.

The bed of the nullah became narrower, the banks steeper and higher. A small trickle of water appeared, sometimes gathering into shallow pools; the jungle looked wilder, the tracks in the sand no less numerous. The elephant's nervousness increased; often she trembled violently, and I thought that only the habit of obedience, not the fear of the cruel ankus, forced her on. Suddenly we heard brush crashing and what appeared to be snorting and bellowing, fifty or more yards away on the left side. The elephant stopped dead still.

The bank stood now as high as the back of our elephant, and although I tried to gaze through the screen of vines, I made out only some dim, dark shapes. Then the native *shikari* spoke a Hindustani word I had already learned.

"*Goru, sahib!*"

Goru means cattle. These were wild cattle, either gaur or mithan, both species of Asiatic bison. I was instantly relieved, because even if the herd stampeded they could not reach us in the nullah bed, and I felt sure they had been alarmed by our scent and would presently make off. This prospect, which at first I had secretly welcomed, underwent a change in aspect as my nerve steadied. My hunting zeal came back and I decided to play the chance for a shot at what might turn out a huge herd leader, a noble trophy for my first sally on the hunting grounds. With this intention, I believe that I prodded the mahout to make him take the elephant forward a few more steps, to afford me a better view. In any case, we did advance a few yards, although I do not remember giving the command.

She stopped again, her head turned, her trunk strangely lifted. Before I saw the cause the mahout uttered a bleating sound and with outstretched arm and shaking hand pointed to the bank. Because I was trying to look over the low growth into the high jungle beyond, my mind still on bison but expecting I knew not what, some time passed before I saw the sight that had put the elephant at bay and paralyzed my fellow riders. Amid a deep silence and stillness it jumped to my eyes. It was a tiger— crouched in the grass and vines, his gaze fixed on us, not ten feet away.

It was he, not us, that had frightened the bison herd. No doubt he had been stalking them when we came up. Why the elephant had not smelled him and balked long before she had brought herself and us into his easy reach, I do not know till this day. Perhaps it was because she had been smelling tigers for the last half hour, and the breeze was off the right bank; and these factors and the strong smell of the cattle had confused her or impaired her marvelous elephant's sense of smell.

My whole present being was focused on the tiger. I knew that we had surprised the tiger in the same degree that he had surprised us. His attentions too had been riveted on the bison. I knew that tigers, encountered suddenly at close range, startled, perhaps fearing that escape is cut off, are terribly likely to attack. This tiger need give but one little light bound to be up here with me. And I almost—not quite—knew that was his intention.

I saw it in his eyes as my rifle was coming up. It seemed to come up so slowly. Even when it started to level, I still thought there would be no time to aim, and I almost—not quite—shot wild. In the last split second, I held—the good teaching of many painful and shaming misses. With a great effort I caught the flat harlequin head full in my sights, and pulled the trigger.

The head dropped. Otherwise the tiger hardly seemed to move.

I have always found the events of the next few minutes difficult to reconstruct rationally in my mind. Possibly they were too close to the wellsprings of human conduct to be readily explicable or easy to confess; perhaps they were only hitched to the whole irrational psychology of big-game hunting. The right word might be vanity; I suspect it is, although I do not know. If so, it is a vanity that lies on the other side of humility, and which the citified, more-than-half-civilized type of big-game hunter, with tender feet and contracted ego, attains only now and then.

This is what I did. In the exaltation of seeing the tiger lying dead, knowing I had shot true and killed him in what might be truly the nick of time, seeing us all alive and unhurt and the elephant getting her nerve back and swinging her trunk again, I decided to go after the bison.

I think it was a little like a roisterer on New Year's Eve deciding to call up the President. I did not need a bison at this point, and I would be far happier not to come to grips with one. I certainly did not want any except an old monster with craggy horns. What I should have was a quiet drink. Despite this, I thumped the mahout in the ribs to make him take the elephant up a narrow path, where the bank stood less steep, a little farther on. He gave me a look of entreaty, but I must have appeared quite fierce to him, for he obeyed. The native *shikari* gasped, and no longer made even a show of brandishing his gun. Bimbo, sitting at the rear, uttered a hushed "Sahib!"

We scrambled up, and there was the herd lined up for us, at not more than seventy yards, and on almost open ground under the trees. I saw the big bull and his cows, and they gave no sign of flight, and I knew they had come to bay to combat the tiger. What I could not know was whether they would take it out on us. Bison are rather dim-eyed, and the smell of the dead tiger was blowing straight toward them from our direction; once they launched a charge en masse, they would not be particular about who it knocked down. Still possessed, I leveled on the bull and almost pressed the trigger. Two things restrained me—a serious doubt as to the worth of his head, as well of the future conduct of his followers.

This act of restraint returned me to my right mind. I signaled the mahout to go back, and all of us on the deck rejoiced to be scrunging down the steep to the nullah bed. How severe a shock we had received and how shaken we remained became evident shortly. The mahout had had the elephant kneel, so that some of us could dismount just below the dead tiger. All hands knew what must be done; the beautiful carcass had to be dragged down the bank and covered with greenery, thus hiding it from the vultures until tomorrow when the skinners could come and take the gorgeous pelt. It took a wrench of my will to hand the rifle to Bimbo until I could get down, and of the three natives, only Bimbo offered to follow me.

I could not bring myself to lay down the rifle to give both hands to the task. Bimbo was stauncher than I, but far from steady, and we jumped at three or four false alarms before we could tug the heavy carcass to the brink and let it slide down.

Now the brush cutting began, and I saw a wonderful change in Bimbo when he got his kukri in his good right hand. I climbed back aboard and kept guard while he finished the job alone.

Just before he covered the head, Bimbo called attention to the animal's tongue hanging out of its mouth. This was plainly a sign of great importance, although I had no notion thereof until he had reported it to John. It meant, he told me gravely, that I would kill other tigers on this trip, a not unlikely prediction considering the maze of tracks. Meanwhile I had noticed another sign that boded well. In telling the tale of the tiger killing—acting it out with an imaginary rifle—Bimbo's boyish face flushed and his dark eyes shone. Plainly I had acquitted myself well in his opinion, and had made him proud of me.

It was a most pleasant development, especially since Bimbo belonged to the military caste of the redoubtable Ghurkas, of strait standards and high tradition. In all fairness, I had made the best shot of my life with the possible exception of my blasting a saladang's forehead at about the same range. This was about ten feet. How could the wildest tyro miss? The proper answer is one that my daughter gives me, when I seek a why or wherefore of her cryptic conduct.

"You'd be surprised!"

IV

After supper, when darkness fell, quite a few natives visited our camp from the surrounding villages. They came by way of the wide-open river bed, not by narrow jungle paths, most of them carrying reed torches that gave forth a strange and flickering light. I sat down with them, in the way that old sahibs, long in the country, were known to do, although it would be unthinkable in most young sahibs, new out from England. With John acting as interpreter, we talked of many things.

Truly, they were greatly afflicted by elephants this year. Patriarchs among them as old as a turtle, as a python, as the lone bull elephant himself, could not remember their gathering in such numbers. Their guru had done puja to make them go away, but it had been weakened by some rival guru, or there was an unpunished murderer in their midst, angering all the gods—even Kali of the bloody breast—or something worse. I did not learn that night what the worse thing might be. Later I was told by a native scholar in Sadiya. Some of the cultivators in the Duars had a lively belief in lycanthropy. It might be that one of their own village, whom they saw every day in the fields, whose woman filled her jars at the river beside their women, only pretended to go to bed and to sleep in his darkened hut. When the cooking fires burned out he crept forth and made the night hideous by the body in which he ran in the jungle— that of a wolf, a tiger, or, worst of all, a black panther.

Tigers too were numerous hereabouts. Happily, most of them were honest tigers, subsisting on deer and wild pig which Shiva had provided for them, and did not pull down the villagers' buffalo, cattle, ponies, and goats. And not since the last sowing had a tiger pulled down a woman or child, let alone a man, although a wolf had carried off a baby left sleeping in the grass only one moon gone. Of course there remained Sakini, the white-faced tigress whose name meant Ogress—not very large, but with an unquenchable hunger for their tender young heifers. How many she had killed in the last ten years only a Brahmin with gold-rimmed spectacles—or a *babu* from Calcutta—could count. It might be that the sahib would kill this tiger. If so, he would be remembered by the people when the youngest elephant calf, squealing over the milk, had grown old and vast.

And perhaps the sahib could tell them why Wilson Sahib, who had slept well until lately, had taken to walking the roads in the pale light of the moon? The guru could read nothing in the auguries to explain it, but perhaps I, another sahib, could throw light upon the mystery. Did I think they were doing something displeasing to Wilson Sahib? How could they find out?

They spoke of this in the same tone of voice as of tigers and elephants. However, when John asked them to enlighten us a little further as to Wilson Sahib, they explained that he had come into their country fifteen years before and at great cost cleared land for a jute plantation. For five years it had appeared to prosper well, then evil fortune had set in: the fences broke down, the bungalow began to fall into ruin, and Wilson Sahib himself took the fever and laid down on his bed and died. I answered that I could not speak for Wilson Sahib, or explain why he went walking on an evening. But I was quite sure it foreboded no ill to the countryside.

Our visitors departed, and I sat alone by the cooking fire, listening to the sounds of the jungle night. They were fully as arresting and mysterious as those of nighttime on the veld. They came clearest in those intervals when the villagers rested from their bell ringing and gong clanging, having discouraged, for a while, the jungle dwellers who had tried to raid their fields.

The greatest number were sounds made by elephants on their unwonted assemblies here. Sometimes there rose quite an uproar near at hand, brush crashing, small trees being broken down, calves squealing, and a confused grunting and mumbling. More frequently it was a clear trumpet note a long way off.

After while there came a distant, nearing sound that brought Bimbo quickly to my side. It was a succession of outcries at short regular intervals, which I would say were prodigious yowls mixed with angry snarls, with a full-throated burst at the end. I have since tried to reproduce it in type. The nearest I could come was a prolonged *ar-ahh-ow-woo-oof*. As it came in close John emerged from his tent.

"That's a tiger," he told me. "He's not hunting—just cross-

ing country—and he's hungry and savage-tempered, and doesn't
give a damn who knows it. Every time he's letting out one of
those caterwauls he drops his head and twists it with an ugly
motion as it's coming up, and it makes the sound seem to roll
along the ground. But he's not coming into camp. He'll come
up fairly close and then turn off."

"Well, I'm glad of that."

But John leaned his rifle handy against a tree and Bimbo ran
like a shot and got mine. When the blast seemed just at hand
and threatened to make the tinware rattle, it suddenly ceased.
I did not know which I preferred: a tiger caterwauling, or stealing along inaudibly a stone's throw from the fire.

We were not quite done with him for the night—or with one
of his striped tribe. Long after midnight I was wakened by a
series of piercing screams that sounded so close at hand, so terror-
ridden and half-human that I jumped out of my bed and grabbed
my rifle and stood in the tent door. By now, though, I had identified the voice, and became the victim of shock and a degree
of horror, rather than fright. Only one living creature that I
knew of was capable of that shrieking squeal, javelinlike in its
sharpness and carrying as far as a rifle shot, and he was some
manner of pig. The discovery made it easier for me, no better
for him. I could not doubt that he was in the claws and fangs
of a tiger, where God knew I hoped I would never be. The
outcries grew shorter and fainter and finally died away.

V

In the wonderful days that followed, we remained involved
with elephants. Almost always we roamed the jungle and the
grasslands on the back of our she-elephant, who bore the holy
name of Parbati, the wife of Shiv and herself invoked in the
fertility rites of certain cults. It seemed to me an odd name to

be worn by an old-maid elephant, a virgin, so the mahouts maintained, according to the signs. If so, she was an unwilling one. We never passed downwind of a herd of elephants without her evincing amorous excitement. It seemed to me that she was constantly maneuvering to get with a bull, meanwhile uttering what were no doubt love calls through her lifted trunk; and the mahout was hard put to it to steer her clear.

I questioned John as to what our modern gynecologists might call the rhythms of elephants. Oddly enough, he did not know and had to consult the mahouts. According to them it was the male and not the female that had mating times and seasons, the height of these being known as *must*, when a secretion from the ear revealed the condition and when, if frustrated, he quite often went berserk. If a wild bull, he was prone to engage a rival in a duel to the death, and long ago I read, in a forgotten book, that a battle between heavy tuskers surpassed in fury and awesomeness any other in the world. If a tame bull, he must be restrained from killing his mahout. I learned also that a mature cow was always amenable to receiving the male, and often, as in the case of skinny, unattractive Parbati, decidedly forward.

Certainly I intended that her libidinous impulses should remain thwarted, while I rode on her back.

On these jaunts we were constantly swinging wide of elephants, but once a small herd seemed so favorably posed for a picture that I could not resist trying to take it. Thirteen loafed in six-foot grass, upwind of us, exciting our riding-beast, while they remained unconscious of her and us. When the mahout had brought her as near as he dared, I slipped off, and with a rifle in one hand and a motion-picture camera in the other undertook a cautious advance. According to the books I could approach within fifteen yards of the nearsighted animals in almost —never quite—perfect safety.

The sally did not prove as pleasant as I expected. It did not lack for thrills—there were many odd rustlings and bendings of the grass—but my total solitude in the presence of the giants aroused some ancient phobias; it seemed unnatural and dismal. Cottar would come straight up to the herd without a second thought. Louis would do so for the hell of it. John would think twice, then manage it with the nonchalance of a pukka sahib. I was only a stray American, and when the elephants began to mumble and mutter and surge about and toss their trunks high above the grass, I wished I had never undertaken the venture. Then I came to a patch of grass higher than the rest. For a short while I could only hear the elephants, making more noise than before, and when again they came into sight they were much nearer than my slow advance could account for. The truth was, they had begun to drift in my direction.

I counted fourteen now, including a very young calf. The latter created a new and unknown potential, so with no more thought of a stunning close-up, I raised my camera high, pointed at the herd, and pressed the button. At once I started to retreat, only to encounter at close quarters two young bull elephants separated from their fellows. I hastened on, and at a good hundred yards, when I could fairly assume that the bungling incident was over, I came suddenly on the herd leader, out of sight until now in a high thicket.

He stood easily nine feet and his tusks showed long and white. He had taken his position on the flank of the herd, where, had I known elephants well, I would have looked for him. John told me later that he had gone there to stand watch against stalking tigers, but our mahout laughed at that, saying that the old paterfamilias hung off from his charges for the almost-human reason of escaping before the squealing of the calves and the interminable gossip of his cows. My time to laugh had not yet come. For the present I was seriously wondering whether I would have to shoot with a ball too light to knock an elephant down, unless aimed expertly for the small brain behind thick plates of bone.

The bull had heard me, or else had caught my scent. He

tossed his trunk, trumpeted, and advanced several angry paces. I scurried away sans dignity or reluctance.

A far-off aftermath is worth recording to show the state of mind of a high-strung imaginative man during his first close brush with a herd of wild elephants. When my photo film was developed, it proved absolutely blank. Obviously I had forgotten to remove the cap from the lens.

This brush was at bald midday. Very shortly I was fated to meet with a herd of elephants in the gray, creepy, and tricky moonlight. Supper was over. John had gone visiting to a native village, and I had good reason to fear that some bottles of arrack had come into the picture. Very likely I would see no more of him for a day or two, when he would return a sorry wreck of the gay, engaging man who had set out. By the same token, I was left without an interpreter and must suffer a kind of muteness till he returned.

Our affair began with loud crashing of brush, squealings, trumpetings, and other noises patently nearby. I could not explain these "other noises"—to this day I do not know what elephants do to create the uproar that they raise when they feel like it. Often there is a drumming sound, and sharp reports as though tree limbs and young tree trunks are being snapped off. It is all the more startling because, when they wish, elephants can move through the grass or even through thick jungle like big puffs of smoke.

The commotion grew greater, but I thought it would soon grow less as the herd passed on. Instead it suddenly ceased, and the Indians sitting around their cooking fire began to get to their feet. The next moment, it seemed, we had visitors.

The elephant herd, evidently a large one, actually surrounded our camp. They made their presence known at first by soft sounds, then an increasing amount of trumpeting and mumbling, and, as they pressed closer, by their tall shapes in the moonlight. I told myself not to be frightened. My mind began a lively search for sensible explanations for the herd's behavior and for opinions as to developments. Surely the animals had been attracted by our two tame elephants. They wanted some sort of communion with them, but they would not come into the firelight, in respect to us humans. However, that respect was not fear of any sharp sort, or they would not come this close. That they could smell us perfectly clearly and see us quite well I had not the least doubt.

I had been sitting alone in front of my tent. A few seconds after their coming, Bimbo brought me my heaviest rifle, and before a minute was up all the men in camp had gathered about me and were crouching on the ground at my feet. And these were frightened men. They did not attempt to hide it, and anyway they could not, because I saw their faces. I had no illusion about their putting confidence in me: I had the only gun that conceivably could kill an elephant, and they craved what protection it offered. Unlike me, they were not trying to belittle what they thought was danger, or talk themselves out of their fright.

The truth was, as I had garnered before now, the word for elephant, *hathi,* was one of the soberest words that our natives spoke. In daylight they went freely into the scrub jungle—to gather fuel and jungle products and to graze their buffaloes—and showed little fear of tigers, and not much of bison, although I had noticed they did not like the proximity of wild water buffalo. When elephants came in hearing they became jumpy and big-eyed, and always seemed to be scanning nearby trees to use as a retreat in case of trouble.

I remembered this, and felt growing apprehension over this visit. The elephants did not appear angry, for though I heard a good deal of trumpeting there were no savage blasts. Still I could not feel much confidence that some little thing would not set them off, in which case a living tornado might sweep away our camp and some human lives. The beasts were drawing in a little closer, and I could not forget they were wild dwellers of the jungle, and the men who knew elephants better than I did were not very far from panic.

One of the native *shikaris* had his old smoothbore. When he brandished it, I called an emphatic "No" which he well understood. Then Bimbo made a little motion with his hand to suggest that I shoot the big rifle, and I gave some thought to firing it in the air. However, I dismissed the idea for the time being, on the grounds that it might start a stampede.

It came to me then that of all the touchy or frightening situations I had gotten or blundered into, this one would have given old Cottar the most concern. Of the rest, he would have had implicit confidence in his ability to shoot his way out. Indeed I could remember, this very moment, incidents of his ivory-hunting days, wherein large herds of elephants menaced his camps, and of occasions in which natives or fellow hunters had been killed. Those were African elephants, larger and more aggressive than the Asiatic variety, but these about my camp were big and bold enough.

The notion of shooting to scare the beasts begot a better one, which was to build up our fires. God knows I had been slow in arriving at it, to say the least, but why had not the natives thought of it? The simple reason, which I discovered shortly, was that all the cut fuel had been burned, and to get more required a short sally into the deeper shadows. The men did not want to leave the glowing coals and the comforting proximity of the gun. Bimbo ran out as soon as he understood my sign language and I heard the strong blows of his kukri; but I had to swear at the others to get them moving, and one native *shikari*, not the one who had been with me at the tiger shooting, but another, a troublemaker whom I had lately commanded not to shoot his piece, remained by the fire, muttering. I drove him before me, threatening him with my fist, then followed the band to our log pile and guarded them the little I could.

At once the flames began to lick and crackle, the light to spread, and the ring of jumping shadows to draw back. Listening to the cheering sound, I could not hear the elephants, and wondered at their silence. When, a moment or two later, I looked for their big dark shapes in the moonlight I could not find any. Suddenly all the natives were beaming, nodding, and smiling.

We humans and our tents and cooking pots and our strange smells and ways had not awed them enough to force their retreat from our humanity-drenched campground; and why should we, when they loomed so mighty and we showed so short? But a mere bonfire, yellow flames leaping high and glorious only to die in darkness, had caused them to draw back, huddle together, and steal away. In this silent place, I felt the wonder and pity and poignance of life as sharply as in a great and roaring city.

V I

I believe, although I cannot prove it, that two other wild elephants paid us a call a few nights later, in a far more cheeky fashion than the herd, and in fact made themselves quite at home.

I had risen in the middle of the night and stood at the door of my tent. Glancing at the pickets, I saw four elephants standing there, plain in the moonlight, mumbling and touching trunks and communing in elephant fashion. I assumed that the two in addition to our regular number were tame beasts brought into camp by mahouts since I had gone to bed, one of them the costly trained *shikari* elephant that John had engaged for my brief use, and whose arrival he had been expecting the past few days. The other could be a companion beast ridden by the mahout's friend for company's sake.

I yawned and went back to bed. In the morning only two elephants stood in their pickets, the old maid and the young blade. When I told John of the incident, he said I had dreamed it. Since all of my nights on earth I have been subject to continuous vivid dreams, I let it go at that.

The big *shikari* elephant, standing a clean nine feet, arrived the following day. I did not keep him longer than John had arranged, since his rental was appallingly high, and his special training and use was for high-style tiger hunts, in which hundreds of beaters drive baited tigers to the guns. However, in the few jaunts I made on his high back, seeking bison and buffalo or perhaps another catch-as-catch-can encounter with a tiger, I came into closer quarters with a wild bull elephant than I had ever been, or wanted to be afterward.

Again we advanced up the dry bed of a nullah, affording an easy road through high grass, although it was not the same as Tiger Nullah, and had lower banks. My mind had fixed on tiger, from seeing a good many tracks, and I had slipped soft-nosed ammunition into the .404 Mauser. The mahout perched on his beast's neck; behind me rode Bimbo. As usual, I had the only gun.

Striding around a blind bend, our elephant stopped dead still. This was no wonder, considering what was standing there, on the yard-high bank. It was the biggest bull elephant I had ever seen, and almost near enough to slap one of us with his trunk— a slap that would surely be fatal.

This was no chance encounter. He had smelled us—he could not help it, the way the wind was blowing—and had belligerently waited for us. In that first wild stare I saw plenty of other corroborative evidence of his evil temper—his slow sway back and forth, the look in his eyes, and his curled trunk. The latter was a sign to frighten the most tried hunter. The elephant can clobber and kill with his trunk—it is his quickest weapon, but he uses it only on men and tigers. In battle with his peers he draws it out of harm's way between his tusks and fights with these and his feet. If I had thought clearly enough, I would have read this sign to mean that his fury was against our elephant, not against us riders. Actually, that would have been little comfort if hostilities began.

What was the cause of his wrath? Did it rise from chronic ill temper against all big bulls—for surely he was a lone bull, famous for irascibility—or was he in must? I never knew the answer.

Nor do I know what saved us from being attacked, knocked off, and perhaps trampled. When the boys pleaded with me to shoot—they knew the word perfectly well—I held my fire; still I do not know if this was the wise course, or if mere luck saved me from the consequences of a terrible mistake. If I had it to do over, I would aim for the bulge in his forehead and try to knock him down. Every good big-game hunter I know would have done just that. My impulse was to wait until he lunged in attack—and that might be too late.

Meanwhile our elephant stood like a shape in stone, his trunk curled up, his head a little turned, ready to meet the other's rush. I believe that this, rather than luck, was our saving factor. This was no common bull—so the aggressor thought. He smelled different and he had men riding on his back. Even if the wild bull were must, he bethought himself.

With a big, peevish grunt, like an old hog's, the king of the jungle turned and paced away.

Immediately the fright of my companions passed off. The color came back into their gray faces and they laughed together and gave me big happy smiles. I did not join in their composure, and indeed when I tried to laugh I could only make a series of raucous noises. Actually I had been deeply shocked and could not at once get over it, as had these young Asiatics who lived for the moment. It did not help matters to discover that my rifle had been loaded with soft-nosed bullets, a fact I had forgotten until now. It is very doubtful indeed if such a bullet would penetrate the immense frontal bone of an elephant's forehead.

The incident had one very happy consequence. After Bimbo had told John the story in detail, this conversation occurred between them, which John translated on the spot:

"Bimbo, why didn't the mad *hathi* attack?"

"When the mad *hathi* saw that the sahib was not afraid, he grew afraid."

For the first time in my life, as far as I could remember, I had been able to conceal a terrific emotion from my companions. Actually I had not tried to do so; it was an odd by-product of my effort to control it, not to yield to it, not to be forced by it into doing the wrong thing. Still, Bimbo would not have been deceived if he had not held my brief in the first place. I began to see that I had gained a most loyal and valiant follower.

Fourteen

IT was no passing thing on Bimbo's part, his quick, heady devotion to me; and by watching him and questioning John I found what I thought was the root of it. He was not at all like the self-effacing worshipful follower of Kipling's tiger-killing sahibs. He never told me that by my favor it would rain. Indeed, I could not persuade myself—although it would be flattering—that he considered me an especially great *shikari*. His young and rash affections seemed to be stirred as much by my boggles as my triumphs. The main clew lay in his calling me the Old Sahib, not always in approbation, sometimes with pique over my blundering into danger, but always with a filial-like respect.

When not quite forty I had grizzled hair, and no doubt that made me appear venerable to this boyish Ghurka of twenty.

He grieved when I left him in camp, not only from missing the excitement that he loved, but in fear I would meet with danger, with him and his kukri unable to come to my help. Sometimes he scolded me in Hindustani; although I did not understand a word, I would always listen soberly, and then pat him on the back. When, while watching over the bait alone, I was "hit on the head by the male bamboo" and, shivering and half delirious with the fever, I started for camp down the white moonlit river bed, it was Bimbo who saw my light flash a half mile away and came on the run, a lantern in one hand and his big knife in the other. I will never forget how he cried, "Sahib!". He did not carry me but he definitely towed me all the way to camp.

I resolved to take him with me on all my daylight jaunts and night watches, greatly to my pleasure and comfort. One pleasant detail of our communion was food and drink. I have already mentioned that Bimbo was the only truly high-caste man in our outfit. Indeed his caste was so high that he must not eat of the meals prepared by my cook; and of course the mere touching of food by an alien or even his shadow falling on it was enough to pollute it. The fact remained that in the blind he drank from my tea flask and gobbled every edible I handed to him from my lunchbasket, even if it was beefsteak. The Hindu rejection of the best meat in the world and the Jewish refusal and the Mohammedan horror of pork had always stuck in my craw, and this communion did us both good.

However, these night watches, sometimes exciting, often weary and boresome in the extreme, produced no tigers. We were hunting them according to an old accepted method. It consisted of buying a cow, fastening it with big ropes or chains, watering and feeding it until a tiger found and killed it, then watching over the carcass in a *machon*—a rude platform built in a tree

forty or fifty feet from the bait. It was not as unsportsmanlike
as appears at first blush. In the first place it was a grueling test
of patience and endurance. In the second, if the hunter wounded
a tiger that escaped into the jungle, it was the hunter's bounden
duty to follow him and finish him off, before he vented his fury
upon some hapless native. The pursuit invariably led into heavy
cover. There the beast was certain to come to bay, and if he
were able, to attack by surprise. More hunters had been killed
following wounded tigers than in any other phase of the chase.

But the tigers here, although numerous, made a habit of not
returning to their kills. At least they hung off until they noticed
something unfamiliar in their surroundings or actually recognized the presence of human beings. Then they would creep
away and kill again.

We saw an interesting variation of this habit one day when
the cook, going in the dawn to our spring, about two furlongs
from the camp, found the carcass of a newly killed sambur stag
lying in the nullah bed. The tiger had not carried off his prize
or eaten of it, possibly having encountered it and killed it after
he had made his night's meal, but more likely because the cook's
approach had surprised him and frightened him off.

It hardly seemed possible that he would return to the bait in
broad daylight this close to camp. The proposal was made that
we move the carcass farther up the nullah, and chain it down near
a tree more suitable for a *machon*. I rejected it, partly on the
grounds that the killer might not find his kill, or any other tiger
might encounter it before it was consumed by vultures. Besides
that, I had a feeling almost as creepy as some of those that came
over that never-forgotten jungle brat, Louis De Fosse. I felt that
if I were the tiger, I would be greatly concerned about the fine
fat buck I had laid low and then had had to leave in inglorious
retreat, and I would not sleep well till I retrieved it and carried
it away into the thick of the jungle.

I was not sorry, and actually relieved and almost glad that no tree hereabouts would support a *machon*. I did not like the device: it seemed to separate me from the scene of action; it was uncomfortable and tiring and, so far, not very effective. Besides, we needed this stymie against its use to invent and take a chance on some other. The bait lay just under an eight-foot bank, grown heavily to grass. Just across the nullah rose another bank, about fifteen feet high. Why not dig a small cave in the latter, screen its opening with vines, and lie in ambush there?

I had no intention of waiting till late afternoon to begin my watch. Indeed I did not wish to leave the deer carcass unwatched for a single moment. So when the cave was dug and screened, Bimbo moved in my rifle, tea flask, headlight, edibles, and a battered copy of Sherlock Holmes stories I had found in the empty bungalow of the tea plantation. When he and I took our seats, the hour was no later than nine.

The camp hands had been told to do their usual camp work, make no unusual noises, and by no means come strolling up this way. Again I was trying to imitate Louis' way of thinking. The tiger had no doubt heard our wood chopping and the like both day and night, and was used to it, while silence might make him thoughtful and afraid. Then, if I had known how, I would have made a little puja to the jungle gods, for of all my formal tiger hunts—running into the striped beauty on the nullah bank had been an informal meeting—this one was more my own, with fewer other fingers in the pie, more the product of my own brain than any of my others, and I dearly wanted it to win.

Opening the book, I began to reread *The Red Headed League*. The story had lost none of its magic, and an hour passed almost before I knew it. Bimbo was sitting with his back to the cavern wall, sound asleep. Presently a vulture volplaned down, lighted in the nullah bed beside the kill, spread his wings, and hissed.

He was the first of at least sixty. They sailed in from all directions, and how the word had passed I could not guess, unless other watchers from the skies had seen the first's descent and their greedy race to this scene had signaled still others. I watched them in dismay. I knew those rapacious beaks and knew of nothing to prevent their reducing the fine bait to a naked skeleton in a matter of minutes.

Soon I saw, to my great relief, that the feast was not as ready as they thought. They seemed unable to tear the tough buckskin, and could attack the carcass only at its various orifices. Moreover, they fought so fiercely among themselves that they made little headway here. Usually two immense king vultures remained perched on the buck's body. The others either made a grisly, squawking, scratching, biting, clawing pile, a sight I had never seen before, or else stood in a dense black throng, lifting their wings and hissing. I thought of trying to frighten them off, only to be struck by a happy thought. It was that if the tiger lay only a short distance back in the grass, he would hear the uproar, and might attend to the matter himself.

I was starting to open my book again when a marvelous growling snarl, so loud and fierce that its source was unmistakable, burst forth from the grass. The vultures hopped away and took wing, becoming airborne wonderfully swiftly, considering their heavy bodies. They were hardly clear of the scene when the tiger sprang down the bank. There he stood, full in the sunlight, black striped against golden yellow, almost too splendid and beautiful to believe.

I had seen a leopard in midday glare, but all my tigers had shown themselves in the dim jungle. I could have, but I did not yet, remember the green-head mallards beating in against the wind under white clouds. I had used to think there was nothing so vivid in the world. Ducks were the big game of small game—tigers were the big game of the whole earth—and there was a relationship between them. The thrills then and now, which I could not try to compare, had been cut from the same cloth.

I looked through the vines and saw the tiger forty feet away. He stood proudly and imperiously, turning his head, gazing in all directions. For this more than anything else I had crossed half the world, and the price was fair. And since it was right for Bimbo to see him too, I laid my hand on his knee. He wakened without sound or sudden movement, and he peered through the screen, and a little thrill ran through his body, and I could know that his eyes glowed.

I aimed at the shoulder, held closely, and touched off. But I had wanted to make puja to the jungle gods—perhaps they had taken the will for the deed—and they did not propose to drop the curtain on this event without affording Bimbo and me an extra measure of excitement. I had not known that the ceiling of earth-dug caves often needed bracing. As the gun roared, fully a bushel of sand and dirt poured down on our heads. At once the dust blinded us, so that we did not know whether the tiger was alive or dead, running away or attacking.

But the silence held and deepened. The dust settled, and we looked out. There lay our trophy beside his kill, splendid and beautiful even in death. For he is a wonder of creation. For all big-game hunters who stick to the game, who follow the dim spoor, he is the ultimate Golden Fleece.

II

My ideal of a big-game hunter is one who never "blows up" under any circumstances. I think that Stewart Edward White was like that—stories are still told of his nerve—and some of the famed *shikaris*, sahibs of the English public-school tradition, must have seemed as imperturbable as the Great Sphinx. I do not count Cottar, for he was not a sportsman; he was the Long Hunter. Anyway, Cottar did explode frequently, with terrific gusts of profanity and rage, although it never affected his shooting in the least iota.

I had thought I was making progress along this line, at least that I was growing hard to shake, when an incident in the high jungle sent me back to school.

Bimbo and I had been keeping our eyes open for a magnificent specimen of the Asiatic bison, the gaur. I had visioned hanging the head at the opposite end of my trophy room from the sala-dang, so that the two great black bulls could confront each other. I had decided to shoot a solitary bull or none—a condition that would add greatly to his appeal, what might be called the glamour of the trophy. He must also be old, long divorced from the herd, with blunt, thick, craggy horns. One day, riding the spinster elephant, we came on such a bull. He was all alone upon a scene that will always live in my memory. The trees were tall, with naked or vine-encurled trunks. He stood in short grass of emerald hue, and the interlocking boughs made a perfect canopy of pale green with golden flakes, high as a cathedral ceiling. The bull loomed black with immense horns.

I shot from my seat on the elephant pad. This is not as effete as it sounds, since Parbati had not been trained to stand to a charge. She had a nervous temperament, and a hunter trying to shoot a charging adversary from her jolting back would be better off on the ground, where he could take a solid stand, whirl, or shoot right or left. Still the principle was wrong. It smacked a little of the royal and viceregal shoots, which were a world removed from shooting rabbits in Indiana cornfields, or even from our hunts in the spruce forest where I had lost my maidenhead. I was deep-rooted in the American frontier, a member of the most democratic body on the earth, with no fitness for the role of a pukka English sahib, who could shoot a driven tiger between teatime and dinner and shrug it off. Perhaps I was oppressed with a faint sense of guilt when I pulled the trigger.

The forest king crashed down. All my shots lately had turned out so, I thought with satisfaction. With great calmness I slipped off the elephant and, although not the reasonable facsimile of a pukka sahib, still a rough imitation of one, I walked toward the fallen bull. Of course I had ejected the empty shell and thrown a live one into the chamber. Also I had ordered Bimbo to wait till I had made sure that the bison was finished—perfectly good *shikari* manners, since he had no extra piece.

When I had drawn within forty feet of the black shape, it suddenly came to life. With a snort of fury the huge beast sprang to his feet. I was on my third expedition to the shooting grounds of the Old World. Five times before then I made extensive hunting trips to our own North; so my conduct now becomes difficult to explain, and somewhat painful to confess. I flung up and shot without aiming, missing the huge target completely. At the same time I began to walk backward very rapidly, almost running, the picture of a man in a complete funk.

I was saved not by any recovery of self-control. Although if the bison had charged me, as was his will to do, I might have rallied in time to drop him almost at my feet, I have no inward assurance that I would not have fired wildly and missed again and been gored to death holding an empty gun.

It was no flagging of his kingly spirit that deprived him of revenge. He had made one great surge toward me when the weaker flesh succumbed to the affliction of his wound, overwhelming his warrior heart. His legs gave way under him and he tottered and fell.

I came up to him in great humility. I would hang his noble head not as a trophy but as a memorial to a great king of the wood, and I would tell my friends about him and how, when he had risen and turned to fight, I had been cowed by his ferocity and might, in spite of holding in my arms the dealer of a two-ton blow. I thought more instead of less of this strange, savage, and yet somehow magnificent game which I and so many other men played for winnings and causes unknown.

I would never again speak lightly of it or act lightly toward it, any more than would old Cottar or Dean Cochran, or Mauf

Hamilton in some Happy Hunting Ground. In spite of all my failings, with these I was somehow akin. But except in an emergency I would never again hunt with an armed guide. To give my adversary that much more of a chance was, I knew, the thing above all others that would finally mark me as a big-game hunter. And I resolved that after taking a wild water buffalo, one of the eight noblest big-game animals in the world, I would not seek any more horned game, except as we needed meat. I had the moose, the woodland caribou, the Cape buffalo, the saladang, and now the Indian bison. From now on I would devote my hunting days to the great felines, especially to the great and beautiful and terrible tigers.

III

Bimbo's loyalty to me stood out again in connection with the procuring and care of the scalp and skull of the bison. At the same time it was the occasion of a wild and funny fluke of coincidence.

The bison being a wild ox, his death caused a flurry of piety among our Hindu camp hands. I think it was three-fourths cant and hypocrisy. Certainly the farmers hereabouts showed no love of cattle when they were goading or lashing their cart beasts —but that fact would not save my trophy when the men refused to touch it, on religious grounds. John had another, scarcely better reason for not doing the job. While he would gladly oversee it, he never liked to put his hands to any camp work, patently on the theory that such was unworthy of a sahib and he would lose face. Since he was an immensely complex man, with many self-contradictions, numerous strengths as well as frailties, and since I was often a fool and always far from an angel, I did not press him.

Not knowing myself how to proceed, I was hard put for a

solution when one little man with a big knife stepped forward. It was Bimbo, and he told John he would save the *burra* sahib's trophy no matter the wrath of the jungle gods or even of great Shiv's, whose avatar was the bull. And this was the first time I had ever been called by this title. It meant the big sahib, and inference was plain that John thus became the *chota* (little) sahib. Truly I did not gloat over the comparison. John had been trying hard, lately, to stay sober and do his job. But I did rejoice greatly that the highest-caste man in the outfit should be least afraid of losing caste by standing duty.

Bimbo laid a copper coin on the flank of the carcass, then went to work with his kukri. At his first chop he broke a piece out of the blade as big as a half dollar, and although I thought he changed color, he continued as doughtily as before. Then occurred the stunning and incredible coincidence. When John and I were helping him turn over the huge beast, one rear leg that had been pinned under the body kicked out with terrific force and struck Bimbo full in the chest. It rolled him over like a ninepin.

He rose, brushed his clothes, and to my amazement, he looked relieved. John explained to me later that Bimbo considered this a rightful degree of chastisement by the gods, not too much or too little. He had got it and it was over and now he could go ahead with a clear conscience and composed mind to complete the task. There was no more thunder on the left, and all went smoothly.

Matters did not go so well with our tiger and buffalo hunting. While I shot a splendid leopard, the best I had ever seen except the king of the leopards that had come before my *boma* on an African night, we saw only young bull buffalo, and the tigers merely killed the cattle we tied out, feasted once, and failed to return the next evening to give me a shot. Bimbo told me, through John, that if I should meet the *shikari* god in the jungle, I must speak civilly to him and give him some tobacco, and on no account to treat him harshly, hairy and ugly though he might be.

"A little like an ape," John explained. "I think he derives from Hanuman, the monkey god."

Also, if I saw two fires at a great distance slowly moving toward each other until they joined, I must leave the country at once and sail forth upon the black seas, if indeed I had time to do so, for this sign meant that the high gods had decreed my death.

When my contracted time with John had only two weeks to go, we received an exciting report from a nearby village. A heifer had been killed just after sunrise only two hundred paces from a farmer's byre, the killer having fled without carrying off or eating of the carcass. There was no doubt in the cowherd's mind that this killer was no other than the tigress named Sakini, or Ogress, and who was sometimes known—so that her dread name need not be mentioned—as the White-faced One.

Used to excitable natives, John questioned the visitor closely. He told him that the tigress's white face had been seen in this neighborhood several times of late, and that the tracks left beside the dead heifer were indistinguishable from those of Sakini.

"I think he knows what he's talking about," John told me in English. "I believe it's your chance to do the villagers around here a turn they'll never forget, and you to win the name of a great *shikari*, and, if you and the tigress should happen to kill each other, to have a little shrine made to you, where the natives would bring flowers and fruit and maybe some rice cakes and even junk from the bazaar. But don't get killed without doing her in too. The natives hereabout don't care for heroes, or gods either, that don't get results."

We sent back word that the carcass was to be guarded from vultures and not to be moved until we arrived. As soon as we could get ready, the mahout, Bimbo, and I rode over on our spinster elephant—for we had long since sent back the high-priced tusker—and John sped ahead of us on a pony. The farmer greeted us volubly, shrill with excitement, and led us to the scene. There lay the heifer where the tiger had felled her, almost in sight of the byre, just within the scrub jungle flanking the grass. But a difficulty became immediately apparent. There was no tree nearby large enough to support a *machon*, and no hill in which we could dig a cave.

"Well, we can dig a pit," I proposed. I had dug pits hunting wild geese in the stubble fields of eastern Oregon.

"That's an excellent suggestion," John replied.

My own enthusiasm declined as Bimbo, the mahout, and the eager farmer proceeded with the digging. The pit must have a shelf, and be deep enough that my companion and I could sit in comfort, without our heads showing. Also, I must have room to stand up and shoot. When it was dug to John's satisfaction, Bimbo cut a little trough through which we could watch the bait without revealing our presence. John now gave orders for the mahout to lay off about a half a mile, and if he heard me shoot, to come for Bimbo and me, and under any conditions to come for us two hours after sundown. He himself made ready to take off for camp on pony-back.

"What if this tiger comes in from the rear?" I asked John.

"He may not see you. If he does, he'll take off."

"That's only your opinion; you can't guarantee it. He's a bold tiger, and he may not like to have people lurking about his kill. It seems to me he might claw one of us out of the hole. I want this pit fortified in some way."

We discussed cutting poles and laying them across the opening, but they had to be far enough apart to permit me to rise and sit down again. Then one of us made what appeared to be quite a brilliant suggestion.

"I saw an old cartwheel beside the byre. We can lay that over the hole."

The natives went for the cartwheel and rolled it happily to the scene; it proved just the right size. However, its wooden spokes were too close together to permit easy passage. Without a second thought, John ordered Bimbo to take the ax and cut out one of the spokes. Now Bimbo and I could rise or sit down with the greatest ease, but the pit seemed almost as unfortified as before.

"You're sure you'll be all right?" John asked.

"I guess so," I answered, sitting on the earthen shelf beside Bimbo.

"Then cheeri-o!"

John rode off on his pony. The mahout took his elephant to a convenient retreat. The farmer looked at Bimbo and me with a very odd expression on his face. Then he shook his head and he too made off. As the stillness closed in I began to feel a distinct embarrassment. There is such a thing in this world as the making of a priceless ass of one's self, and I was greatly afraid I had done so.

I wondered what Bimbo was thinking. I did not want to lose face before him, and as far as I could tell I had not. He sat in his usual silence, with his wonted patience, and appeared his usual cheerful self. Actually, I thought, there was nothing really wrong with the setup, for its extravagance was more apparent than real. If the tiger came straight to the bait from the direction I gazed I could see him in plenty of time to stand up and shoot.

Still I could not rid my brain of a nightmarish expectancy of a ruffed face suddenly appearing in the mouth of the pit and a striped front leg terminating in four hooks lashing down between the spokes.

I wished heartily I had never got Bimbo and me in this fix. I would retreat now, if I could do so with the least grace. The prospect of sitting here till two hours after sundown—from just about noon until half-past eight—was depressing in the extreme. In a few minutes I could expect the vultures to come coasting in. I would be almost glad of their gruesome company and perhaps they would signal the tiger's approach—if and when he came at all.

But the first of the foul birds, lighting greedily, immediately took off with a fast forced beat of his wings. I waited in vain for others.

It seems that, at that moment, I should have known that the tiger was nearby. I thought of it—thinking of him lying somewhere in the scrub, possibly moving about in the underbrush— only to be unable to credit it. It seemed to me far more likely that as the vulture volplaned down he had sighted Bimbo and me in the pit, had paid no attention to us and, as a kind of "delayed take," as in an old-fashioned comic movie, he had suddenly realized the oddness of the sight and had beat a sensible retreat. The fact remained that I no longer felt foolish or bored.

Not even this ridiculous cartwheel over our heads, let alone cattle lowing, dogs barking, and children playing about the nearby homestead, prevented me from knowing that Bimbo and I were on a tiger hunt—that the carcass laying there was by a tiger's killing—that the tiger was a bold and crafty female famous in these parts—and at any moment she might return.

It happened that Bimbo had a better view up the little trough than I did. He was keeping a good lookout when his hand crept to mine and pressed it lightly. Later I could not remember a more brotherly gesture from anyone, and I thanked my particular stars that I had been able to make such a bond with him that he, a native in race-conscious India, could signal me in this way. Now I glanced into his face. He nodded slightly and leaned out of the way so I could look up the trough.

Into the open stalked the tigress. She was about forty feet distant, and this was scrub jungle with thin shade, and the sun was high, and she glimmered. Anyway, she was the most gorgeously striped tiger I had ever seen, wild or in a zoo, almost incredibly bright gold and raven black. A tigress has different lines from a tiger. I think this partly caused the effect of stunning beauty that she conveyed. She was indeed Blake's tiger—of awful symmetry.

She walked up to the bait and stopped and looked around. As her piercing glance started to sweep over the cartwheel, her head stood still, and her gaze fixed on it, not yet in suspicion, but in deep curiosity; maybe she knew it had not lain here when she had felled the heifer. And now I knew that she was surely Sakini, the Ogress, the White-faced One. The hair around her mouth was not white, but definitely of paler shade than the rest, and the Y-shaped stripe that usually runs up the cheeks and forks to fence in the eyes was absent. Actually such paleness here is common and may even be general in tigers, but the missing stripe called attention to it and gave her face an unmistakable uniqueness.

According to the lore of old *shikaris,* the hunter should try to avoid firing at a tiger when the animal's eyes are fixed on him, because when the ball hits, he habitually rushes in the way he is gazing. I thought of it in the way a man's brain works in a crisis —a kind of instantaneous and simultaneous perception of things known. But I could not act upon it—I was afraid that any instant the tigress might become alarmed and dart into the thickets. So I readied my gun and stood up.

I did not stand very tall, but I have since thought that my sudden appearance on what seemed empty ground must have astounded her. Certainly it angered her, because her ears laid back and her lips drew in a snarl. I have always wondered if she recognized me as a man. She saw men almost every day, but none were sunk halfway into the ground. Before she could choose a course of action I had leveled and fired.

At once I dropped back, half falling, into the pit. Even so I saw the start of that wonderful lightning dash which tigers as well as lions can make, when they come to kill. I did not see the rest of it. Her course was not straight toward the pit but slightly quartering, and she probably passed about eight feet away. I heard the light drum roll of her feet, then all was silence.

Bimbo and I crouched motionless, in terror and shock. We did not know what had become of the tigress, whether she was near or far, and when we began to recover, we peered with greatest care through the wheel spokes before we dared start to emerge. I came out with my rifle held in front of my breast, ready for a quick shot. I could hardly believe it when the seconds passed and nothing more happened. I had entertained such lively expectations of an immediate attack. Soon we were both out, and the scene seemed just the same as before, but the tiger had come and gone.

Had I hit or missed? I was not at all sure, nor could I get Bimbo to tell me. Wildly I acted it out, in my deep anxiety digging myself in the side with my finger to signify the bullet striking, at the same time speaking words he could not understand. He gave me a faint smile, then paid me no more attention as he searched in the grass. Presently he came out with a joyful "Sahib!"

I hurried to him and he showed me red drops where the tigress had stood, and a trail of them leading off in the direction of the thickets. Then he looked at me with an eager expression whose meaning I knew only too well.

For the first time in my dealings with tigers I was confronted by the situation which the oldest and most tried *shikaris* dread— the necessity of following a wounded tiger into thick cover. Some say there have been amateurs who welcomed it. There is the story of how certain dashing cavalry officers of a famous British regiment had deliberately shot tigers in the belly, knowing they would only wound them and thus could have the sport of trailing them and meeting, in almost every case, a lethal attack, but I did not believe it, simply because such actions would comprise deliberate cruelty, with which I could not charge our kinsmen and allies. I thought of such attacks, remembering only too well what I had heard of their cunning and fury, and my nerve ran out of me, and I did not know what to say.

What other course was open? I need not even consider waiting till tomorrow, when John could join me with his lighter rifle, meanwhile giving the tiger time to stiffen up or die. This very evening natives would move here and about in their daily traffic. If one of them came into view of a wounded tiger at bay, there would be the making of a full-scale tragedy. I might be able to send for John now and get him here late in the afternoon, but it would require writing some sort of note with such materials as I could find in the farmhouse and the luck of his being in camp to receive it. But if Bimbo and I had to slog it alone, we had better go now, when the sun was high and bright.

It came about that I gave Bimbo a nod, at which he rejoiced. I do not believe that he wanted me to engage a wounded tiger. He just couldn't bear for me to show the least white feather or fail my obligations as a *shikari*. In any case his high approval of my course did me much good. With me on his flank, my gun held with both hands slanting across my breast, he began to follow the spoor.

It led us into ugly, brushy country. I hardly know how I went on, I was so wrought upon by fear. Only when I had seen K'nini in the leopard's claws had I felt it deeper, colder, more devastating—and that had quickly passed, while this was prolonged. If the tiger were alive and able to fight, he would almost certainly charge. We would not know from what direction to expect him. He would have the advantage of cover, and our danger would be greater than K'nini's and mine that day, because now we had no Cottar to guard us, and our quarry was a tiger who could kill with one stroke, not a leopard.

A great many—in fact most—of the crises that lie in the cards of big-game hunting are never dealt. Therefore it remains no more or less than a classic sport, although its perils are perfectly real and of a strangely spine-chilling sort. So it was today.

After creeping along about fifty yards, Bimbo saw an anthill, common in this region, and sprang to its top. At once he uttered a joyful cry, pointing wildly. I sprang up with him, and fifty yards farther on there lay on almost empty ground the gaudy body of a tiger, and I would have shot again, if Bimbo had not touched my arm and shaken his head. "Daid," he said very distinctly in English, holding his lips oddly. Then he and I yelled and shook hands.

There remained only the glorious aftermath. We saw the farmer coming on the run, and we beckoned to him and he almost danced with joy. He called to another native, who ran and got a cup, the use of which I could not imagine until he put it beneath the death wound, squeezed out some blood, and drank it on the spot. No doubt it was medicine of great power.

Two Bhutanese who had been lurking about the byre came rushing up to cut steaks from the dead heifer. They were coarse-faced, burly fellows, each of whom looked twice Bimbo's size, but he would not stoop to scaring them off with his kukri, and instead chased them out of the neighborhood with a little stick. The mahout came, with a wonderful beam on his face, and was so highhearted that he easily induced the spinster elephant to come up to the fallen tiger and to kneel. There were ten now, and all of us shared the joyous task of heaving him aboard; and even so it was harder—or at least more awkward—than we had thought. Meanwhile we talked in loud, half-hysterical tones, not caring whether we understood what one another was saying, only wildly happy to be fellow humans on this marvelous occasion.

But the cattle watched lazily and with indifference, not dreaming how many of their lives Bimbo and I had saved.

Fifteen

LIKE many imaginative men, I have a lively belief in the Unseen.
I have no doubt whatever in the reality of telepathy, prophetic
dreams, and other aspects of psychic phenomena, despite the
prevalence of fakes and fakers. In fact I myself had a prophetic
dream, so rich in detail that it was like a sneak preview of a
slightly distorted film of the minor event to come. I have never
been able to put any credence in the conjure constantly practiced
in the neighborhood of my Georgia farm, mainly because it is
childish and of ambiguous results. But I have nevertheless known
several Negresses with curiously witchlike powers.

All the natives in my camp believe firmly in puja—a word
meaning magical practices as well as religious rites—and although

John professed disdain, I felt that he had been very strongly impressed when the dead bison had taken a swift kick at Bimbo. In fact, in these ancient jungles I found myself wrought upon by superstition more than at home. I propitiated devils by knocking on wood, became more attentive to what might be signs, and took care not to invite disasters and practical jokes by loose talk in the hearing of the gods. So when it happened that I had a brush with puja in direct connection with my hunting, I certainly did not believe in it, but found it at first novel and decidedly discomforting, and ultimately an interesting experience to rack up with my others.

The affair began with John's discharging the native *shikari* with whom I had had slight difficulties on the night of the visit of the wild-elephant herd: he had been a troublemaker from the first. About five nights after this I became worried about two things—the poor results I was having in the field and the low morale of the camp hands. When even my audacious and grinny Bimbo began to look glum, I questioned John.

"Something's gone wrong," I said. "What is it?"

"Well, it's been more than a week since you took a skin or scalp. The tigers aren't returning to kills and you've seen nothing worth taking in the way of a buffalo."

"I've seen no game at all but barking deer. I think it's moved on to another jungle. Some more ought to drift in soon."

"Will you be able to see it? The boys don't think you will. Now I've said this much, I'll have to tell you the rest. The native *shikari* that I fired complained to the village guru and the johnny has made puja against you to the *shikari* god. According to the reports we've had from the villagers, a film has been put over your eyes so you can't see any more game."

"That's the most complete tommyrot I ever heard."

"I know, but the boys believe it, and I wish you could get a trophy to buck 'em up."

I wished it too, and hunted long and far in the next few days.

As luck would have it, I not only failed to get a trophy but saw no animals of note. These great green jungles seemed forsaken by all that could rank as big game. I came so close to seeing it, without actually laying eyes on it, that it took a deal of common sense, an actual focusing of the mind on reality and a refusal to treat with mumbo-jumbo, not to begin to wonder if I were bewitched. Once I saw the grass move where a tiger fled from his kill, although I caught no glimpse of his striped hide. Once I found buffalo tracks daubed with wet mud and piles of steaming dung and heard them breaking through reeds within a stone's throw—a big herd of buffalo in a place handy to find them—without sighting a cow or calf. Once I came on wild elephants in thick scrub jungle and heard them on all sides of us and saw what I thought was a snaky trunk, but when I looked hard at it, it disappeared.

In recounting these events, the wheels of my brain check and I ask myself whether I am drawing a low bow—if I am omitting a few animal appearances that I find it convenient to forget for the sake of a good story. When I have searched and found the answer, it is always no. However, I would have dismissed the story as trivial or at least put it among my anecdotes except for its rather magnificent and completely factual climax. There is an anticlimax too, which I smile over now, even if it seemed somewhat impressive at the time.

When the puja had been in effect something over a week, I planned a day's jaunt on the wild and enchanting Baldy River. I rode the spinster elephant, with the mahout on her neck and Bimbo perched behind me; and we took along one of the trackers, to break our run of bad luck. As we advanced up the wide, almost dry, rocky bed, I thought I saw a large boar lying on the opposite bank. He was about the color of the ground and I could not be sure of his outline, but when I pointed to it, Bimbo nodded rather doubtfully. The camp hands like wild-boar meat, even though the lowest caste among them would never dream of eating domestic pork. Besides, he might have big tusks that I could keep or give a friend—and, best of all, his taking would be a solid fact to explode the myth of the curse the *shikari* god laid upon my eyes.

I took careful aim and pulled the trigger. The rifle did not fire. In haste I threw in another shell, with the same result. This was the first time that the reliable Mauser had ever failed, and by far the most odd and puzzling circumstance in the present affair—the only one that jarred me a little. Perhaps in my nervousness I had only taken up the slack in the trigger and had not applied enough pressure to trip the firing pin. The rifle fired on my third attempt and the bullet raised a little cloud of dust on the opposite bank. When I looked for my hog, I could not find him. He had either made an escape worthy of legerdemain or he had been an odd-shaped shadow to start with.

The elephant trudged on, her trunk dangling. My companions and I were deeply depressed. We ate our lunch and considered returning to camp, but the wild country ahead beckoned me on and the steep hills of Bhutan made a wonderful purple wall on our right hand. My watch said three o'clock. And a minute or two after that I noticed that my flashlight, carried in a knapsack slung on the elephant's pad, had come on. I supposed that a rubbing motion of the animal's thigh had depressed the button. It was not a very likely explanation but the best I could find. Meanwhile the boys were giving one another wondering glances and speaking in low tones. Obviously they thought that we had received a sign.

11

About fifteen minutes later there occurred something far more notable, indeed a sign of the unfailing wonder of the jungle and the wild. Out of the wooded bank ahead of us there strode an immense bull elephant. He walked on to the river bed, into the brilliant sunlight, and his tusks glimmered, and he curled his trunk, and the scene of majesty of might was one to remember always. I went through the motions of wiping my eyes, meanwhile jabbing Bimbo in the ribs with my thumb. This was to banter him for ever believing in the guru's curse.

We were riding into a cross wind. Still the elephants caught each other's scent, and our amorous spinster evinced so much excitement that we had to take her down the current a short distance, until the bull went on his way. And now we were approaching the point of no return in daylight. We must either turn back now, or make the last mile or two into camp in the whispering, thrilling darkness.

Such a feeling of optimism had come over me, like a presentiment of a great event, that I ordered the mahout on. The boys approved; I could see it in their flushed faces and shining eyes. In half an hour we came to our great reward.

As we rounded a curve we looked over the reeds to a noble sight. It was the black shape of a huge bull buffalo, solitary, ominous, advancing slowly with his massive horns laid back. These were fully four feet long, marking him as an old bull, and a great trophy. In fact he looked even larger than the massive buffalo of which I had caught a brief glimpse in Indo-China. Of the four ruminants of the world, by far the largest of the horned beasts and ranked among the kings of wild nature, I had already taken the Cape buffalo, the saladang, and the Indian bison. This, the wild water buffalo, did not stand quite as tall as the latter two, but taller than the African buffalo, and his horns were the largest of all; and he had a somber splendor all his own.

The wind blew across us now, but if we followed the curving river bed he would surely scent us. So I had the elephant kneel to let me off so I could skirt the bend, staying well downwind of him, and come out in his fore. Bimbo uttered a soft sound. He wanted to go with me. I could not look after him with one gun and was forced to shake my head.

In a few minutes I had completed the maneuver. Crouching in low grass, I saw the black giant come forth from a screen of trees, walking in steady, powerful strides. The grass was almost shoulder-high but it would shorten soon, and then I would have a clear shot into his heart chamber. But with that shot, if I made it, I would be done with horned game. Each of the four walls of my trophy room would have its central adornment, more meaningful to me than bossed shields or crossed swords borne by distant ancestors.

Then upon the scene entered the unforeseen circumstance. The mahout had not understood that I wanted him to wait downwind of the quarry, but had pushed on around the river bend. Instantly the bull scented the elephant and no doubt the riders on her back, for with thrusting muzzle and laid-back horns he whirled to face her. Catching a glimpse of her, he again turned and began to walk rapidly in my direction. As he merged into short grass, I took a close, hard aim and fired.

I felt that I had hit, although the bull gave no sign of it. Nor did the roar of the rifle have any visible effect on him. As he broke into a thundering run it was still to escape the enemy he had scented. At first his course was not straight toward me, rather at an angle that would cause him to pass me at a few yards' distance, and this helped to steady me for a second shot. Before I could get it off, he caught sight of me in breast-high grass, and instantly recognized me as another enemy. Stopping a brief instant, he bellowed and came on.

This was the wild water-buffalo bull, the unyoked sire of patient plow beasts of the paddy fields and drawers of wagons, and even his dwarfed offspring will sometimes fight tigers. He came to clear his path or avenge a wound, and in all the wild-beast world I could not imagine a more magnificent charge.

I had time for only one shot. It need not be meticulously placed but it must go home. It was no job for a tyro, because it needed all the steadiness I could muster, the schooling of the North Woods, the tundra, the veld, and the jungle. You would think it would take no feat of will to take a steady aim at the huge target, but it did; as the bull bore down, bellowing, his hooves drumming, his horns laid back, and his eyes wild and green, I was hard put to it to hold. I did, however, with great belligerency, and saw his heaving shoulder in the sights, and pressed hard. The bull crashed down.

Running up to me, deer-fleet, Bimbo found me entranced. He put his hand on my arm and spoke to me quietly and I saw the pallor in his face; the whole scene had a sudden greater meaning than before, although I knew not what.

III

It came to me too that this scene marked my farewell to the jungles of Mowgli, and at the same time it ended a phase of my life. I would return hereabouts, but to a different scene, in a different state of mind. I would not hunt the run and ruck of India big game but take a new and particular course, as thrilling a prospect as that of my first trip to the North Woods. Only an experienced hunter could follow it with success. Many a sahib sportsman had tried and failed.

But I have mentioned an anticlimax to the thrilling climax of the charge. I put it down with some misgivings, since it is so pat, like the sometimes forced contrivance of a novelist, but it is a true part of a true story, and I have no choice.

When we had covered the carcass with boughs and made our exultant ride into camp, our elephant stepping high, we found John waiting for us with what I thought was a bad conscience.

However, he was perfectly sober, and the darkness managed to conceal from him the flush on our faces and the sheen in our eyes.

"No luck?" he asked.

"We saw a big elephant," I answered.

"What time did you see him?"

"What does that matter?"

"Well, I'm just interested. I never believed a minute in that bally curse, but I just wanted to prove it was all bilge. Did you see him before three o'clock?"

"As a matter of fact, it was just after three."

"Then it doesn't prove anything. In fact, it's bloody odd. For just after tiffin I went over to see that guru bloke, and for the sake of the boys' morale, I gave him three rupees to take off the curse. He got some piles of cow dung and some milk and said some incantations. He finished up at exactly three."

I V

A few days before meeting the water buffalo an English-speaking forest warden stopped at our camp and looked at my trophies. He greatly admired my bison, and the pelt of the white-faced tigress Sakini, not for her size but because of her brilliant coloring and her ill fame as a cattle killer. He said that my other two tigers were good specimens, about four-year-old males, and any tiger larger than a cub was a splendid trophy. But he wished I could have taken a great tiger, one of the giant tigers that grew hereabouts—a Royal Bengal tiger that bred in this country, next door to the province of Bengal. Such tigers were the largest, best-furred, and most ferocious of any tigers in southeastern Asia.

"I took a giant tiger in French Indo-China," I told him. "I suspect that is one man's share. There don't seem to be many giant tigers in this reserve. At least we have seen only one track that looked as if it might go with a nine-foot tiger."

"They are scarce in all jungles. It is not in the jungles where you should look for giant tigers, because when a tiger gets big and heavy and slow, he leaves the jungle. He has to, because he can no longer catch deer and wild pig."

"Where does he go?"

"He goes to the scrub jungle around the villages, where he can kill plow and milk beasts, goats, ponies, and sometimes men."

"Do you know any villages entertaining such tigers?"

"I know of a dozen such villages, all within thirty miles from here, dotted over the grasslands they use for grazing cattle. There must be fully a dozen Royal Bengal tigers living in the scrub and grass jungles, especially the reeds besides the river bends, and some of them have been there—as the natives say—'always.' Actually it must seem like it. I have no doubt some of them are thirty years old."

"Why haven't the tiger-hunting sahibs come and killed them?"

"Most sahibs don't know about them. If they're told, they don't believe it. They think they have to go to a maharajah's preserves. Those that do look into it, find that the country is not suitable for beating; it's too open and spread-out and the animals can slip away in any direction. Even so, quite a few sahibs have tried shooting them from *machons,* almost always without success."

"Why didn't they succeed?" I asked.

"Because, growing old, these tigers have grown cunning. They will kill a tethered cow, but never come back to it. They will come up, hang out in the thicket, identify a *machon* or a blind or see some little change and go their way. Why not, when the plain abounds with cattle? Each tiger kills an average of two cows a week—a hundred a year. Often they go only a hundred paces from their lairs and drag the carcass into the nearest reed patch. The natives have tried traps and poison, always in vain, and now they shrug and say, 'No man can fight the gods.' The less pious and resigned have another saying about their cattle raising. 'One for me, one for the tiger.' It may be quite possible that in the long run, the tigers will take half their herds."

"My friend, do you think the tigers will still be there two years from now?"

"Why not? I have no reason to doubt that the plain has been infested with giant tigers for the past fifty years. If you could take even one of them, you would do the villagers a mighty favor and you would have a trophy to match the finest ever taken in the royal shoots. If you are lucky enough—or persevere enough —you might get more."

The forester went his way, and when John came into camp I told him what he had said.

"It's no news to me," he replied.

"It seems to me you should have told me about them before now."

"What would be the use? You couldn't get them. I never take parties there and let them waste their time. Those cattle killers are devils of cunning, and extra dangerous besides. One of them is a man-killer called Kala Bagh. As it is, you've got a wonderful bag."

He stopped, and turned his gaze away—not that he had failed to tell the truth, but for other reasons that we both knew well.

"Yes, but two years from now I expect to return to hunt the giant tigers."

John was still a long time, went to mend the fire with his own hands, and at last returned and blurted out what he had to say.

"I don't suppose you'd consider hiring me again."

"I would consider it, yes."

"I don't deserve it; I know that. I've gone on too many drunks in the villages, made you too much trouble. But maybe you've noticed I've done better the last two weeks."

"A great deal better."

"If you give me another chance, I'll do my level best not to touch booze from the day you come till the day you leave."

"How does it happen?" I asked, after another long pause.

"Didn't you tell me every man is a fool or a physician at forty? I haven't got too much time."

I thought it over, and concluded it was a good answer. There was no unction in it and no bunk. Besides, I had not known many drunks that had escaped the rubbish heap except through self-respect.

"Under those conditions, expect me twenty-two months from now."

Before the night was over, I had the germ of a plan, the merest glowworm of an idea, of how I might outwit those giant tigers. But I did not confide it to John. Moderation in all things, I thought—especially in trusting those who sometimes drown their whole brains in a bottle.

So the hunt ended in happiness and triumph, and in thrilling hope of the future. I bought our two elephants a huge meal of sugar cane; I crossed with silver the dark, friendly palms of the camp men; and the hour came when I said farewell to Bimbo. He gave me the kukri he had broken on the neck of the bison bull. I gave him money to buy another. At last he gave me his hand, then turned and walked away in his little blue suit, and I dreamed I would never see him again, and it was a true dream. Still, we had had great days together, beheld the jungle in the dawn and the dusk and the sun-steeped stillness of midday, and we sat in the same hole when Sakini, the Ogress, the white-faced shining tiger, came forth to her kill. That was only one of our great moments. . . . And Bimbo, you have also eaten beef with me in the dark of the blind. But I won't tell the Brahmins.

5. Pursuit of the Giants

Sixteen

AS the time drew near for my second voyage to India, I bought another rifle. This was no less than the double-barreled .470, made by the great George Gibbs of Bristol, and the grandest piece of ironmongery I had ever seen. Its long cartridge contained a five-hundred-grain bullet propelled by ninety grains of cordite, the latter in contrast with twenty-six grains of ordinary smokeless powder in a twelve-gauge shotgun shell. If well placed, its bullet should put to a mercifully quick end such heavy beasts as buffalo and saladang, which would frequently live long when hard hit by a .404. And if I happened to engage an elephant, the piece was the right size. Because I was so taken with the Mauser I meant to continue to use it as my main arm when

hunting giant tigers, for which it was barely heavy enough, if not on the light side. But if I must follow wounded tigers or go into the grass where the charge would be sudden and short, I meant to carry or be backed by the terrific double.

John MacDonald met me at Ranguya station under the Bhutan hills. It seemed to me he looked fresher and better than I had ever seen him, and overjoyed at the prospect of the adventure awaiting us. As he rode in a truck to the grasslands, peopled by handsome Nepalese herders, countless cattle, and, without doubt, a scattering of the greatest tigers found anywhere in southeastern Asia, I told him of the tactics I intended to adopt in hunting the huge and gaudy beasts.

"The forest officers told me that they will kill tethered cattle, make one meal, and never return to the carcass. If they simply abandon it, my plan's no good. But if they attempt to return to it, which is certainly tiger nature, and come up and survey the scene only to be warned of the hunter's presence, I think I've got the answer. Anyway I've come ten thousand miles to see."

"It has to be jolly good," John said thoughtfully. "These tigers are mind readers—or they're equipped with radar, or something uncanny. If your plan is to tie the cows in the open grass where you can see for a hundred yards, it won't work. They'll kill there, but they certainly won't come back."

"We'll tie the cows in scrub jungle by the watercourses. We'll dig the pits—I prefer those to *machons*—ahead of time. When the tiger kills, and I come to watch, we'll tie up another cow close to the carcass. When the tiger comes back and begins his survey, he'll see her. Will he see anything else?"

"What do you mean?" John's eyes began to glitter, for he knew what I meant.

"What's the nature of a tiger? To kill. He's a far more passionate killer than a lion. When he lays eyes on the live cow, those big adrenal glands are going to start shooting, and he's going to forget all about taking care. Instead of surveying the scene, he's going to come in one terrific rush. Is he, or isn't he?"

"I think he'll work around downwind from the cow. That's tiger nature, too. For that matter, he usually approaches the bait from downwind. But I don't think he'll look for pits or for any change in the scenery, and when he gets set, I believe he'll come. And what a sight that will be!"

A shocking sight, I thought. But I had dealt with this aspect of the situation, and had reached a conclusion about it. Neither of the two cows tied out would suffer a more cruel death than that administered to cattle in an American stockyard. Unlike goats and dogs, which are sometimes tied for leopard bait, cattle and buffalo never seem to suffer from fear when being tied in the jungle. Since the tiger does rush from downwind—Louis had told me that—the victim never knows of his presence until the second of doom. The lives of two cows would be a small price to pay for the death of an inveterate killer of two cows a week. I did not like such moral juggling—I felt something of a hypocrite—but the fact remained. Simplifying a little, I decided to let the tiger kill two cows so that I might kill the tiger. If thereby I saved a hundred cattle for the herds, that was all to the good.

In the rear of the cart were about five chains heavy enough, it seemed, to hold an elephant.

"What are you going to do with those?" I asked.

"They are for tying out the cows, chaining 'em out, I mean, so when they're killed they can't be dragged away. You haven't any idea of the power of a tiger, and neither had I, till I took a scouting trip up here and talked to some of the herders. This trip is going to be an eye opener for both of us."

That proved to be something of an understatement.

II

At the camp John had laid out I found two old friends. One was our spinster elephant, which he had again been able to hire, still scrawny-looking and nervous, but with a kind of charm about her. And I think she remembered the sugar cane I had given her, for she threw up her trunk and opened her mouth for another tidbit. The other friend was her good mahout, who shook my hand and grinned. We needed no baggage elephant on this trip, as we had pitched close to a village lying only a few miles from a truck road, and native carts could do the little hauling that we needed.

It would have seemed odd to some tiger hunters to be camping amid a wide grassy plain, broken only by a scrub jungle along the watercourses and occasional reed beds generally lying at the bends of the slow rivers. However, I found myself quite at home, perhaps because the countryside reminded me of the prairie on which I spent my early childhood in northern Indiana. There I used to play at hunting lions and tigers, and had been able to believe that bears could be found there. It seemed now that I was watching a childhood dream come true.

John had arrived a few days before and had already ridden about the various villages, inquiring for tigers. In our immediate plain, their killing grounds in easy reach, dwelt four giants. These were not vagrant tigers: they had settled down in defined neighborhoods, living a life of ease. They had dwelt there for many years and hundreds of natives knew them by sight, and they had killed and dragged to their lairs cattle past all counting. John had some of the herdsmen stop at our camp and tell me about them, as he interpreted the rush of words; and this interpretation and the tense look that came into the brown, well-molded faces stirred me deeply and excited my fancy in an odd way. It seemed I had a chance to be not only a tiger hunter but a dragon-killer. Except for their terrible reality, these tigers hanging out here year after year, taking their steady toll, suggested the tales of *in loco* dragons of Dark-Age Europe and of medieval romance, and made me think of famous wild boars that afflicted whole countrysides, and beyond that, into the mists of classic myth, of Hydra, Gorgon, and the Minotaur. The cattle drovers of Attica must have been very similar, in their ways of living and thinking, to the sun-browned herdsmen of these plains.

One of the four tigers was called the Grandfather of Tigers, or, more simply, the Great Tiger. John proposed to me seriously that he might measure, pegged out unskinned, ten feet from tip to tip. If so, there have been a few, a very few, greater tigers taken in all the history of *shikar*. Almost all of those reported as larger had been measured along the curves, not a straight line, or showed only skin measurement. In old days in India, sportsmen had spent years trying to get a true ten-footer, often without success. This tiger was the oldest on this plain. Men could remember tales of him told when they were boys. He killed cattle, plow buffaloes, and ponies, but had never been known to tear down a human being.

Two tigers dwelt in the same patch of jungle, both immense, and so alike that the people had never learned to distinguish one from the other. Undoubtedly they were brothers of the same litter. However, a few dissenters maintained that one was slightly larger than the other. An equally large tiger, still not as long or as burly as the Grandfather, lived six miles away, and was especially famed for killing heavy buffalo. Legend had it that in respect to strength he was a Hercules among tigers. John had not been able to find the source of this belief, but he never doubted it, and we were fated to discover, to our great amazement, that it was true.

The herders did not regard these tigers as essentially evil.

They knew it was a tiger's nature to take to cattle killing when he grew stiff and heavy. They paid their guru to make puja, whereby the killers might die, or go away, or be killed on the horns of a plow buffalo, for often the bulls were brave, and the old-man tiger need fumble only once. However, the holy man had his work cut out for him, to bring about any of these consummations. Although the titulary god of the country was of course Shiv, whose avatar was the bull, many believed that his wife was not Parbati but Kali, who was Durga, the Dark Mother, whose avatar was the tiger! Nor did they evidence the slightest hope that I, some sort of sahib from far away, could in the least alleviate the affliction. Other sahibs, far better outfitted and more pukka-looking than I, had tried without result.

So I foresaw from the start that we would not get immediate cooperation from the natives.

However, there remained one tiger who was evil incarnate. True, he did not dwell about their pastures and in fact had no fixed abode. He came and went—some said according to the moon, others said at his devilish inclination. He was not as large as the Grandfather, and about the size of the two brothers, which John reckoned as nine feet and several inches. His name, Kala Bagh, meant the Black Tiger, not on account of his outward color but of his inward nature. It was his way to stalk and kill a cattle herder, which was bad enough. Worse than that, he did not eat of the body, as would the common kind of man-killing tiger. Instead he let it lie while he went and killed a cow. Such unnatural conduct filled their souls with horror.

I had trouble understanding and then believing the story, and asked John to try to verify it. So we heard it from several sources, always substantially in the same form. Apparently this old tiger harbored the mistaken notion that he must kill the herder before he could kill one of the herd, and by what long-ago events he had got it in his stubborn head I could not imagine. John told me that a tiger ranging this area had been officially listed as a man-eater, charged by the game department with killing over twenty men. And although Kala Bagh had eaten none of his victims, John did not doubt he was the one.

What a wonderful opportunity for a hunter! In a quite real degree John shared my excitement and the morale of the whole outfit stood high. Then we encountered the obstacle, the fly in the ointment. When the herders perceived that we were going to use cattle for tiger bait, they became reluctant to sell us any.

In one of my novels, the audacious Captain John Smith was heard to observe that "religion was like rum, a little of it warming and comforting, but too much raising the Devil." You might have thought that the natives would have given us, with no thought of silver, all the cows we needed—that is, an American utterly unacquainted with natives might make such a prodigious miscalculation. But even John was surprised by their refusal to sell us cattle, even at well above the market price, considering it might bring about the saving of hundreds of head. It was another epidemic of piety, such as had gone through our camp when I killed the bison. This one, however, swept the whole countryside. Each herder tried to outdo the other in priggishness. Actually each one thought secretly that I could not kill the big tigers anyhow, and by this act of slavish propitiation of the gods not his herd, but his neighbor's, would catch it next.

It might mean we would have to send to distant villages for the cattle we needed, a troublesome and expensive operation. John's immediate hope lay in a colony of low-caste herders dwelling not far from these pastures, perhaps not as pious as our immediate neighbors, or more amenable to that heart-warming piece of philosophy, reflecting the common sense of the human race, that what they did not know would not hurt them.

III

Before John went to deal with these less sanctimonious Hindus, he put me on the trail of the Grandfather of Tigers.

It was a trail the like of which I had never seen and could hardly believe and I refer not merely to his tracks, which looked as big as my two hands.

He had killed an old plow buffalo close to a byre, and about a mile from the scrub jungle where he had his ancient abode. The herder declared that the bull was the largest in his herd, and I had no reason to doubt the statement when, in due course, I saw the carcass. It was certainly that of an old bull, and it looked as big as a big horse, and I guessed its weight at twelve hundred pounds at least. The great tiger had carried him more than a quarter of a mile, and not by dragging him. Dragging that heavy body over the rough ground would of itself have been a Herculean feat, considering that about eight men who came to build my blind could not move it a single foot. This incomparable tiger had carried it the whole distance.

This is one of those statements that one finds difficult to make, because of the feeling that it will collide with a wall of disbelief. But it is true. I myself saw the trail, not of a dragged body, but of four legs dragging on the ground beside the tiger's pugs. He must have gripped the carcass at the base or close behind the neck, and walked along with his head up. I would have gone a long way to have seen that sight with my own eyes. I wish that all Americans who doubt the power and the glory of the wild beasts over which man won dominion in the Million Years' War could see it, as well as those who have lost the power to wonder.

But even the Grandfather of Tigers could not accomplish what he had set to do—to carry the kill into the scrub jungle where he lived. Suddenly, it seemed, he came to the end of his strength, for he had dropped the bull, and as far as I could tell, made no further attempt to move it. Would he return to it? It was certainly possible, and surely the chance was worth playing—a few hours of patient watching that might give me a shot at one of the great tigers of the world—but I could not believe it. I had heard a good deal about wild animals and thought much about them and begun to try to postulate their behavior, not in the mystic way that Louis did but according to some unproven but provocative premises. For the Grandfather of Tigers, long king of the country, the dropping of the buffalo was an admission of defeat. I thought that he would want nothing more to do with it, and would go forth and kill again.

Even so, the men dug a pit and fortified it with some rails, and left me sitting there throughout the late afternoon and early evening. I wore a headlight on my cap and when darkness fell I was slightly hopeful for a while, but nothing came of it, and then the elephant came for me, and I went to camp and to bed.

In the morning John and two helpers came in from the low-caste village with three cows—not nearly enough to ease our worries, but enough to let us start hunting. Although he was not sure he could get any more, he thought it rather likely, when the rich and liberal owner of a large herd returned from the Bhutan bazaar. We tied out two in favorable places, keeping one back to use in our stratagem. Both remained untouched the first night. On the second night a big cow, picketed on the bank of a big, dry river bed, was torn down and dragged the length of the chain. One quarter had been half-eaten, such a light meal that I doubted if one of the giant tigers had made the kill.

The tracks verified my guess. The killer proved a middle-sized tiger, probably a female according to the herders' guess, and a newcomer to the country. We had already dug a cave in a high bank about sixty feet from the carcass, and a guard kept vultures away until three o'clock in the afternoon, when I entered the blind alone. I made no arrangements to tie up a live cow. We must save what stock we had for a chance at a monster.

Quite to my surprise, no vultures gathered to the kill. I could not imagine why, since no cover lay nearby that would hide a tiger, and the ghastly birds could surely have no fear of me, in my well-screened blind. They passed over and looked down but did not light.

It struck me that the bait was rather poorly placed—more

than a hundred yards from the scrub jungle. The purpose had been to bring it close to the steep bank offering a site for a cave, but the result was that the tiger must walk that distance in the bald open to reach his kill. I could not conceive of his doing so in broad daylight. Hence I resigned myself to a long watch after dark.

Not only lowly vultures sometimes fail to run true to form, or live up to reasonable expectations. About half-past four I was gazing calmly down the river bank, not looking for anything, lazily watching, when my nervous system gave me a pleasant jolt. It was quite like a shock of electricity, and I became a different man, alert, intensely alive, far more capable and aggressive than is my wont. The whole scene sharpened because of its central figure. It was that of a middle-sized tiger—probably a tigress, judging by her racy lines—advancing calmly down the river bank.

I suppose she never knew what hit her. The shot presented no difficulty and I made it easily, for although this was a beautiful and worthy trophy, she was not one of the giant tigers that I craved. There were two interesting and significant incidents of aftermath.

When the skinners who had heard the shot came up and began removing the brightly painted hide, the vultures gathered in force, lighting only thirty feet away, croaking and hissing and grimly waiting, and the rocks that the men threw could not make them fly. I wondered how they knew that this river bank had suddenly become a safe landing place.

The other evolved about the native herders' attitude toward the tigress. It appeared patronizing to say the least. Most remarks about her consisted of scornful comparisons between her and the giant tigers that regularly butchered their cattle. In the name of the gods, she was scarcely fit to be called the cub of one of that great ilk.

"Would one of the giant tigers have mated with her?" John asked in the Nepalese tongue.

"Well, no," an old village headman answered. "Our tigers have outlived their days as husbands, and their only passion now is to fill their bellies with our good kine."

"When they grow old and die, who takes their places at the banquets?"

"There are always fresh tigers from the jungles—"

"This is a fresh tiger. Whether cublike or not, she was still able to kill a big cow and she had come here to live. I think you had better thank the sahib, instead of boasting of your great tigers before the gods."

The headman thought this over.

"Yes, I spoke too rashly. He has done us a service, beyond a doubt. Our only sorrow is that he cannot do us another and a greater one, by killing one of the giants. They be devil tigers."

"We've come a little farther," John remarked when the herders had left, "but not much."

IV

That night, the night that John and I took our comfort in a fresh, beautiful skin on the drying racks, the cow that we had tied across the river from our camp was killed by a giant tiger.

We looked at his tracks and at the half-eaten carcass. We thought he was one of the brother tigers that lived not far away, and to incite me to do my best John ventured that he would peg out about nine and a half feet, half a foot over the minimum measurement of a Royal Bengal tiger. I did not need this incitement. I was already too excited and I needed calming down. I needed to be told that regardless of his size he was still only a striped cat, and that I was a writer of some small note, and that if I did not get him, I would probably have a chance at another, and I must retain a proper sense of values. I told myself all this, although it was no use. By two o'clock in the afternoon I had become so nervous that I had to bluff every hearty word and jest that I made.

The blind in this case was in the style of a *machon*, although only eight feet off the ground. That was in easy hooking reach of a giant tiger. Thinking of that calmed me rather than excited me further—God knew, not from any bravery, but from the feeling that I was not playing it slicker-safe, and if I lost the tiger, my shame would thus be somewhat reduced. I entered the blind, my headlight fastened to my cap, at half-past two. Until then the human traffic up and around the scrub jungle had been too heavy to cause any likelihood of the tiger's premature return. Vultures had not entered the thickets and the meat remained intact.

Almost at the last minute we decided not to stake out a live cow beside the carcass. Even now I am not quite sure why I gave over the plan. Possibly yesterday's luck had caused me to consider it unnecessary, and certainly I was aware that we had only one live cow remaining. John did not know if the men we had sent off to the low-caste villages could get any more, and discretion urged that we save her for a greater need. But I should have learned by now to be suspicious of discretion. It often parades as common sense, a different thing entirely, and frequently an undue respect for it ties a man's hands and blinds his eyes. There is a time to go all-out, and bet all the chips in the stack.

I kept seeing people, near or far, until the sun set and the buffaloes had streamed back to their byres. As soon as the shadows fell I pressed the button of my headlight to find out if the mechanism was in order, but I did not wait a while and try casting it on the bait. I suppose I feared that the tiger might be coming in that very moment, and he would see the glare, and take fright. By temperament, I hold Chance in deep distrust. My mind is always conjuring up stratagems by which she can undo me. I am a man of little faith; if I give the Devil an inch I think he will take an ell. Most of the failures in my life have been caused by taking such extreme precautions against some dangers that I overlooked others. How this fits in with an occasional sudden disorganization of my mind into a reckless disregard of all dangers, I cannot explain.

I intended to sit until ten, when the elephant was to be brought along side my *machon* so I could step onto her pad without touching the bloody, perilous ground. The tiger tried to return about eight. In coming upon the scene, he crossed the wind, and the reek grew incredibly strong. It was the kind that people say they can cut with a knife, and you felt it would drip like dew off the leaves.

For nearly half an hour he haunted the scene, and haunted was the right word—for he lurked about it, presenting overwhelming evidence of his presence, but never showing himself. His smell grew stronger or weaker according to the distance and the breeze. I could not be sure that I ever heard him, although I believed that I did—a sound like the rustle of a few leaves or the crack of a twig underfoot. I had rarely endured for so long a period such intense excitement. My heart was thudding to shake my breast and I had actual difficulty in breathing. There was still light enough from the pale western sky to show his outline, if he should come, and my expectancy rose and fell, from a wild certitude to a dark pessimism. But I wished to high heaven I had tied out a live cow. The situation had come out perfectly right for the trying of our experiment, except that John and I had botched it.

The tiger moved from shadow to shadow, from thicket to grass clump. Still he did not go away; the smell faded only to revive. He craved the meat and that might take the edge off his caution, and my blind had been meticulously built, perfectly screened. And then a shadow looked a little different from the rest, odd-shaped, of another tone, and that shadow moved.

From the deeper darkness into the lighter, from utter invisibility to the most meager, half-guessed visibility, the tiger came up to the bait.

I leveled the rifle, braced it with my left arm, and felt in my right pocket for the battery switch. My headlight came on, but it cast no strong yellow beam through the opening in the blind, a clean swath picking the tiger in all his black-and-gold brilliance out from his sheltering shadows. Instead there was a yellowish smear two feet from my eyes, beyond which I could not see at all.

The blind had been too well screened. It was the same story of misdirected caution that had kept me from trying the light beforehand. The shaft struck leafery that refracted and dispersed it. I turned off the light and clawed at the hole and then tried again. When trying to shoot at a giant tiger in Indo-China, the second trial had won. But I had been steadier then, not so frantic, nor so oppressed by the inkling of defeat. The light remained dim and broken and bad. Still I thought I made out the form of the tiger and I took quick aim and fired.

He uttered a great growl that might mean he had been hit. Then he ran away, in great clumping leaps, heavily as a buffalo, it seemed, on the sun-baked ground. Then there was nothing to do but sit, too depressed to curse myself or my luck, and wait for the elephant. Happily she was not long in coming.

"Kill?" the mahout asked.

"No kill."

We went to camp, where I briefly told the story to my pale-faced, very quiet companion. We would search in the morning for blood sign, he told me. Even if we found none, I must not be discouraged, for he had managed to buy two other cows, which we would tie out tomorrow. I went to bed, where for hours I could not sleep, and when at last I did, it was with the heavy disconsolate sleep of a moping dog. When, in the morning, we started for the scene, a couple of cattle herders followed us on foot. They showed no fear whatever of a wounded tiger.

We found his heavy footprints, and followed them a ways, but could not find one drop of blood.

"It be true that the sahib can kill the common jungle tigers," one of the herders remarked when we gave up the search. "He has killed one that lately left there, thinking to dwell in our grass. But he cannot kill our great tigers, and if he is wise he will go back to the jungle, which is better than going back to his own place with an empty bag."

To my surprise, John turned dark red in the face and I feared he would strike the man. He did not, but he showed me something I did not quite want to know. In my pursuit of giant tigers, I saw that both of us together had become profoundly and inextricably involved.

V

On the following day we tied one of the cows at the scene of my failure, and since the blind was already built and only needed careful redressing, we had time to move camp to what John thought was a more advantageous site. This was more central to the various tigers than the first camp, nearer to the low-caste village where he had succeeded in buying cows, and to a meat supply in a scrub jungle frequented by barking deer. Also it was somewhat off the beat of the Nepalese herders, who had started the practice of dropping in, acting very wise, and lowering the morale of our camp hands. However, it lay over five miles of sun-baked plain from the grass and thorn thicket where dwelt the Grandfather of Tigers.

The new camp had one pleasant feature I had not anticipated. Among the young women—in America they would have been counted young girls—who came to our stream to fill their water jars was one who delighted my eyes, a truly original and authentic beauty. About fourteen, tall, with a grave and stately walk, she was pale-brown in color, with blue-black hair and long black eyes, and features that I thought had a Grecian cast. If an imaginative man encountered her in the jungle, he would think he had met a wood nymph. Her form too, although too well hidden, was symmetrical and wonderfully lithe.

I thought it odd and pleasant that this out-of-the-way corner of the earth, the haunt of striped giants, a kind of gorgeous ogre, should also produce rare human beauty. She was already married, and to a graybeard. In fact all the young girls who came to our stream had superannuated husbands—probably the patriarch's third or fourth take, John thought. There seems to be tragedy behind almost every beauty of India, and this was the tragedy of child-brides, soon worn out and gone to the Ghat from child-bearing.

I did not speak to her. I never learned whether she was a high-caste girl, like most of the daughters of these herders, or one of the low-caste villagers, or even a so-called Untouchable. Sometimes, when no one was in sight, she gave me a shy smile. Once, under odd and still puzzling circumstances and in the presence of a multitude, she did more than that.

The cow we tied lived out the night, nor was the carcass of the first cow ever touched again. John feared that my wild shot had scared both of the big-brother tigers out of their ancient abode.

The day brought thrilling news. The Grandfather of Tigers had killed the cow we had tied out only the day before, and devoured more than half of her carcass. I went there on the elephant, a long, hot five miles, John beside me on the pad and one of the camp men leading another cow for sacrifice. I had not visited this scene before, and except for the bloody remains of his kill I found it hard to believe that the great tiger, full of years and cunning, would be bold enough to come here. The meat lay beside a cane thicket less than two furlongs from a farmer's house. Children played, dogs barked, and buffaloes wallowed in plain sight of the blind. This had been built in a big, lonely tree, again about eight feet off the ground, and I was fascinated to find parallel grooves in the bark, far higher than my seat, where the Great Tiger had sharpened his claws.

The farmer told us that he owned the land on which the giant lived, and that his cattle herd was the giant's pantry. He did not go there every day, or even once a week—he seemed to know that this would exhaust the stock—and neighboring herds furnished most of his gigantic meals. However, he killed every cow not shut in the byre when darkness fell, and enough cows and buffaloes on the grazing grounds to keep the farmer poor. The latter was a tall, lean man with an anxious face I will never forget. The gods had afflicted him, he said, and although he had paid large sums to the gurus, and given them ghee, and rice, and fowls without end, still the affliction only grew in weight with the passing years. Now he knew it would remain upon him until his last breath.

"It may be that the sahib will kill the tiger," John suggested.

"It may be the tiger will weaken, and one of my worthless dogs will tear him down."

"Do you not fear for the lives of your children at play?"

"Not in the daylight. When the sun sets I bring them within doors, and lock those doors. This is a good tiger, a worthy tiger, a most honorable tiger, in respect to sparing people. But I would not trust my own mother with him after sundown, for all that he has been our boarder for twenty years."

I could hardly believe this last figure, and asked John to make sure that the tiger tracks were the same I had followed to the buffalo kill. He was positive of it, and told me solemnly that for the first and the last time in my life, I had been given a chance to shoot a ten-foot tiger.

"Ten feet pegged out unskinned," he went on, sweat on his forehead. "A tiger unsurpassed in the whole length and breadth of India. You could hold up your head among the great *shikaris*.

It would count more than being elected governor of your state. I myself would consider it equal to winning a place on the king's birthday list. When you are too old to hunt any more you could still boast—"

"Don't say any more," I interrupted him. "It's rugged enough already."

A good many farmers and herdsmen had come to see me take my stand. One who had gone to a mission school shook hands with me and gave me a pleasant "Goot lok." On all the other faces was the same look of strain—an ounce of hope lifting against a crushing ton of incredulity. Yet every man salaamed to me as he started off, and I answered every salaam by pressing both hands together. I supposed they were saluting my try. Even that suggested great audacity against the gods.

V I

Pleasant domestic sounds continued until sundown. Then the children went into the house, the dogs stopped barking, the cattle and buffalo that had streamed into byres settled down for the night. The only life in sight was the cow we had tied, and that was a tranquil life. She shook her ears and chewed her cud and had no evil dreams. I began to feel deeply depressed, without being able to find the cause; it seemed the forecast shadow of a coming event. To get rid of it, I tried my headlight, making sure there were no obstructions to its beam, and surveyed all avenues of approach to my blind. Then I smoked a cigar to settle my nerves. When I threw the stub away the day had dimmed to a cheerless dusk. Failing fast was my hope that the tiger would return in time to give me a shot in the failing light without use of my lamp.

I clung to it until I could barely see the cow, not thirty feet away, and the time was long past that I could make out my front sight in line against her. A sudden attack of depression, in which were involved loneliness and self-dissatisfaction and what seemed an intimation of bad luck, caused me to lean back in the blind, my head against the rail supporting the dressing of the blind. I had been careful to make no noise. I did not think of any other harm I might be doing. I remained in this position about five minutes. And I had barely leaned forward again, disgusted with my own moodiness, when there came a great outburst of sound.

I have since tried to describe it, both to others and myself. It was a tearing sound, very dry, a little like canvas being ripped, although a hundred times louder. Almost instantly I knew what it was, simply because it could be nothing else—a tiger of great bulk and weight running through the patch of dry, high cane. It lasted, I think, about three seconds, and then instead of one still shadow below me there were two shapes in violent motion, one greatly larger than the other. They joined together and stood high and then both of them sank. I stared, and my scalp drew tight, and my neck prickled fiercely, because I could no longer see the cow. She was down and covered by the tiger. Except for the tiger's approach and the brief, all but instantaneous noise of struggle, neither made any other sound.

Straining hard, I could make out the tiger's shape, but I could not possibly be sure of sighting on his shoulder without the glare of light. Leveling my gun, I turned on the switch. And now I knew the likely damage I had done when I had leaned back in my blind, and that was to blow my chance. I knew the bad fortune that had been laying for me. My cap, with the lamp fastened to the brim, had become turned a little on my head, so that the beam no longer burst out in the direction of my gaze. Instead it fell a little to one side, making a brilliant circle on the bare ground, and leaving the tiger and his kill in complete shadow.

There was nothing to do but lift my hand and wrench the cap straight. The tiger saw the motion, and was in the act of leaping when the shaft revealed him, enormous and gold and black. My heart told me, instantly, taking no time at all for the communication, that if I could get him he would be my greatest prize. I knew it without thinking as I fired. And as he passed in a black shadow out of the field of light I could not remember aiming.

Once more I heard the swift, heavy clump of feet, the same as a few nights past. It stopped or it died away somewhere out in the dark, and I felt cold and stunned and sick. In vain I flung the beam about me. I saw the yellow reeds, the sunburned grass, the dead cow with her head twisted back over her shoulder, nothing else but the encircling gloom. There was no sound anywhere. I had never known a night more silent. The strong smell of the tiger still hung over the scene, but it was swiftly fading.

My actions of the next few minutes are hard to believe, extremely difficult to explain, and impossible to defend. I know only, from experience, that a man like me, with a hex like mine, immediately after firing what he profoundly fears is a wild shot at one of the greatest big-game trophies in the world, is not in his right mind. In deep gloom, really in a kind of despair, I climbed down from the blind and began to flash my light on the ground looking for blood sign. Holding the rifle in one hand I became incapacitated for a quick shot. I knew this was the wrong thing, still I felt no fear. All that I knew was, I could not see any blood.

I went a little farther from the dead cow—in the direction that the tiger had run, I thought, but I have no sense of orientation and felt immediately confused. I was standing there, an easy mark for a wounded tiger, when I heard the men coming with the elephant. They had heard me shoot, and they came in hope of seeing a dead tiger, the Grandfather of Tigers, lying still and impotent in his gorgeous paint. In the most reckless action of my life, I hurried to meet them.

My motive was plain enough. I could not bear for them to see the dead cow, for there she lay, indisputable proof that the tiger had come within thirty feet of my blind, killed, and departed.

Already a cunning lie was shaping in my brain, which I would tell as soon as we could reach John. For that I went plunging through the high grass.

But I told my lie sooner than I had thought possible. It happened that the mission-taught native, championing me with the herders, hoping to gain face himself if I shot the Great Tiger, had waited with the mahout and a companion for the sound of my shot.

"Sahib, is the tiger dead?" he asked, when the elephant had kneeled to let me mount.

"I don't know. I caught a glimpse of him, about a hundred yards away, and like a fool, I fired. It's quite possible that I missed."

He did not answer; only hung his head.

What of the dead cow? She would certainly be found by the farmer in the morning, intact or half eaten. I had only to say that evidently I had missed the long, reckless shot, and the tiger had returned and killed after I had gone.

We had hardly started on our way when the prospect of meeting John tonight, and watching his face in the lantern light, as I told my lie, became too painful to entertain. And the camp was five bleak miles away!

"Do you know of any house nearby where I can spend the night?" I asked the English-speaking native. "I want to come very early to the grounds to see if I killed the tiger."

The native did know of such a house. It belonged to some sort of native official. It was clean, he told me, quite fine. The owner was his friend, and I would be greatly welcome. So we went there, and the householder received me with honor, and presently showed me the bed on which I was to sleep—of handsome solid wood, a blanket folded on its boards, without spring or mattress. So I lay there, my bones and muscles aching, my thoughts bringing back every incident and moment of the event, and my eyes summoning up that one great picture—the tiger springing as the light hit him, the avatar of all big game, ever unobtainable, the monster in black and gold.

But I slept at last and wakened just before dawn with a vivid dream. It was that I had killed the greatest of the sambur stags, but I could read no significance in it, and hardly any hope.

At once I asked for pen and paper and wrote a note to John. I wanted to break the news to him by long distance, so he would have time to digest it before I saw his face. I wrote briefly that I had shot at the Great Tiger and that I believed that I had missed, but the mahout and I would search the grounds to make sure.

He and I started out, the English-speaking native behind me on the pad. When we came to the scene we met the farmer. No longer worried-looking, he was in fact triumphant in a baleful way, believing that his worst expectations had come true. He reported that a tiger had come in the night and killed my cow. He did not know what tiger it could be. Also I had left my sun helmet in the blind, which his son had climbed and retrieved. Had he seen anything from that eminence, I asked? If so, the lad had not told him.

Tasting defeat, almost certain of it now, I asked the mahout to search the area about the blind. But I could hardly persist with the undertaking, so dreary and hopeless-seeming, after seeing quite a large band of natives cutting grass not a hundred yards from the blind and in the direction that I thought the missed tiger had fled. Their sharp eyes would not miss a seven-hundred-pound carcass of such bright hue. Still I told him to make a little circle. We must do that for my story's sake and for my pride.

We had hardly started when the mahout uttered a wild shriek. It was not of terror but of utmost joy, and his hand had a palsied shake as he pointed. In a second more I soon saw what it was. Only fifty yards from the blind lay the body of the Grandfather of Tigers, shot straight in the shoulder, and he was by far the largest tiger I ever hoped to see. Whether or not I ever took another trophy, I had become a big-game hunter. I had won the palm.

VII

This was the great thing, but there were little things of high joy.

One of them was my calling one of the grasscutters. He approached suspecting no great wonder, then suddenly saw the tiger's body in the grass. He shrieked and wildly began to beckon his companions. They came on the run, and great shouting ensued, and many eyes grew big with disbelief. A crowd began to gather. Where it came from, I have no idea—it seemed that every little path had people in it, hurrying in our direction.

The farmer came, chattering with excitement, then ran to his house at high speed and returned with a piece of cane sugar about as big as a domino, which he gave to me and which I ate then and there. By him, and for the first time, I was given quite an impressive title. He had sounded it, and thereafter all the natives employed it when they spoke of me in the third person, although they continued to address me simply as sahib. The title, Burra Amerik Shikari Sahib, meant, freely translated, the Big American Hunter Master. But I said to myself, "You sonofabitch," just to keep a good balance.

The mahout came and the elephant kneeled and all hands demanded a part in lifting the enormous tiger to her back. We grunted and sweated a good while before we pulled him up, an inch at a time, and finally balanced him. And then the sight of his huge head and terrific burly shoulders and front legs hanging from one side of the pad caused a gasp of wonder to rise from the whole throng. Meanwhile, with the help of the English-speaking native, I had borrowed a pony. I meant to ride ahead of the elephant and pull John's leg. It would be boyish and foolish, but marvelous fun, and I could not resist.

He saw me coming, the elephant and her followers still out of sight, and hurried to meet me. He looked pale and drawn and he spoke in a rush of words.

"I've taken a long walk and thought it over. It's not your fault —everyone misses sometimes—but we've got to go back to the jungle. The natives won't sell us any more cattle. They'll see us in hell first. I don't think anybody can kill these tigers."

"I killed a tiger," I told him calmly.

"What?"

"He's a small tiger with big feet."

John knew that was a sell, and he looked at me, and for a moment I thought he was going to weep. Then he pulled me off the pony and roughhoused me a little, a lapse in dignity I had never expected but which was nevertheless heart-warming. Before long he saw the elephant emerge from the scrub, half a mile down the lane, the tiger shining even at this distance, and about sixty men walking behind. And this was only the beginning of the festival that took place that day, at our camp in the grass.

An anxious moment arrived when John had placed pegs in front of the tiger's nose and at the tip of his tail, and I had gotten out my steel tape. It turned out that I need not use the word "practically" or any of its equivalents. Without the slightest bluff or exaggeration the distance was a solid ten feet. This meant he had the same length as "the Bachelor," a tiger famous all over India that had been killed by the great Jim Corbett. Unlike the other tigers described in his book, this giant was not a man-eater, only an inveterate cattle killer. The chapter reads as though Corbett pursued him and finally shot him simply because of his huge size, making him the trophy of a lifetime. I kept no record of the Great Tiger's other measurements, chest, forearm, and the like; however, his immense bulk persuades me that he equaled the Bachelor all along the line.

The crowd continued to increase with constant additions of men, women, and children. They sat in rows and clusters, in some instances perhaps representing different castes. And John as well as the camp men seemed in their glory, and some of their sallies as the skinning went on might not have been of a delicate sort, to judge by the way the tittering girls and young wives half-veiled their faces. Then came a wonderfully pleasant surprise. Indeed it was in the way of being a marvel, an experience to treasure always, and so rare that John was dumbfounded, and one I am sure that many self-appointed authorities on India would categorically deny.

A little apart from most of the crowd, with some of her own village, sat the tall, pale-brown beauty whom I had seen bringing full water jars up from our stream—this last, according to Indian folklore, an augury of good fortune. I asked her if I might take her picture, although hardly hoping for her assent. The back-country Indians still retained a lively fear of the camera, and seemed to think that no one could "take" their picture without removing something from them. Perhaps they feared losing some soul-substance. However, this rustic Artemis rose and stood before me with every grace.

Some people in the crowd began to call to her. When I asked John what they were saying, he made an astounding reply.

"They are telling her to bare her breasts, to make a more beautiful picture."

These kindly folk, her neighbors and kinsmen, knew that she was most beautifully endowed in this respect. She stood serenely as I snapped the picture, and I felt that of all the compliments in their power to pay me, this was the most memorable and the best.

Seventeen

HAD I supposed that my great upturn of luck in killing the Grandfather of Tigers would usher in a series of brilliant successes, I had reckoned without my host.

True, we suffered no more from a shortage of cows. All the herders seemed glad to sell us what we needed, taking their chance on the wrath of Shiv and their guru. Usually, though, these stood untouched night after night. Frequently when we found them with broken necks and the telltale perforation of big fangs in the throat, as a rule the meat remained intact and the tigers never returned to the kills or paid any attention to the new baits tied out, which meant that I stood many a long watch in vain, mainly in pits and caves. The most likely explanation we could propose was that these kills had been made when the killer had already gorged, an easy thing considering the vast number of cattle roaming these plains.

Sometimes we predicated a cunning almost superbeastly to account for the tiger's giving me the slip. Perhaps the dressing of the blind had looked strange and foreign. Possibly I had moved or made a suspicious sound, or the moon had gleamed on my flashlight lens or my gun barrel. On several occasions I smelled tigers, or thought that I heard them, only to have them drift away unseen.

Once, when we had put out a bait for the tiger reported to possess Herculean strength, we found the evidence of this strength. John had chained the cow to the big arched root outcropping under its tree. When the boys reported no sign of the animal, we went there to find the root torn out of the ground, broken off, and cow and chain carried away into a thick morass of reeds where pursuit was impossible. I named that tiger Dragoman. Those who had seen him declared him not as long or as bulky as the Grandfather of Tigers, but surely he was as strong; indeed of a strength almost beyond imagining in an animal weighing no more than six hundred pounds. I suspected then that he was fated to be my hoodoo. I could hardly expect to win the blue ribbon and the red as well.

The next big skin on our drying rack was not of my taking. Riding our elephant through thick scrub jungle, happily with my big .470 double across his lap, John had been suddenly called upon to meet the full-powered unprovoked attack of one of the two brother tigers whom we had begun to call the Heavenly Twins. John did not have the patience or perhaps the stability to put up with the long watches over bait, but he was what we call a good man in a pinch—aggressive, quick, and capable. He had shot fast and straight.

The tiger had run off wounded and come to bay. Together John and I followed him and finished him off—a fine specimen, nine and a half feet pegged out unskinned, although lacking the heavy pelage of the Great Tiger. Why he had attacked remains a mystery. It is certainly not a common thing for a tiger to make an unprovoked rush upon an elephant. Buffalo were grazing at the edge of the thorn thickets, and John ventured that the tiger mistook his mount for one of them, but this explanation predicates faulty vision—one of the last faults with which anyone can charge a tiger. Perhaps the high-strung beast came on the elephant suddenly and attacked by instinct. Perhaps he liked elephants no better than a nameless immortal liked Dr. Fell. Possibly he saw John and simply took a notion to kill him.

My imagination makes one more leap. If this tiger was indeed one of the brothers, which all the evidence indicated, then the chances stood fifty in a hundred, a heads-or-tails toss, that I had fired at him and missed him about three weeks before. The shot had caused him to growl in rage and to forsake his kill, to which he had never returned. Now three weeks is not a long time to remember an affront and a humiliation, especially if one is a great, proud, yellow-and-black beast of the wild. Perhaps ever since then he had nursed a deep rancor against measly men who came into his brushy domain and sat about eight feet high.

It came my turn to be humiliated in about a week. A very large tiger, the equal of the Twins, had come into scrub jungle on the river bank about a mile above camp. John and I might have thought he was Kala Bagh, whose time to revisit these scenes had almost rolled around, had not a farmer who had caught sight of him said he was a longer, leaner, and redder animal than that evil slayer of cowherds. We tied out a cow for him, which he promptly killed. But this dispatch had caught us short. The cow we had meant to tie beside the kill broke her tether and escaped, and we could get no other this late in the day to take her place.

I decided to sit over the half-eaten carcass, again on a low *machon*. Leaving instructions for the elephant to be brought for me at ten that night, I got in the blind about four o'clock in the afternoon. At sundown I made a disheartening discovery. The mechanism of my headlight was broken and no amount of tinkering with it would make it come on.

I should have quit the blind then and there. But the dream of another big tiger in my bag would not let me waste this hour between sundown and dark, the hour most likely for the giants to rise from their beds and come, ill-tempered and surly and hungry, back to their kills. Deciding to wait it out, I kept a close watch until the hopeful hour passed by and it grew too dark to shoot without a light, and the night lay thick except for gray patches of moonlight between the trees.

My watch said half-past seven. Two hours and a half more of impotent waiting became tedious to contemplate. Depressed and lonely, I wished I had left when I had a chance. Well, why not go now? My tree stood no more than fifty yards from the dry river's edge, and once I gained its white moonlit shingle I could see in all directions and walk to camp without fear. And almost under the tree lay an inviting patch of moonlit ground.

I did not stop to wonder if this was one of the rash, impulsive, notions to which my nature was given. Without thinking any more about it, I took my rifle in one hand and scrambled and fell to the ground below. And I had hardly gained the brilliant patch of moonlight when I smelled tiger.

He had come, and he was standing out there in the dark, certainly within a hundred feet of me—a distance he could cover in four light bounds. I remembered the tiger that had charged John and his elephant. It seemed that I thought of all I knew about tigers, and there was no comfort in any of it, and I did not know what to do. And then I recalled with bursting sweat that a bed of grass, sixty feet wide and six feet high, separated me from the open bed of the river.

Perhaps I had known brief seconds of sharper fear than this, never as prolonged a state of intensity. It was not fear really;

it was terror of only too stark a sort. My very cold sweat made it worse, for I thought of the tiger smelling it. Knowing I was afraid, he would lose the little fear that stayed with him after dark, and he would attack. What would keep him from it? I had got in his way, between him and his meal. I thought of shooting to frighten him, but what if it didn't, and instead tripped the trigger of his nerves? Then he would be on me before I could work my bolt.

I knew I must leave this little gray island. Since I could not possibly get back in the blind without dropping the rifle from my shoulder, I must head for the tall grass. As I did it seemed to me that only a lucky chance would bring me through, and the odds were against me at last.

It was by no means a false alarm. As I gained the edge of the grass the tiger growled, a sound he would not have made if not belligerent, and he was torn between attacking and hanging back. I went through the grass, shouting and wildly whirling. It was a dreadful experience.

When I confessed it to John later he quit his job then and there, declaring that he was starting at once for the settlements, that I could pay him for his services so far or to hell with it. He was not going to stay on the shooting grounds with a fanatic who took such chances. He meant a fool, and I knew it, but deep in my soul I had never doubted my deserving the title, anyway. It took all of my persuasive powers and many promises to get him to change his mind.

II

My next adventure with a tiger was notable mainly because it took place vividly, in good light, and because I witnessed the behavior of a hunting beast on first sighting his prey.

The survivor of the Heavenly Twins had killed a cow we had tied in the same scrub forest where I had shot and missed. We tied a live cow by the half-eaten carcass, and my blind was a shallow cave in a low bank, its mouth screened with vines. I got into it with my smokes and tea flask about three, but left my hope behind, so many long watches had I stood in vain. However, not many more remained. In only a week now I must catch the train at Rangiya, heading for Calcutta, there to take ship to Rangoon. After a month's stay in that cleaner, greener land of which Kipling sang so well, hearing the temple bells, traveling the road to Mandalay, visiting the fabulous ruby and sapphire mines at remote Mogok, I would set sail around Malaya into Hong Kong, and across the Pacific to San Francisco, and then home. My tickets were bought and reservations made. I knew of nothing that could upset that schedule.

I was thinking of it, just now, partly because so little else induced thought. Hunting tigers in the grasslands became terrific sport only because its few-and-far-between moments of crises were so high-powered; its tigers were so great, so cunning, and so dangerous. But in the waiting time between engagements, the jungles of Mowgli and the Mois beat hollow these scenes of scrub woods, thorns, reeds, and grass, where there were no monkeys, few birds, almost no deer and wild pig, no peacocks, not even varanus lizards and cheerful jungle cock. I had read myself out of books. On the other side of the dry river I could make out a herd of buffalo, tended by a brown boy of about ten, but they were the only living things in sight.

Then suddenly, through the thorn wood, came walking a tiger. He had appeared from I knew not where. He seemed to be sauntering along, making in the general direction of the bait, perhaps sixty yards away. But this rather casual coming did not in the least militate against his distinction and beauty. This was no little or middle-sized specimen, no stray, but one of the Great

Tigers, almost certainly the surviving twin of the famous pair. He lit up that dim piece of scrubby woods. It was like a visitation from beyond.

He did not yet offer me a clear shot, and before I could get at it he caught sight of the live cow. If my theory and practice of hunting the great tigers of the grasslands had needed any more vindication, it was given to me now. His whole aspect changed. He stopped, then he took half a dozen rapid strides forward. He did not scan the scene; instead he poised to charge.

The thought came to me that I should wait. A few seconds more would bring him within a pebble's toss of my blind, and I would see the kill in daylight. Also he would lie still a moment then, his fangs in the heifer's throat, and I could take a sure shot. Still I do not believe that my impulse to shoot at once, before he began his rush, arose from the instinct to save the cow. I wish I could think so. Instead I think that ever mysterious and fierce passion of the chase, the unbrookable lust to kill quickly, now, to possess the beautiful and splendid quarry without an instant's delay, flung my rifle to my shoulder and curled my finger around its trigger. I saw him in the sights and squeezed steadily and hard.

He made one leap, then broke into a headlong run toward the thickest wood. It did not look to me like the rush of a mortally wounded beast, but instead like intelligent flight. Had I missed? It is so easy to miss; even a tried old hunter can do it—Oom Paul might have done it sometimes, so might Jim Corbett. I feel sure that Cottar did do it, once in a blue moon. I had no long string of hits behind me. I had broken my good string in this very wood only a month ago. If I had missed again, the people would remember the death of the Grandfather of Tigers, but my memory would be dimmed by a final failure.

I got out of the blind and looked about for a blood trail, but when I could not find it, I did not enter the thickets alone. This was my pledge to John. It happened that he had waited that day with the mahout, and in half an hour he appeared. The sun had set and the shadows gathered fast.

"What happened?" he asked when he saw the live cow.

"I shot at the other twin. He ran off into the thickets. I don't know whether I hit him. I thought I had a good aim."

"Why didn't you wait till he was on the cow?"

"Maybe I was trying to save her." I wanted to believe that, and half did. Not until later, when I went over the whole event, step by step, could I recall the moment of high passion in which I had moved.

"I daresay you got him. Anyway I'm going to pass the word around for the natives to stay away from the woods until we can take a good look. That will be the first thing tomorrow. The light's getting too dim to try it tonight."

I agreed to that; it was sensible. John glanced about for a blood trail, evincing no pessimism over finding none, for he did not take time for an extensive search. We mounted and went to camp, John and the mahout in seeming good cheer. Indeed they remained so throughout the evening meal and the brief loaf until bedtime, and I fought the blue devils alone. The fact was, they and the other camp hands had every confidence in my having shot true. But had I been capable of a similar confidence, I would not have been here; it would not have been necessary. Neither would the skin of the Grandfather of Tigers have been drying on our rack, nor the head of the great saladang adorning my trophy room, nor the skin of the great Kodiak lying on the floor. I supposed it was all fair, all part of the game. I continued to worry, and to wish to high heaven I had waited to make sure. I read some poetry by the flickering fire, then I went to bed and to sleep and into swiftly weaving, vivid, but untroubled dreams.

After a predawn breakfast and a short ride, John and I had an exciting half hour in the first rush of sunrise. We found a blood trail plain as day, and followed it about a hundred yards into wicked bush, and even experienced two or three mild false alarms. But at the end of the trail we found what I most craved: the great tiger lying dead. The thrilling discovery had one touch of sorrow. That came when I felt pity and poignance along with the exultation of victory.

When we knew we were near the blood trail's end, when it went in and did not come out of a small, thick patch, we still had trouble finding the dead tiger. That was because he had crawled into a kind of hole caused by the uprooting of a tree, fallen in some storm of long ago, and which was all but covered with greenery. He had felt his life's swift waning—the ball had entered his chest cavity—and he had gone there to die. I could not dream his deeper motive, he who had lived so boldly and so proud, a life with the power of a hundred common lives, but I felt it was a strange, dark end.

Yet out of the strange mixture of pity and exultation the kill aroused I derived a certain gain. By now I had hunted enough big game so that when I told of it, or wrote of it, I would receive a respectful hearing. Never again would I remain silent when hunters urged the adequacy of light rifles against heavy game. These made for straighter shooting at long ranges. But let the hunter take more time and care in the stalk, and then hit as hard as he can, for surely noble quarry deserves a quick dispatch. That is the least we can give.

III

One night, arriving in camp close to midnight after an especially weary and profitless watch from a screened cave dug in a bank, John, getting up to keep me company while I ate supper, gave me a belly laugh that I sorely needed.

"I'll never forget this trip," he said in a meditative tone. "One bugger digs holes all day, and the other bugger sits in 'em all night."

This was a thousand times better than the pain I gave both of us, when on another night I came in late and told him at last I had been given a chance at Dragoman, only to lose it.

It was my last chance at a baited tiger before taking off for Burma. He came in the gray moonlight to an untouched kill and stood, a huge shape behind the carcass, for a matter of five seconds. Instead of turning on my headlight and firing aggressively, I waited for him to begin his feast and thus give me a sure shot. Instead he sensed my presence, leaped, and made off.

This is the simple story. Actually I have gone over it, detail by detail, a thousand times, and it remains one of those actions, the like of which all but the most self-mastered men commit, for which I cannot forgive myself. I can account for it only on the ground of nervous fatigue. I had sat too many hours in too many holes in the ground; I had stood too many anxious and impotent watches, and had ridden too many miles atop my elephant through the hot grass under the Indian sun. The aggressiveness that may or may not be native to me, yet which now and then appears in my behavior, did not show up. I became like a baffled and stomach-sick Roland, when he had failed in the crucial moment to grasp the fairy Morgan by the forelock.

Tomorrow I must set forth for Burma. Today I would officiate with my rifle at a deer-and-pig drive that our neighbor villagers wanted to make through twenty acres of brushland hardly half a mile from our camp. The men had seen a few barking deer and wild shoats in the thickets, and wanted me to kill enough to let them gorge. I thought it unlikely that they would flush more than a head or two, but gladly agreed to try it. It was the heat of the day; a more barren-looking strip could hardly be imagined in lush India; and the notion that any excitement might develop, let alone of such intensity as I had very rarely experienced in all my hunts, could not even cross my mind.

About two hundred men lined up, with pans and bells and other noisemaking ware. In the center of the line John took his place, riding our elephant, my .470 across his lap. I chose as my stand a kind of bank from which I could see well nearly at the end of the strip of thorn and thicket, something over a quarter of a mile from the beaters. The beat began, with a hearty tintinnabulation. Guests of the maharajah or the viceroy heard its like on a much grander scale at the royal or viceregal shoots; as it drew near it usually meant that tigers had flushed, and would soon break into the clearing before the waiting guns. Sometimes, of course, the tigers broke back through the line of beaters, and then a native or two whose name none of the guests knew was likely to meet sudden death or be merely mauled, which in more than half of the cases meant slow death from lockjaw or gas gangrene. Instead of shooting tigers in this high style, thank heaven I sat over malodorous baits.

But today the natives were only beating out a strip of scrub jungle, for me to shoot them enough deer and wild pig for a big feed.

So I thought as the line came into view. But just a little ahead, there sprang up a big, bright-colored form. I saw it clearly at about four hundred yards; and it was a giant tiger that no one had dreamed lurked in this strip of stunted woods, that had probably come in the last few days. He did not flee in my direction. Instead of fleeing, he turned back and rushed upon the line. It broke as the men tried to dodge the attack, but one man was too late. I saw him go down under the tiger and the brute stop. I knew what he was doing, in the two or three seconds that he stood there, before he rushed on. The last I saw of him he was vanishing in a patch of high grass.

I ran as fast as I could, without losing my breath and hence my capacity to shoot. By the time I arrived on the scene, everything seemed for the moment static; there was not one visible movement whatever. John's elephant had stampeded, throwing him off, and that was why I had not heard him fire in the beater's defense. Now all the others had gathered about the tiger's victim, seeking what safety they could find in the cover of the big rifle, and not one of them made a sound. The victim himself lay in the bloody grass, and his head was thrown a little back, and I did not doubt that his neck was broken. On his face was the look of death.

But there was one noisemaker on the scene, and he made a terrifying noise. A little way into the grass patch, about an acre, the tiger had come to bay and was roaring his rage.

It was a thunderous, reverberant crash uttered at regular intervals of two or three seconds. It sounded something like "Tak-*whoom!* Tak-*whoom!* Tak-*whoom!*"

I said something to John—shouted it, rather—which for long afterward I treated in a light way, laughing at myself for what might seem its melodrama. In those days it was still my instinct to make mock of the highest motives and the best actions that I had ever attained. Actually there was nothing funny, let alone phony, about it. I have since seen that in the height of feeling men do not necessarily curtail their vocabularies or use the language of ignorance. Instead they incline to precise and powerful diction.

Holding my rifle in front of my chest, quick to get to my shoulder, I shouted, "Let's advance!"

But John declined. "I can't do it," he told me simply—and I have never blamed him or ever wondered at it. He had seen at close range the man go down before the tiger's rush, and had seen him mauled, and this beast was no little leopard such as I had faced with Cottar on the day of K'nini's mauling; this was a great Royal Bengal tiger in the transports of his rage. I do not know whether I could have gone in alone. To this moment I have no idea, and when I think I could have I realize it is my wish to think so; thus the supposition becomes suspect. I was trying to rally my nerve when the wounded man uttered a low groan.

I turned to him and saw life in his face and thought there was life to save. If it could be saved, I was the Johnny-on-the-spot, because in camp I had needles ready and loaded with tetanus and gas-gangrene antitoxin. While I stood guard, every second expecting the tiger to rush out, I told John to rally the men and fix some kind of rig for getting the mauled native to camp. Once they received their orders, they were wonderfully quick and competent and cool.

With their machetelike knives they cut two poles and three crosspieces. The latter they fastened deftly with rattan, and fixed other strips of rattan between the parallel poles, making a rude stretcher. This task they completed in about five minutes. Five minutes later we were on our way to camp, while from behind roared the diminishing thunder,

Tak-*whoom!* Tak-*whoom!* Tak-*whoom!*

The wounded native was well out of shock when I administered the life-saving serums. In his shoulder, a little above the heart chamber, were two holes that looked two inches deep and more than an inch in diameter where the tiger had set his fangs; these and the grooves cut by three claws across his breast I filled brimfull with raw iodine. He turned his head a little and gave me one steady, proud glance as the pain bit; otherwise he made no sign. But I already knew he was a brave man. John had told me how, when the tiger stood over him, mauling him, he had struck at him twice with his kukri. Perhaps this was why the beast had not lingered to finish him off.

The spinster elephant returned meekly, obeying her mahout's lightest signal, no doubt ashamed of her cowardly conduct. We loaded her with my trophies and gear, leaving a place for the wounded man to lie down, and with me astride a pony we were soon ready to start for the small government hospital thirty miles away. At the very last, John made a speech in my name to the hundreds of natives assembled to see us off. It was to this effect, although couched, no doubt, in eloquent Hindustani:

The old sahib must now depart, first to the hospital, then to the land of Burma, where he had pressing and unpostponable business. From thence he had intended to cross the Eastern sea to his own land, but that intention he has now forsaken, in order that he can return here and take vengeance upon the tiger, who, if the signs told true, was none other than Kala Bagh.

"Yea, Chota Sahib," said a scarred old native *shikari*. "I saw him well as he smote down Kushru, and of a certainty he is Kala Bagh."

In the old sahib's absence, all the people who lived in the grass-lands must keep watch on this tiger, reporting his kills, his wanderings from one patch of jungle to another, and where he made his lairs. It would not be a hard task, for the number of giant tigers hereabouts had been thinned by three, and they would not forget the color and shaping of this Tiger of Eblis, now they had seen him in action at such close range. And in a little over a month the old sahib would return, and tie out cows where the tiger dwelt, and, by the favor of the gods, slay him.

"Can you say anything to the people?" John asked me.

So I said "Gung ho!" According to Kipling's books it meant "Go in and win," but I was not sure it was a Hindustani saying, and instead it might be Rajput, from the northwest. However, the crowd of natives appeared pleased and the elders nodded wisely.

The whole throng followed my elephant about a mile before they turned back. Eight weary hours later I arrived at the little hospital, hardly more than a first-aid station, run by a Bengali *babu*, to whom I must speak harshly and with the presumption of authority I by no means possessed before I could get tolerable attention paid to the wounded cowherd. But on being told I would report the case personally to the President of the United

States, he began to bustle about, redressed the wounds with considerable skill, and administered sedatives. I remained there all the next day, to keep my fellow company—although we could not speak to each other—and the attendants up to the mark. At the end of that day a sort of circuit-riding native doctor came in, and immediately won my confidence. He examined the patient, found only a slight fever, and told me to continue my journey in good cheer.

"But I couldn't have saved him if you hadn't had handy that fifteen rupees' worth of serum," the doctor told me. "Tell the rich Americans so when you get home."

Home remained a long way off. Just now I was heading for Burma, where the temple bells ring, and after my engagements there I had an assignation here in India with a giant tiger who might or might not be Kala Bagh, who was a great antagonist, worthy to round out what might prove the finest bag of tigers ever taken by a visiting hunter. These limitations excluded the tigers killed by India-born Englishmen, of whom Jim Corbett was the most renowned. And I was not even thinking about some of India's winter visitors, American or English, who had shot driven tigers. No number of their fashionably gotten pelts could equal my rank-smelling four.

Eighteen

ON my visit to Burma I had not intended to hunt big game, and my doing so came about only through an attack of pique. In love aforetime with the very name of Mandalay, I had gotten a letter of introduction from the American Consul at Rangoon to the president of the Upper Burma Club, not as exclusive or as renowned as the Carlton Club in London, but certainly the most redoubtable in all that vast hinterland east of Calcutta and west of Singapore. I had intended to loaf about its rooms for a fortnight, talk to all who would talk to me, and use the city as the locale of a novel.

As it happened, I did not get to meet the president of the club or any of the members. I was received by some sort of

Eurasian maître d' hôtel and allowed to sit at a table and buy drinks. I sat there from seven to midnight, and of the sixty or so Englishmen enjoying fellowship there, not one deigned to speak to me. It could not have happened in a French colony, a Dutch, or—God knows—anywhere in American domain. By midnight I felt so lonesome that I carefully paid my bill, tipped the maître d., and hurried to catch a train.

Although this was a childish way to behave, I had certainly lost the urge to exploit in a book the British sahibs who ruled Burma.

I was left with a two weeks' loaf. So I went to the Forestry Department, and after listening to a few witticisms at American expense cracked by the commissioner, I talked to a warden. Was there, I asked, anywhere in handy reach of Rangoon a big cattle-killing or man-eating tiger, of which he had heard complaints? If so I would like to make a short *shikar* and try to take him.

The warden knew of no such tiger below the Chindwin, but was I interested in rogue elephants? If so, there was one in the hills not far from the end of the rail in southeastern Burma.

"This is a very large bull," the warden said. "He may not be as big as native report pictures him—in fact I doubt it. They give his measurements as exactly ten feet, and there hasn't been a ten-footer shot in Burma in a good many years."

"I don't see how they could say 'exactly,' without climbing up and measuring him."

"Well, they could if they correctly measured his tracks. If it's twenty inches, as they say, the bull stands ten feet. The height of a bull in inches is always six times the diameter of his fore footprint. In any case, he's a rogue. He comes down at harvest and raids the fields, and once he caught and killed an old native woman. He has very thick tusks that have been broken once or twice. There's no price on his head and I can't let you go after him without a license, but I'll find you a chap who knows the country to help you with your outfit, and rent you two forest elephants to carry duffel."

The "chap" he found for me was a so-called "boy of the country"—meaning that he was born and raised in Burma, and some native blood flowed in his veins. I called him Frank, and no one could ask for a more agreeable companion. In due course we detrained at a station on the slopes of the southern Arakan Yoma and rode horses into high jungle as noble as any I had ever seen. With us were skinners and trackers—some Indian and some Burmese—and a cook.

Known as Burra Hathi, meaning the Big Elephant, our quarry ranged a neighborhood of about a hundred square miles. Finding him in this expanse did not seem likely, especially since five days went by without our seeing his tracks. We found plenty of elephant tracks, some eighteen inches in diameter, and one of nineteen inches, and every day we heard the giants crashing in the bamboo forests. We saw an abundance of other game, including the biggest bison bull I could imagine—perhaps a record head—and we heard tigers almost every night. But the boys thought that Burra Hathi was away visiting. If so, I was still glad I came. I did not need the big elephant's heavy tusks to make the jaunt a success. Except for him, I would never have seen this jungle, unsurpassed on earth.

On the seventh day, Frank, a Burmese tracker, and I sat on the top of a bare-topped hill, searching the distant hills with our glasses. We found a big herd of bison feeding in the park land and, farther on, a few middle-sized elephants. Then, speaking through Frank, the tracker asked to use my binoculars. I adjusted them to his twenty-twenty vision.

"Burra Hathi!" he said quietly.

Frank spoke to him in the tongue of the country and, after a short palaver, turned to me.

"Singu says there's no doubt of it. He can see the heavy, stubby tusks, and the beast's great size. He's feeding in some dwarf bamboos, and I believe you can get a shot at him by mid-afternoon."

Following Frank's careful directions, I too found the bull in the lens. He stood taller than any Asiatic elephant I had ever seen and looked as imposing as the great bull who had bade me good-by to Africa. We hurried to camp and had lunch, although, as Kipling had once put it, we "sat not long at our meat." With only the big double and a camera, and four additional natives for such work as came to hand, we struck out for the ridge where we had seen the quarry. And in an hour's hike we found him again, far down the hill from us and loafing in a clump of trees.

The wind blew uphill, and all other conditions looked favorable. The bull would be impossible to approach in silence, but this was not necessary; he was used to the sound of deer and pig scurrying through the dry dwarf bamboos. However, I found us making more noise than I liked, and when we drew within two furlongs I asked Frank and all the natives except the tracker to stay here and wait my shot. The tracker had orders to stop at a given signal, whereupon I would go on alone.

I had only one gun. I did not feel I could take care of two people, and, as usual, there blew a cold chill down my backbone asking if I felt certain of taking good care of one. It must be remembered that elephant shooting, if done with the least decency, becomes very close work. To shoot a ball into the vast body would seem to me an inhuman and barbarous act. Unless it destroyed the functioning of the heart, the quarry would live for hours—and possibly for days—before he recovered or died a useless and cruel death in some distant jungle. The great ivory hunters, Cottar, Lord De La Mere, and the rest, crept up within fifty feet, preferably thirty, and placed the bullet, shooting from the side, just in front of the orifice of the ear. That was the only shot sure to reach the brain.

And the tyro had better damned well do the same, I thought, especially when not backed by another rifle. An elephant cannot run as fast as a man on open ground, but in thick cover his relation to a man is that of an enemy tank to an infantryman. True, there is a shot from the front that tried and expert elephant hunters may make. It must strike near the top of the trunk at a certain angle that will carry it under the heavy plates of bone. I knew better than to consider such a shot.

Down the hill the tracker and I went, and it was getting steep, and the dry bamboos made a loud and unavoidable noise. Still the elephant browsed among the trees, occasionally breaking off a limb with a riflelike report. I could see his dark shape and sometimes catch a glimmer of his tusks, but at fifty yards, and then at forty, and then at thirty, I could get no clear view of the side of his head. At this point I left the tracker and went on the chill and lonesome way.

When the distance between us shortened to fifty feet, he broke another limb, but instead of swishing it about in his trunk, he let it fall. And the next second he came striding out of the clump of trees. I never knew the reason, nor could I guess at his intention. Perhaps it was mere restlessness; possibly he came to investigate sounds that did not strike him as familiar. Moving swiftly along the hillside, I got out of his way. Then I turned and faced him.

I felt an acute sense of danger, a sharp fear for my life, and at the same time a kind of solemn awe. I had not dreamed that any walking thing could be so big. Never before had I seen a full-sized bull elephant at truly close range. Actually this bull was not as tall as the bull that had told me good-by to Africa; he belonged to a slightly smaller species. But here in the low growth at a distance of thirty feet, ten steps, he seemed immensely vast. The forest warden had given his height as ten feet. I did not doubt it now, although the largest Asiatic bulls I had seen so far had stood about nine feet. Also he was broader and bulkier than any of those bulls. He was as tall and wide and long as a study room in which one sits, yet he was walking swiftly.

That was what stunned the mind—the sense of living power, not measurable or explainable by piston thrusts; the miracle behind all other worldly miracles, animating the titanic form and driven by a mind between the widespread alerted ears and behind the coiled trunk and the small, red, angry eyes. The huge muscles worked. The enormous thighs drove forward, and the monstrous feet lifted and set down. The smashed bamboos made a noise like a prairie fire. Out shot the questing trunk.

But I had a clear view of him now. I knew his Achilles heel, the one spot in which a little man with a little gun could deal him the death stroke. I aimed in front of the orifice of the ear and pulled the trigger.

Of what happened next I have no clear remembrance. Perhaps the heavy recoil incapacitated me for a second or two, like a blow in the breast. I had a sense of terrific sound and cataclysm, then of intense silence. When vision returned to me, the elephant had disappeared. I could only believe that he had fallen and turned a backward somersault down the steep hill into the blind thicket.

I followed him there—the kind of thing I had hoped never to do again—in wild abandonment of all care and common sense. I thought that he might still be alive, and would rise and escape before I could get sight of him and put in a second shot. At once my foot slipped on the steep slope and I slid and tumbled. It was the leg of the elephant that checked my fall.

He never moved again. But if he had had one move left in him, when I collided with him, he would have certainly devoted it to me.

It would have been a fitting end to my career as a big-game hunter. I had craved trophies out of all reason, had taken too many reckless chances, and the percentage in the hunter's favor, as Cottar would have put it, had caught up with me. My story sense told me it would have been a noble end for Burra Hathi, the big elephant of the Arakan Yoma, the great rogue who had ravaged the native fields and once taken human life, to strike once more in his death throes, and to give up the ghost in the fullness of revenge.

II

My companions came down to me, and cut away the thickets for a clear view of our prize. And when they had gazed awhile in awed silence, I thought to measure the front foot, thereby to calculate his height. As it happened, one edge of the hoof had dug into the ground, and I asked Frank to have the men lift it up to clear it. There were seven of us, but our combined strength could not move the foot the least fraction. When we had cleared away the dirt we tried it again. Still we could not budge it.

But the foot measured exactly twenty inches in diameter, proof that he had stood a clean ten feet. We tried a shoulder measurement, holding out the tape to get a straight line, with the same result. In due course we cut out the tusks. They were eighteen inches in circumference and weighed just short of sixty pounds apiece. African tusks no heavier than this would be considered common; in the case of the Asiatic elephant they were ranking trophies. Both had been broken twice, otherwise I thought that each would have weighed about seventy-five pounds.

Wishing for a longer stay in beautiful Burma, in due course I made for Calcutta. From there, going north before I turned eastward, I touched a city named Parbatipur—the city of Parbati —and instead of Shiv's wife I thought of a spinster elephant, still unmated, still frustrated, waiting for me at Rangiya station in the Duars of Bhutan. Away in the grass another dweller of this region, whose name might be Kala Bagh, raged and killed. An inkling came to me that we would settle our affair before long.

The natives in and about our grounds had done a wonderful piece of trailing. Throughout my absence, they had lost track of the man-mauling tiger that they called Kala Bagh for only two periods, both brief; and they had kept an almost complete count of his kills: six cattle, one buffalo, one pony, and, oddly enough, three goats killed in the same night and probably the same minute. For a five-week term it appeared a bloody record. And the great tigers of the grasslands had been piling up that kind of slaughter for years.

But among the grinning throng that met me coming up the road stood Kushru, able to herd cattle and watch the grass spring up behind the rains, and bearing impressive marks. I caught the feeling that he had gained face.

Kala Bagh had lately been reported as dwelling in Dragoman's old lair by the buffalo pool. We tied for him here, and he killed, only to drag the bait out of our reach into a reed bed. Then our trackers followed him to the former abode of the Heavenly Twins, where for four nights I sat late, without a glimpse of him in the thorn or a whiff of him on the breeze. Then we learned he had returned to one of his old lairs, amid a high grass jungle at a river bend, too boggy for elephants to enter and a long, long haul to camp.

When we put out a bait for him here, I knew that my great tiger hunt, surely one of the major chapters of my life —worthy of mark and remembrance in the life of any man —was drawing to its close. May had come to India, afflicting the land with heavy heat. We could not take our elephant out of the shade except in mornings and later afternoons, lest she fall from sunstroke. We had no punkas to dry our sweat, no ice to cool our throats. You could hardly believe that anything called a breeze could be so baking as the stir that crept over the grass in the late afternoons. Overdue at home and in my long-neglected office, I must catch the next liner from Calcutta to Genoa. Anyway I was tired out by long and lonely watches, and weary returns to camp under the hot stars.

A little brook, of the sort I had been raised to call a "crick," wound beside the marshy jungles. On the opposite side stood a steep bank, fit for digging a blind. The bank was naked. I thought nothing of this at the time, although possibly the fact had an interesting bearing on the outcome of the adventure. We screened its opening with vines and tied out a cow.

The tiger killed her the first night, and in the morning we brought a bullock. So wildly leaped my imagination that I thought of Keats' urn, and of the festival of sacrifice that had emptied the little town; after that aberration, I had the comfort of thinking that this was my last offering to the dragons of the countryside. We tied him by the bones already picked by the early birds of death. Then John told me that if the tiger returned, I must take the head shot and kill him instantly, because if he rushed into the marsh we could not follow him on the elephant and bring him in. Actually, I took this under consideration, planning to do so if I could. If they had to wade to their knees and enter blind reeds, I believed that our staunch herders would somehow find him and retrieve his gaudy hide.

I went into the blind at two o'clock. The wait until four stretched long. Then there rose out of the grass a most hopeful and thrilling sound, the full-throated growing snarl of an angry tiger. Kala Bagh, if it were he, had just wakened from his heavy sleep. Now he was ranging up and down the grass jungle, scaring the deer and pig that he had grown too heavy to catch, and every few steps giving vent to his evil temper. Now it is not a common thing for tigers to sound forth in broad daylight, unless they are courting, fighting, or brought to bay. In fact these giant tigers, unlike the young ones of the jungle, very rarely break the silences of the night. The thought came to me that this present tiger was an especially savage individual, mean as the devil—which pointed to the possibility of his being

Kala Bagh, famed in that regard. I had a hunch that he was. I felt rising excitement.

It rose with every roar, and then it bounded up to an intense pitch when the roars ceased. The silence closing down so deep and ominous meant to me that the killer had seen the cow.

About five minutes passed. I watched the bank of reeds down-wind from the bait, believing that the tiger would attack from that direction. If he was stalking her now, his blood was up. He knew the sharpness and, I could say—not very accurately, but reaching for something—the wonderfulness of existence, intensified a hundred times over common life; and the excitement that fired his blood and shortened his breath and raced his heart and blazed in his eyes was not a whit more than I felt, waiting in silence and immobility in my ambush. This was the reward, the goal. The trophy became only its symbol. The cow chewed her cud, and wiggled her ears.

Then the charge came. I knew it first by a great tearing sound in the reeds. The tiger bounded forth, blazing, and in two or three seconds smote the cow. My eyes were on them both, alerted and finely sharpened by the crisis. The light fell in a limpid sheet from the burning sky and the arena lay full in the open, yet I have never been able to determine with what actual strokes the tiger killed. One instant they were together; the next the cow lay on her side, her neck twisted back, and the tiger crouched over her with his fangs set in her throat.

I thrust the end of my rifle through the curtain of vines in the pit mouth. This caused one of them to bend sideways, obscuring my view. By the time I had reached slowly and cautiously and pulled it aside, the tiger had changed position. Now he stood over the cow, watching her with a catlike vigilance for any sign of life; if she showed any, he would strike again. And now the cow's shoulder halfway concealed his head. I had no choice but to take the shoulder shot, holding and pressing hard.

As the bullet struck, the tiger rushed, leaping the narrow creek and mounting the bank. I could not tell at first whether he was charging me or running blindly, and my hand raced at the bolt. And just as I was thinking he would pass to one side of me, he veered in his course directly toward me.

But, great engine of life that he was, death-dealer to great oxen and buffaloes and perhaps men, he could not live long enough to carry out his aim. As he came to the steep part of the hill he leaped and toppled back. I thought of putting in another bullet, only to see it was not necessary. The ball in his chest cavity had overwhelmed him, and he coughed once and died.

I still do not know what his aim was as he veered toward my blind. It would thrill me to think that he had caught sight of me, recognized me as a man and an enemy, and came to kill his last kill. However, the bank was naked except for the vines screening my cave, and these might have caught his eye. He might have mistaken them for the front of a thicket into which to dive. But the latter is no more likely than the former, and I choose to think that he died a warrior's death.

Was he Kala Bagh? The natives thought so, but were never able to present any convincing evidence. That he was the tiger that had attacked Kushru there could be no doubt; for with a yell of joy Kushru himself found the mark of his kukri in the tiger's breast. It was several inches long, and a new-healed scar.

News has reached me that Kala Bagh comes no more to kill the herders of the grasslands. Many people say that he is dead, and some of them make propitiation to his spirit, lest it return to take possession of a human body whose spirit has just fled. Of the great tigers, the giant tigers that had preyed so long upon the herds, the Grandfather of Tigers and the Twins are slain, as is another mighty cattle killer and a medium-sized tiger, new from the jungle. Many more heifers and bullocks grow to full size, and old cows and bulls often die of old age.

But Dragoman still kills, according to report, and drags his prey into the darkest thickets. From the jungles nearby others come in, constantly recruited, to keep the herders lean and wary and cause them to be generous with their gurus and their gods.

Of all the people I knew on the hunting trails, news of the death of only Mauf Hamilton and Cottar had reached me. As far as I know, John MacDonald still builds *machons* and digs holes for visiting hunters, but though he may deal with better marksmen, he will never find a more patient sitter. There remain K'nini, Frank, Bimbo in his blue boy's suit, Dean Cochran, Francis and Louis De Fosse. I spent great days with them, and wish I could sit once more with them beside the campfire.

Someday soon I might return. There is nothing to stop me but the memory of the drama and the excitement and the magnificent adventures and the wonderful luck of my other trips, which I fear the hunting gods would not pour out to me again— at least not in such abundance. So lately I have returned to hunting ducks, my big game of small game. And seeing under white clouds a flock of green-head mallards arching their wings and showing their bright feathers ameliorates, although it does not cure, my fevers.

And with what joy I think upon the caribou and moose in the spruce forest, the grizzlies roaming the Northern wild, the vast red Kodiak of the windy barrens, and, on grounds far away, lions, leopards, rhinos, buffaloes, wild elephants, the great saladang, and, most splendid and beautiful and thrilling, the arrogant, gorgeous tigers! Throughout this century at least they will share the planet with us. They will increase the fascination of our world. For everyone, for all of us in some degree, they will raise the pitch of life.